DRAGON IN
THE TROPICS

A BROOKINGS LATIN AMERICA INITIATIVE BOOK

The Latin America Initiative at Brookings focuses on the most critical economic, political, and social issues facing the region. The books in this series provide independent analysis for a modern Latin America.

Titles in the series include:

Javier Corrales and Michael Penfold
Dragon in the Tropics: Hugo Chávez and the Political Economy of Revolution in Venezuela
2011

Albert Fishlow
Starting Over: Brazil since 1985
forthcoming 2011

Abraham F. Lowenthal, Theodore J. Piccone, and Laurence Whitehead, eds.,
Shifting the Balance: Obama and the Americas
2011

A BROOKINGS LATIN AMERICA INITIATIVE BOOK

DRAGON IN THE TROPICS

HUGO CHÁVEZ AND THE POLITICAL ECONOMY OF REVOLUTION IN VENEZUELA

JAVIER CORRALES

MICHAEL PENFOLD

BROOKINGS INSTITUTION PRESS
Washington, D.C.

Library of Congress Cataloging-in-Publication data

Corrales, Javier, 1966–
    Dragon in the tropics : Hugo Chávez and the political economy of revolution in
Venezuela / Javier Corrales, Michael Penfold.
        p. cm.
    Includes bibliographical references and index.
    Summary: "A study of the Venezuelan revolution headed by Hugo Chávez, first elected
president in 1999, with emphasis on how Chávez took a frail but still pluralistic democracy and turned it into a semi-authoritarian regime, achieving political transformation at
great cost to the country's institutions, including its oil industry"—Provided by publisher.
    ISBN 978-0-8157-0497-3 (pbk. : alk. paper)
    1. Venezuela—Politics and government—1999– 2. Venezuela—Economic policy.
3. Venezuela—Foreign relations—1999– 4. Chávez Frías, Hugo. I. Penfold, Michael.
II. Title.
    JL3831.C68 2010
    987.06'42—dc22   2010043335

9 8 7 6 5 4 3 2 1

Printed on acid-free paper

Typeset in Sabon and Strayhorn

Composition by Cynthia Stock
Silver Spring, Maryland

Printed by R. R. Donnelley
Harrisonburg, Virginia

It will not do to leave a live dragon out of your plans
if you live near one.

J. R. R. TOLKIEN

Contents

Acknowledgments

A number of institutions and individuals made this book possible and, in the process, helped us become better researchers and writers. Mauricio Cárdenas at the Brookings Institution embraced this project from its inception. Mauricio's close reading and criticism of earlier drafts was a source of inspiration and original ideas. His offer to sponsor a book incubator at Brookings was nothing less than a splendid gift, allowing us to obtain priceless feedback from world-class experts such as Cynthia Arnson, Miriam Kornblith, Abe Lowenthal, Alejandro Grisanti, Fidel Jaramillo, David Myers, Moisés Naím, and Michael Shifter. At different stages in the writing of this volume we also received comments from other, equally generous colleagues: Francisco Rodríguez, Boris Muñoz, Ricardo Hausmann, María Victoria Murillo, Enrique Ochoa Reza, Jon Eastwood, Larry Diamond, Virginia López, Kurt Weyland, Steve Levitsky, Christopher Chambers-Ju, Maxwell Cameron, Aníbal Romero, Michiel Baud, Barbara Hogenboom, Sergio Dahbar, and Daniel Altschuler.

Over the years, Amherst College has provided ample resources for our research on Venezuela. The Research Fund at the Institute for Advanced Administrative Studies (IESA) in Caracas provided valuable financial support to help us finish the writing. Adriana Arreaza, Ramón Espinasa, Maikel Bello, and Asdrúbal Oliveros supplied invaluable data on oil, poverty, and the economy. Carlos Sabatino, Tara Shabahang, Mariana Urbina, Alejandro Cáceres,

Luis Pulgar, Ricardo Suárez, Daniel Mogollón, and John Yarchoan offered superb research assistance and were great students. Henry Gómez Samper edited and proofread our drafts with a dedication that went far beyond duty. And we are grateful to Andy Anderson for his help designing the map in chapter 5. During our fifteen years of research on Venezuela, many other institutions have lent us vital support: the Carter Center, the Center for Research on Latin America (CEDLA) at the University of Amsterdam, Columbia University, the Fulbright Foundation, the Open Society Institute, the School of Government at the Universidad de los Andes (Bogotá), the University of Southern California, and the Tinker Foundation. We also acknowledge colleagues with whom we have co-authored academic papers, chapters, and books on Venezuela: Imelda Cisneros, Rosa Amelia González, Manuel Hidalgo, Francisco Monaldi, Richard Obuchi, Daniel Ortega, Roberto Vainrub, and Carlos Romero. Without the support of these friends and institutions, this book would have remained mostly a collection of unpolished ideas whirling in our minds.

Last, we would like to acknowledge the help of staff at the Brookings Institution Press who worked closely with us to bring the book out into the world.

1

Introduction:
The Chávez Revolution in Perspective

This book spotlights one of the most sweeping and unexpected political transformations in contemporary Latin American politics. President Hugo Chávez Frías, in office since 1999 and reelected in 2000 and 2006, has transformed a frail but nonetheless pluralistic democracy into a hybrid regime, an outcome achieved in the context of a spectacularly high oil income and widespread electoral support. Hybrid regimes are political systems in which the mechanism for determining access to state office combines both democratic and autocratic practices. In hybrid regimes, freedoms exist and the opposition is allowed to compete in elections, but the system of checks and balances becomes inoperative. More specifically, such regimes display the following features:[1]

—Government negotiations with opposition forces are rare.

—Die-hard loyalists of the government are placed at top-level positions in state offices, such as the courts, thereby undermining the system of checks and balances.

—The state actively seeks to undermine the autonomy of civic institutions.

—The law is invoked mostly to penalize opponents but seldom to sanction the government.

—The incumbent changes and circumvents the constitution.

—The electoral field is uneven, with the ruling party making use of sinecures that are systematically denied to the opposition.

Undeniably, the rise of a hybrid regime in Venezuela occurred in the context of significant electoral support. Venezuela under Chávez has conducted plenty of elections—thirteen as of September 2010—and *chavista* forces prevailed in all but one. This widespread use of elections is certainly impressive, and many consider it a sign of democratic vitality, even though electoral institutions have been openly manipulated. This electoral majoritarianism has been used by the president to justify concentrating a broad array of institutional power, including ending term limits. As a result, Chávez's "Bolivarian Revolution" (so-named by Chávez after Simón Bolívar, the Venezuela-born South American liberator) has reduced accountability, limited alternation in office, and expanded the powers of the executive like few other electoral regimes in Latin America.

These are all typical features of an "electoral autocracy," a term that became popular early in the new century to describe hybrid regimes in which one dominant party or ruling coalition overwhelms the rest.[2] Scholars have noted a rise of hybrid systems across the globe in the latter part of the 2000s: the Chávez regime represents the most pronounced case of hybridity to emerge in Latin America since the 1980s. Other nations in Latin America have in the recent past lived through somewhat similar experiences. Oftentimes labeled "neopopulist," majoritarianism combined with weak political parties has led to strong personalistic rulers as recently as Alberto Fujimori's regime in Peru during the 1990s.[3] But *chavismo*, the term that is conventionally used to denote the methods and goals of Chávez's particular type of hybrid regime, exhibits three additional features that are less typical of other similar experiences in Latin America.

First, there is a heavy and unconcealed militaristic bent, far greater even than under Fujimori. The military is present in the cabinet, in the management of the ever-growing number of state-owned enterprises, and in running subnational government programs. *Chavismo* essentially contravened and maybe even ended the trend in Latin America until the late 1990s of containing rather than expanding the role of the military in governance and spending in areas that have little to do with national security.

Second, in terms of economic policy, the regime is heavily statist. Other than offering a major fiscal stimulus and cheap imports, the state does little to promote private investments and imposes some of the most severe regulatory restrictions in the world. State control has expanded in basic industries ranging from power and electricity to telecommunications and ordinary sectors such as cement and hotels. Expropriations have expanded from a few abandoned lots to major profitable industries.

Third, the regime has adopted a distinctive foreign policy: an active commitment to balance the influence of the United States and to export a somewhat radical political ideology of statism across the region. Chávez has become one of the world's closest allies of Iran, one of the world's leading buyers of weapons from Russia, and one of the world's most openly confrontational leaders, not just toward the United States but toward any head of state whom he dislikes.

In short, in terms of policy and discourse toward his detractors—at home and abroad, in good times and in bad times—the Chávez administration is nothing less than a fire-breathing dragon in the tropics. Latin America has seen few comparable political dragons emerge in its recent history. To be sure, over the past decade many of the region's leaders have deployed some of these practices, but none has undermined checks-and-balances institutions and co-governed with the military to the extent that Chávez has in Venezuela. A number of countries have veered to the left in economic policy, especially when compared to the 1990s,[4] but none has achieved the same degree of state control of the economy as in Chávez's Venezuela. And although some countries have abandoned the policy of close rapprochement toward the United States that prevailed at the close of the twentieth century,[5] none since Cuba during the cold war has embarked on such a world campaign to counter American influence in this hemisphere and elsewhere.

The chapters that follow provide an in-depth review of how this major political transformation took place in Venezuela. We chiefly synthesize studies produced by both of us over the past fifteen years. As academics, both of us have focused much of our careers on the study of Venezuela. We both wrote doctoral dissertations on Venezuelan politics prior to the "Bolivarian revolution" from a comparative perspective (Corrales compared Venezuela to Argentina, Penfold to Colombia). Since Chávez came to office, we have separately and jointly published academic journal articles, book chapters, commissioned reports, and newspaper op-eds. With this book we seek to summarize a number of key thoughts generated in our research and policy experience, render them accessible to a less specialized audience than that for our earlier writings, and update them to take into consideration new developments and research.

Explaining *Chavismo*

We have several goals in mind. One is to provide an explanation for Venezuela's political overhaul. Conventional accounts of the Chávez regime generally focus on some combination of three principal factors: the role of (decaying) liberal democracy since the 1970s, (failed) economic reforms in the 1990s, and (overpriced) oil in the 2000s. Some scholars have argued that Venezuela's legendary democracy—one of the first successful "pacted" transitions in Latin America—turned into a rigid "partyarchy" in the 1980s. During this period two parties, Acción Democrática (AD) and the Social Christian Party (originally Comité de Organización Política Electoral Independiente, or COPEI), dominated the political field. Far too many actors across all income categories were excluded by an agreement among these parties' leaders that over time restricted access to democratic institutions and failed to manage economic development once oil fiscal resources started to decline. This led to demands for new and more participatory political institutions, a tide that brought "revolutionary" Chávez to the fore. Others have argued instead that Venezuela's experiment with market economic reforms in the 1990s led to harsh austerity policies that expanded poverty without restoring growth, leading to a demand for a more leftist-populist-nationalist type of economic development. Finally, a new wave of high oil prices in the early 2000s supplied the means for the Chávez regime to deliver on these society-demanded changes. In a nutshell, many scholars think that the failure of liberal democracy and economics explains the demand for the type of regime now in place, while oil provided the figurative and concrete fuel.

We offer a slightly different interpretation of events. First, on the role played by political institutions, we don't dispute the degree of exclusion that preceded Chávez, but we contend that it was the dramatic institutional opening in the 1990s, rather than continued institutional closure, that created the opportunity for regime change. In the 1980s the old pacted democracy entered into a deep social and political crisis, leading to political decentralization and reform, which allowed for more than twenty governorships and more than 300 mayors to be directly elected by the people by 1989. Political decentralization triggered two profound political earthquakes: it allowed new political forces to emerge and capture state office—especially Causa-R at the outset of the 1990s and Chávez's own Movement of the Fifth Republic (Movimiento Quinta

República, or MVR) in later years—effectively ending the country's stale "partyarchy."[6] Decentralization also eased the stranglehold of the leading traditional parties, AD and COPEI, thereby ushering in an unprecedented party fragmentation. We are convinced that the wedge opened by decentralization and party fragmentation was one of the most important underlying institutional explanations for why Chávez—a consummate newcomer—managed to win state office in 1998 and easily overwhelmed the political system in a matter of a few years. The main point is that greater democratization rather than less democratization made possible the entry of new political actors; and party fragmentation permitted this new political force, once in office, to consolidate power in a short period of time.[7] Without decentralization (which opened the doors) and party fragmentation (which cleared the path), Chávez would have faced possibly insurmountable obstacles at election time and, certainly, as a policymaker.

With respect to economic reforms, we agree that poverty and erratic economic performance prevailed in the 1980s and 1990s, but we disagree that "neoliberalism" was the key culprit. Market economic reforms never really took hold in Venezuela. Attempts to open the economy by Carlos Andres Peréz in 1989 and, after some delay, by Rafael Caldera in 1996 faced formidable political roadblocks that prevented deep implementation. Other than trade liberalization and a few privatizations, most economic activities, especially on the export side, remained largely statist. Moreover, there is no evidence that the majority of the population repudiated market economic reforms as vehemently as Chávez did when he gained power democratically.[8] We are persuaded that Venezuela's economic ailments resulted from factors other than "neoliberalism," namely, the persistence of dependence on oil, which caused macroeconomic volatility; political party fragmentation, which triggered policy incoherence and infighting; government mismanagement of the economy, which led to greater contraction of the private sector in the 1990s; and the Asian crisis of 1997, which devastated Venezuela's economy just around the time that Chávez ran for president. To blame market reforms for Venezuela's economic ills up to 2003 is an exaggeration; other, more serious, economic ailments mattered more.

Our position on oil is a bit more complicated, so we devote an entire chapter to this topic. We do not dispute the growing consensus in development studies that high dependence on mineral or land-based natural resources generates multiple forms of political and economic distortions—the so-called resource curse, or "paradox of plenty," arguments. But we think that oil alone fails to explain the recent course of Venezuelan politics, and even less, the direction of regime change. Oil has been the key economic factor in Venezuela since large-scale production started in the 1920s, and in subsequent decades the country experienced all forms of political regimes (dictatorships, democracies, and semi-autocracies), institutional arrangements (unipartisan, bipartisan, multipartisan, antipartisan), and economic policies (import-substitution industrialization in the 1950s and 1960s, heavy investment in large utilities in the 1970s, unorthodox economic adjustment in the 1980s, aggressive market reforms in the early 1990s, timid reforms until 2003, and aggressive fiscal spending since 2003). Oil has been invoked over and over again to explain the status quo, even though the status quo has changed repeatedly during the last 100 years.

We propose instead that the explanation for the rise of Chávez's regime lies in what could be called an "institutional resource curse": oil, certainly, but in combination with a number of institutional arrangements, is what explains key regime change. In particular, Chávez was able to obtain direct political control of the state-owned national oil company, Petróleos de Venezuela, S.A. (PDVSA)—which reflected the erosion of checks and balances already under way prior to the Venezuelan oil boom from 2003 to 2008. This institutional grab by the executive branch allowed it to distribute oil rents to the population without any intermediation from other political actors after 2004. Without this prior institutional change, which also involved deep constitutional reforms that strengthened presidential powers, the oil boom in Venezuela under Chávez might have had a different political effect, one less empowering of the president and less detrimental to the opposition. Our focus is therefore on identifying the type of institutions that, in combination with oil dependence, led to a transformation of regime type and policies after Chávez came to power.

A focus on oil and related institutions, rather than oil alone, is a departure from the common treatment in current (generally quantitative) studies of the resource curse, but it continues a venerable tradition in research on Venezuela and in qualitative studies of development in general. For instance, some of the best works on whether countries succumb or escape the resource curse—however it is defined—tend to stress variations in institutional features among petro-states.[9] Likewise, some of the best studies of Venezuelan politics over the years emphasize the role of institutions, not just oil, to explain the origins of democracy in the late 1950s, policy incoherence in the 1980s, and regime change in the early 2000s.[10] All of these studies consider variations in state-based variables, party-based variables, or both. This book builds on the tradition of examining oil and institutions interactively rather than separately.

We do recognize, however, that regardless of institutions, oil dependence generates a demand for "rentism" on the part of economic agents that is perhaps more pronounced than in other societies.[11] We define "rentism" as the drive of social, economic, and political actors to extract fiscal resources for private rather than public gains through lobbying for lessened competition. This behavior creates a strong bias toward favoring distorted policies aimed at protecting the extraction of these "rents" by a broad array of actors. Moreover, oil is no doubt the fuel that has powered the Chávez regime, as it does any incumbent in petro-states enjoying an oil windfall. But again, understanding why the regime has taken on its current shape and, more important, why it has moved in a particular direction (why the dragon protects certain political assets and not others, and spews fire at some targets and not others), requires us to know more than just the fact that fuel has been plentiful.

Additionally, focusing exclusively on oil, as the resource-curse literature often does, fails to explain one of the most noteworthy features of Chávez's policies: the decline in the country's oil sector under his watch. Considering that both in rhetoric and in practice the Chávez regime places oil at the heart of the country's development strategy, allowing this sector to decline as much as it has since 1999 is astounding. If anything, one would think that Chávez should cherish the oil sector unfailingly. Furthermore, considering the concentration of power in the executive branch, one would also think that he should have no trouble protecting this asset. Yet most indicators reveal a serious deterioration of Venezuela's oil economy since 1999. Chávez is not the first president in Venezuelan history to be mesmerized by the promise of oil, but he has become the one who has allowed the sector to decline the most. The mystery of the Chávez regime is not that it has relied on oil as much as it has, but that, despite this excessive reliance, he has allowed the sector to decay. In our chapter on oil we try to explain this decline: again, to explain this decaying trend in the oil sector (not just in regime change) we propose an "institutional-resource-curse" thesis.

Politics under *Chavismo*

Another objective of this book is to demonstrate that to understand the current political system in Venezuela, it is necessary not just to look at the demand side (namely, citizens' preferences), but also the supply side: ways whereby strategic actors at the state level managed to manipulate policies and formal rules in order to prevail politically. At its core, *chavismo* could be conceptualized as a political project that seeks to undermine traditional checks and balances by building an electoral majority based on a radical social discourse of inclusion, glued together by property redistribution plus vast social handouts extracted from the oil industry. Like previous populist movements in Latin America, *chavismo* is a politically "illiberal" project because it uses electoral majorities to erode horizontal and vertical accountability.

Robert Dahl's classic idea of liberal democracy combined high contestation and high inclusion; judged in these terms, *chavismo* may be deemed definitely deficient in the former and problematic in the latter criterion.[12] At the level of contestation, *chavismo* has increasingly undermined political competition for office by placing state resources and security services at the disposal of the ruling party while denying them to its rivals. At the level of inclusion, *chavismo* has mobilized new and nontraditional actors in the electoral arena (which clearly strengthens democracy), but also has deliberately excluded comparatively large segments of society, labeling them "oligarchs," "contemptible," and "enemies of the common people." Judged in terms of accountability and treatment of the opposition, this regime is a long way from Dahl's conception of liberal democracy.

Underlying these changes in contestation and inclusion is the complete erosion of checks and balances. Consider one example of this erosion: very few court cases are known where societal actors have sued the state, let alone won a case against the state. Under *chavismo*, the concept of limits on the power of the majority—which all scholars who study the quality of democracy posit as being a minimal condition that regimes must meet to qualify as such—has collapsed in Venezuela.

Authoritarian leaps have always been commonplace in Latin American politics, as elsewhere in the developing world. In the 1980s in Latin America, new checks emerged on these tendencies, and for a while they actually worked. Furthermore, the radical left lost steam with the collapse of European communism, the military retreated from politics and experienced budget cuts, civil society became stronger and drew on international support, the region's press gained strength and autonomy thanks to new media technology and new markets, and a general climate against mistreating the opposition and respecting human rights prevailed worldwide. Moreover, radical right-wing movements that had sponsored either paramilitary groups or military governments came under increasing scrutiny from human rights organizations. Accordingly, traditional means by which concentration of power imposed itself in the region—coups, insurgency, repression, terror, outright bans on political liberties—were neutralized by these international and domestic barriers.

But the Venezuela case shows that rather than being laid to rest, autocratic impulses can simply adapt to both worldwide and domestic countertrends. Rather than retreat, political movements aimed at concentrating power can discover and conceive new ways to expand, even in the context of seemingly tougher barriers to such expansion. *Chavismo* adapted to this situation, as described in chapter 2, by selectively discontinuing certain institutions, co-opting others, and creating new ones. Hence, we focus significant attention on the regime's clever manipulation of state and civic institutions to show how a project that seems to be a throwback to Latin America's past can overcome adverse circumstances and forge a new future.

The Domestic and International Political Economy

We also want to explore how this new regime requires us to rethink questions not just about radical politics, but also about development in general. Chapter 3 thus focuses on economic development issues—more precisely, on the heavy use of statist policies to manage economic affairs. We argue that even though Chávez brought forth a new form of politics in Venezuela, he recycled old economics. Chávez's political economy until 2008 could be labeled a modified return to import-substitution industrialization (ISI), defined as an attempt to use broad protectionist measures as a way to boost local production. State intervention has been maximized, often with the intention of expanding self-sufficiency. As with previous cases of ISI in Venezuela and in Latin America in general, this set of policies has led to extraordinary inefficiencies and, once again, to an expansion rather than a contraction of imports. In addition, in an attempt to socialize production, oil rents were used to expand the role of the state through nationalization, often in areas that were well beyond what leftist governments elsewhere in the region were advocating. This modified ISI strategy in the context of an oil economy—more statist and more favorable to imports than previous versions—has allowed the regime to attract voters and build adherence from unexpected sectors and special-interest groups, which helps to explain its electoral successes following 2003. Since 2008 Chávez's economic policy has become more radical, showing more blatant disregard for market forces. Although it is too early to tell what this new economic radicalism will bring, all signs thus far point toward a longer economic crisis than in most other countries in the world affected by the 2008–09 global recession.

In chapter 4 we discuss oil policy. Oil is central to *chavismo*, this much is clear. But we go beyond this obvious point to elaborate on two less understood aspects of the role of oil in consolidating this regime. First, rather than accept the point that oil explains the rise of political and economic institutions under Chávez and the features of his regime—hybridity and state-led economic policy—we argue that political institutions shaped the way in which the regime came to use oil to its advantage. More precisely, Chávez's overhaul of institutions within politics and within the oil sector in the 1999–2004 period, which led to the erosion of checks and balances and the restructuring of PDVSA, allowed Chávez to convert the oil sector into, in essence, the regime's checking account. Without this prior institutional overhaul, the impact of the 2003–08 oil windfall would have been dramatically different, namely, less beneficial to the incumbent. The second puzzle we discuss in chapter 4 is the decline of the oil sector under Chávez, which is evident from any available indicator. This decline is also the result of new institutions established by Chávez with the purpose of treating the oil sector less as an investment than as a social ministry. But it is also a symptom of the regime's most important chronic and potentially damaging weakness: the combination of distorted economic policies and ever weaker state capabilities. Oil is the ideal sector to illustrate this process of dwindling administrative competence, precisely because it is the one sector where the process is most salient and also the least expected, given the importance of the oil sector to the government.

In chapter 5 we turn our attention to foreign policy. Except for a plethora of op-eds, not much has been written analytically about the implications of Chávez's foreign policy. We argue that, to some extent, a key feature of Venezuela's foreign policy is "soft-balancing"—countering U.S. influence and playing social power diplomacy. Soft-balancing refers to nations' efforts, short of military action, to frustrate the foreign policy objectives of other, presumably more powerful nations; a variation of traditional balancing behavior, the concept is a core tenet of realism. Whereas "hard-balancing" involves efforts, typically military in nature, to reconfigure the international system—for example, to end the predominance of a great power—the goals of soft-balancing are less ambitious: chiefly, to raise the costs of action for the more powerful state. However, we insist that not every aspect of Chávez's foreign policy counts as soft-balancing—or *effective* soft-balancing, at least. Some aspects, such as his empty rhetoric, are *too soft*. Other aspects, such as his deals with terrorism-sponsoring nations and organizations or his strong military spending, are *too hard*. Furthermore, he has multiple foreign policy goals (other than challenging the United States) and target states, some of them less powerful than Venezuela itself. Nevertheless Venezuela has displayed all the usual signs of soft-balancing the United States, and so it is worthwhile to study lessons about the origins, practice, and effects of this kind of policy in North-South relations. In line with the rest of the book, we discuss how domestic institutions, specifically the decline in accountability and the concentration of powers in the executive branch, interact with oil to both facilitate and hinder Venezuela's soft-balancing initiatives.

The Social Face of *Chavismo*

Without a doubt, the regime's social policy—both at home and abroad—is its most widely discussed feature, yet it, too, is not always fully understood. Many observers find that Chávez's social policies illustrate a democratic commitment rare in Latin America. We disagree. Certainly, there is no question but that poverty at home has declined under Chávez: there are some estimates that the proportion of Venezuelans living in poverty fell from 48.6 percent in 2002 to 27.6 percent in 2008.[13] These declines notwithstanding, our message is that under certain circumstances, aid is disbursed to *some* of the poor, and more gravely, in a way that ends up helping the president and his allies and cronies more than anyone else. Overall, social policy is conceived more as a key instrument to build a radical political coalition both domestically and internationally in order to sustain the electoral support and international legitimacy of Chávez's hybrid regime. This practice is not necessarily felicitous for democracy, although from a superficial perspective it might seem to qualify as progressively distributive.

Nevertheless, beyond a doubt the Chávez regime has channeled unprecedented funding toward social programs, exceeding by far what is generally achieved by liberal democracies in developing countries and many paternalistic autocracies, even in petro-states such as in the Persian Gulf. We argue that social policy and funding social programs play a much larger role than is conventionally understood. Essentially, this social dimension plays a major role in domestic politics, in economics, in the oil sector, and in foreign policy. Thus, each of our chapters devotes considerable attention to social policy. Whereas a conventional account of Chávez would typically have a separate chapter on social policy, we find it more illuminating to discuss social policy as a factor in each of the various aspects of the regime.

Thus, chapter 2, on domestic politics, discusses how clientelistic practices underlying social policy acted as the regime's co-optation and opposition-disarming tool par excellence. The chapter also offers an explanation for the fact that a regime such as Chávez's—neither fully democratic nor fully authoritarian—generated a higher-than-expected level of spending than many democracies and dictatorships. The type of political competition that is allowed to exist in a hybrid regime triggers an incentive for the government to spend, while the erosion of checks and balances in such a regime permits the state to overspend and to do so in a discretionary way. The combined outcome is a level of state spending that is high, inefficient, and politically biased. Chapter 3, on economic policy, shows that yet another way social spending under Chávez functions is as a form of permanent economic stimulus package and as a mechanism for generating labor demand for state expropriations (social spending is used to lure workers into welcoming the state takeover of private businesses). Chapter 4, on oil, shows that social spending also played a major role in determining how the oil sector was managed. More specifically, the chapter illustrates that the decision to privilege social spending (essentially, operating expenses in the form of cash transfers and massive subsidies) in determining priorities for the oil sector came with a devastating opportunity cost in the form of forgone investments in infrastructure, technology, and production. Chapter 5, on foreign policy, discusses one of the most innovative uses of social spending under Chávez: as a tool to soft-balance the United States, win allies across the region, and silence criticism of the regime from regional governments and even international intellectuals. In short, oil, and the social spending it has made possible, has played a major role not just in politics, but in all the dimensions of *chavismo*. In this sense, social policy has become a powerful instrument for political consolidation and not just an objective in itself.

Reflections

This book thus examines how oil and institutions have interacted to produce regime change, radical populism, decay of the oil sector, and an anti–United States foreign policy in Venezuela. Our wish is that the book will offer something of value to a broad readership comprising the general public, nonspecialist scholars, and policy wonks.

For Venezuelanists, we offer arguments that deviate from some of the most widely held theories on the rise and effects of *chavismo*. For comparativists, we offer enough material to provoke the question of whether *chavismo* is replicable and could anticipate the future of politics in countries suffering from party decay, chronic weak state capabilities, and economic volatility, or whether *chavismo* is unreplicable because it is either too anachronistic or too reliant on oil. For Latin Americanists, we provide material to fuel a debate as to whether *chavismo* is the wave of the future for the region because it points toward a "postdemocratic" regime, as one of Chávez's most influential early intellectual mentors called this political movement, or whether *chavismo* is a dead-end proposition precisely because it is too undemocratic.[14] For those interested in North-South relations, we offer an explanation of soft-balancing that relies more on the political needs of the challenging nation than on the actions of the hegemon. And for those interested in development more generally, we hope to offer some criteria to help assess the conditions under which countries that come to enjoy formidable economic fortunes can actually manage such blessings for the good of society as a whole, not just of the president and his supporters.

2

Power Grabbing and the Rise of a Hybrid Regime in Venezuela, 1999–2009

How did a grassroots movement that began in 1998 as an effort to bring more democracy to Venezuela transform itself into a movement intent on empowering the executive branch above any other actor? The emergence of a hybrid regime in Venezuela cannot be explained easily with functional theories. Such arguments posit the breakdown of democratic institutions as an outgrowth of chronic crises in governability, which prompt political actors— whether in office or in the opposition—to seize and centralize power in order to cope with daunting issues.[1] Between 1999 and 2001, however, when some of the most important changes in the regime were established, Hugo Chávez was enjoying a formidable political honeymoon, with approval ratings and electoral results that were the envy of incumbents in the region.

These early institutional changes that allowed Chávez to increase presidential powers occurred before the 2003–08 oil boom and were not brought about by oil wealth either. Expanding presidential powers did generate a governability crisis: by late 2001, the country became intensely polarized between *chavistas* and Chávez's detractors, and this polarization continues to this day. One could debate whether the governability crisis that ensued was structural or fabricated (we argue that there was substantial fabrication), and this, to some extent, justified some of the executive's growing buildup of powers in 2002 and 2003. Following 2004, however, when Chávez survived a contested recall referendum, he once again had little reason to feel politically threatened or encumbered, as his approval ratings, electoral fortunes, and command of institutions recovered spectacularly, and street protests against the government never again matched the levels of 2002 to 2004. And yet, Chávez responded to this post-2004 stability once again by speeding the pace of power concentration and increasing constraints on the opposition and independent civil groups. None of this occurred in the context of any genuine political emergency.

Our account of Venezuela's transformation into a hybrid regime draws, first, on arguments based on "elite intentions," by which we mean the preferences of elected politicians, based on their own ideologies and their misreading of the preferences of certain constituencies.[2] But we go further, showing how this leap was also an outcome of available "political opportunities," chiefly the presence of economic resources at the disposal of the state, together with institutions of representation that were weak to begin with and were further weakened by deliberate state policies. The availability of economic resources alone would not have sufficed as a condition enabling the rise of a hybrid regime. In the presence of stronger political parties and institutions of accountability, the political impact from an economic windfall would have been different. The movement toward a hybrid regime also resulted from the deployment of state strategies, by which we mean the incumbent's deliberate use of polarization, political "clientelism," impunity from punishment for corruption, and job discrimination.

Advocates of the "Bolivarian Revolution" have never tired of proclaiming a commitment to participatory democracy as an alternative to liberal democracy. Chávez is certainly correct that Venezuela is moving away from liberal democracy, but it is not moving toward greater accountability and participation. Instead, Chávez has shown how a democratically elected leader can manipulate domestic institutions to crowd out social and political groups and, by extension, to crowd out democracy. He accomplished this with different strategies at different stages.

Despite this variety of strategies, a discernible pattern emerges to explain how a hybrid regime came into being under Chávez: usually, the government would carry out a power grab by choosing one or a few, but not all, institutions and attempting to strip them of autonomy, almost one at a time. The opposition would respond in different ways: first by protesting, then by trying to subvert the incumbent, then by staying quiescent, and more recently by opting for more effective electoral strategies—all to little avail. Most of the time, the government would respond by becoming more hard-line and exclusionary, in the end concentrating more power in the executive branch and leaving fewer institutional spaces for any other political group.[3]

Yet, the path toward the consolidation of a hybrid regime in Venezuela since 1999 is a convoluted story, not necessarily following a straightforward sequence of events. In this chapter we try to describe this process in terms of different "acts," a theatrical metaphor, to make sense of the remarkable metamorphosis of Venezuela's regime through various stages over one decade. The backdrop of all of these "acts" has been a deeprooted political polarization that at times has induced the opposition to turn to nondemocratic means to remove *chavismo* from power (such as the failed coup in 2002) and has also allowed *chavismo* to justify the manipulation of constitutional rules for its own political gains (such as banning opponents, allowing the ruling party to spend state money unaccountably, eliminating term limits for the presidency in 2009, or creating electoral laws that are biased in favor of incumbents). In the following sections we provide a narrative of how this hybrid regime emerged and, in the last section, attempt to explain how this regime has managed to consolidate power.

Act I: Creating a Hyperpresidential Constitution

The first in a series of power grabs was the rewriting of Venezuela's constitution shortly after Chávez took office. Chávez won the presidency in 2008 on the heels of a twenty-year crisis in the so-called *puntofijista* system. The term *puntofijista* comes from the Punto Fijo Pact, which was a series of agreements signed in 1958 by the leading democratic political forces of the time, setting the terms of democratic political competition following years of dictatorship.[4] By the late 1990s, the vast majority of the public had become convinced that the *puntofijista* system was corrupt, inept, unstable, and rigid. Chávez had promised to radically dismantle this system, starting with the very same parties that founded it, Acción Democrática and COPEI (Comité de Organización Política Electoral Independiente).

Dismantling the previous system was not that difficult. Economically, the country was in the midst of two "lost decades," the 1980s and the 1990s, in contrast to the rest of Latin America, which had lost only one decade, the 1980s. In addition, a new series of decentralization reforms introduced in Venezuela in 1989 allowed governors and mayors to be directly elected, which created an opening for new movements to emerge and thus shake the power structure of traditional party barons.[5] Economic crisis and political opening are the main reason that new, somewhat anti–status quo forces surged in the 1990s, first the Causa-R, and by late 1990s, Chávez's own movement.

Nobody disputes Venezuela's calamitous economic and social performance prior to Chávez. In 1998 the GDP per capita had already reverted to the level of the early 1950s. Moderate and extreme poverty spread from 44.4 percent of households in 1989 to 57.6 percent in 1998, and extreme poverty grew from 20.1 to 28.8 percent during the same period. This steep fall in economic and social indicators partially explains why voters were willing to support a candidate who promised an overhaul of the political system.[6] A plunge in the price of Venezuela's oil in 1998—to almost eight dollars per barrel, its lowest price in decades—provided the final blow against the electoral strength of the traditional parties. The system was ready for any "newcomer," and during the 1998 election several newcomers contended for office. But the electoral climate favored the newcomer who promised the most punitive policies toward the existing parties. That candidate was Chávez.

As president, Chávez could have started off by focusing on the economy, which everyone knew was in shambles. Instead he focused on rewriting rules governing relations among the branches of government, with an eye toward expanding presidential powers. In what became a trend in the region in the 2000s, Chávez took advantage of the widespread antiparty sentiment across the electorate to call a National Constituent Assembly expressly aimed at putting an end to *partidocracia* ("partyarchy"), the local term for the stranglehold of traditional political parties in Venezuela. Because these parties held some power in other branches of government, it was easy for Chávez in 1999 to justify weakening those branches, if for no other reason, as he put it, than to "stab to death the moribund parties."

One of Chávez's first administrative acts was to sign a presidential decree calling for a consultative referendum under which delegates to a National Constituent Assembly could be elected. The wording for the referendum was drafted by a special commission appointed by the president and led by Ricardo Combellas, Ernesto Mayz Vallenilla, and Oswaldo Álvarez Paz, well-known intellectuals or politicians who had long favored the idea of redrafting the 1961 constitution. At the time, a two-thirds vote was required for Congress to change or reform an article of the constitution or to call a Constituent Assembly, but Chávez's political party, at the time called the Fifth Republic Movement (Movimiento Quinta República), had obtained little more than 20 percent of seats in the Chamber of Deputies and 22 percent in the Senate, so he lacked the requisite votes.

Chávez thus needed a mechanism for bypassing the elected Congress—not just to write a new constitution, but to govern. As a means to bypass Congress, the special presidential commission recommended the use of a consultative referendum, a novel instrument first employed in 1997 during a legislative reform to the electoral law. Chávez embraced this idea. Instantly, a profound conflict flared up between the branches of government: Congress argued that any constitutional rewrite needed to be in its own hands, whereas the presidency demanded a popular referendum. In March 1999 the Supreme Court sided with the executive in a ruling allowing a consultative referendum. In the referendum, which took place on April 25, 1999, about 87 percent of the voters approved the idea of holding a Constituent Assembly and the electoral rules set up by the presidency to elect delegates to the assembly. Some months later the Supreme Court also agreed to suspend Congress while the Constituent Assembly was under way, another of Chávez's main goals. Despite having reservations regarding this process of stripping Congress of power in this way, the Supreme Court did not feel confident enough to block the wishes of such a popular president. Chávez was enjoying the highest approval ratings of any Venezuelan president since the 1960s. And so began the process of using the power of majorities to bully the various branches of government.

Another of Chávez's formidable political feats in 1999 was to gain overwhelming control of the Constituent Assembly. He achieved this by clever institutional manipulation: the presidential commission designed an electoral rule for selecting delegates (a plurality system with different district sizes at the state level), together with a well-thought-out nomination strategy that ensured that no more candidates from his coalition would be nominated per district than there were seats under competition, which was a way to avoid wasted votes. The opposition did the opposite: candidates competed individually rather than under a single political banner, regardless of how many opposition candidates existed in each jurisdiction. These formal rules and informal procedures (unity of the ruling party and fragmentation of the opposition) enabled the government, with only 53 percent of the votes, to obtain control of 93 percent of the seats—the opposition votes became too dispersed among too many candidates to permit more than a handful to make it to the assembly.

Given the ideological homogeneity of the Constituent Assembly, it is not surprising that the new constitution was drafted in less than three months, with negligible input from the opposition. The result was a formidable expansion of presidential powers relative to other branches of government. This does not mean that other aspects of civil society did not receive new rights, but rather that in relation to other branches of government and traditional parties, the president won the most expanded powers. To this day, Venezuela's 1999 constitution remains the most "presidential" constitution in Latin America.[7] The presidential term was expanded from five to six years and immediate reelection to a second term was permitted. The president obtained complete discretion over promotions within the armed forces without legislative approval. The Senate was eliminated, which eroded checks and balances within Congress and between the legislative and the executive branches. The president gained the power to activate any kind of referendum without action from the legislature. Public financing for political parties was banned. Also, the new constitution introduced the possibility of recalling mayors, governors, or the president, but contingent on very stringent conditions.

Venezuela's 1999 constitution produced what scholars denote a "high-stakes" political system: the advantages of holding office and, conversely, the costs of remaining in the opposition were significantly expanded.[8] When the stakes of holding power are high, the incentives for incumbents to give up power to the opposition decline, and the acceptability to the opposition of the status quo shrinks. Immediately after the new constitution was ratified, a demoralized opposition felt the effects of exclusion and was deprived of any means to influence policy.

The political regime that emerged in Venezuela as a result of the 1999 constitution differed sharply from the *puntofijista* system. The starting point of that system had been the newly legalized political parties. With the 1999 constitution, the focus on parties was replaced by a focus on the presidency. Once legislative prerogatives were weakened, it became easier for the president to pack the court and tighten control over the attorney general, the comptroller general, and the Consejo Nacional Electoral (CNE), the electoral monitoring body.

Controlling the CNE, in particular, was crucial in accelerating this process of raising the stakes of office holding and increasing barriers for opponents. Chávez achieved control of the CNE by creating a transition council that governed legislative affairs in the period between the approval of the new constitution in December 1999 and the election of the new Congress in August 2000. This transition council, called the "little congress" (*congresillo*), was made up of members of the Constituent Assembly and non-elected representatives, most of them *chavistas*. Based on a set of transitory prerogatives provided by the Constituent Assembly, the *congresillo* appointed the CNE and enacted a body of key legislation.

In short, Chávez's success in rewriting the constitution in favor of greater presidential powers, and his methods of doing so, raised the stakes of power holding and threatened those in the opposition. For the first time in Venezuela's democratic history, the entire opposition (not just a few marginal opposition groups) developed profound doubts about the fairness of institutions and especially the electoral system.[9]

Chávez did not stop here. The next step was to rearrange state-society relations.

Act II: Polarize and Punish

Taking advantage of his new constitutional prerogatives and the declining autonomy of various branches of government, Chávez in 2001 obtained from the legislature "enabling powers" to rule by decree on a series of policy areas, mostly property rights in the hydrocarbon and agricultural sectors. Before this, in August 2000, he had obtained control of the nation's new unicameral legislature, the National Assembly, when all existing electoral posts, including that of the president, were subject to new elections, the so-called mega-elections of 2000. Chávez's loose political coalition, called the Polo Patriótico (Patriotic Pole), obtained over 59 percent of the vote for the presidency and 60 percent of seats in the National Assembly. Using his grip on the legislative branch, Chávez also threatened to use his power to change the education law to give the central government greater leeway over the hiring and firing of teachers and the curriculum in both the private and public systems. This move touched a historic nerve in Venezuela, where a successful struggle had been waged for the autonomy of private schools between the 1940s and late 1950s, and for public schools and the universities since the 1960s.

The enabling law, the erosion of institutions of checks and balances, and the proposed education reform provoked an immediate allergic reaction from broad sectors of society, shocked at what they perceived as gratuitous power grabs.[10] The opposition, made up of multiple sectors that did not always agree on many political issues—business and labor groups, civic organizations and parties, new parties and old parties, parental associations and teachers, and many former *chavistas*—began to organize national protests, including a two-day general strike in December 2001. By 2002 the country was experiencing the worst polarization in Latin America since the days of the Sandinista regime in Nicaragua in the eighties. Rather than pull back, the president responded to this rise in discontent by becoming more defiant, more dismissive of detractors, and more unwilling to reverse course.

For two years, from 2001 to 2003, the opposition seemed to gain the upper hand in this state-society conflict. The ruling coalition suffered defections in record numbers from the cabinet, the legislature, the voting ranks, and even the military. Interior Minister Luis Miquilena, a skillful political operator who had crafted Chávez's rise to power, led a large disaffected faction within *chavismo* that became more vocal about the lack of consultation over key legislative changes. On November 13, 2001, in a cabinet meeting that lasted almost fourteen hours, the president approved forty-nine laws, most of which had not been discussed with any social, business, or labor organization. The abrupt nature of these decisions created a political schism; a group within the National Assembly headed by Alejandro Armas and Ernesto Alvarenga organized a special commission to review the content of the new legislation. But the damage had been done already. Civic organizations, political parties, business groups, and the media reacted by stirring up discontent against the president. Luis Miquilena quietly left the government. Across the country, opposition marches and civic stoppages became commonplace. Some groups within the opposition, particularly those linked to the business community and the traditional parties, openly started plotting against the government, courting upper-rank officers to participate in a potential coup. A large international campaign by opposition forces was initiated to erode the democratic legitimacy of the government. Perhaps following precedents from Argentina in 1989 and 2001, Brazil in 1991, Guatemala in 1993, Ecuador in 1996 and 2000, Paraguay in 1999, Peru in 2000, and even Venezuela in 1993, where opposition forces compelled elected presidents to resign through massive street protests, Venezuelan opposition forces thought they could do the same against Chávez.

On April 11, 2002, nearly a million people marched on the presidential palace in one of the largest civic demonstrations in Venezuela's history since January 1958, after the dismissal of the dictator Marcos Pérez Jiménez and the transition to democracy. As the marchers, surrounded by loyal supporters, neared the palace, violence broke out; 19 people were killed and over 150 wounded. Military leaders refused to heed President Chávez's call to suppress the protest, and Chávez reportedly resigned as president. The next day Pedro Carmona, head of the Federation of Business Chambers (FEDECAMARAS) led a coup, with support from a small military faction, swore himself in as a "transitional" president at the head of an ultraconservative government, and announced the scrapping of the 1999 constitution, the dissolution of the National Assembly, and the recall of governors. But early civilian supporters, who had been shocked at the undemocratic nature of the first set of laws, soon abandoned Carmona, now shocked at Carmona's undemocratic laws. The military immediately pulled back, labor groups distanced themselves from Carmona, *chavista* supporters took to the streets, and—unusual for truncated presidencies in Latin America since the 1980s—the departed president was restored. Army units led by some of the same leaders who had challenged Chávez restored him to power in less than seventy-two hours.

This series of coups, as we prefer to call them (Chávez's coup against institutions of checks and balances, the military coup against Chávez, Carmona's coup against the constitution and elected officials, and the civil-military coup against Carmona) left few leaders in Venezuelan politics guilt-free. Yet the events ended up tarnishing the opposition's reputation more than that of any other group. Although civilian protests and interbranch crises leading to truncated presidencies had become commonplace in Latin America by 2002 and bolstered non-incumbent forces, in Venezuela the crisis bolstered the presidency and the military. This was in part because the nation was so polarized: Chávez still enjoyed substantial support, and the military, to avoid escalating societal tensions, opted for formal restoration of the status quo ante rather than for a call for new elections. Civil conflict was averted, but polarization actually sharpened. *Chavistas* became more hateful of the opposition, and the opposition more resentful that the status quo had been restored rather than reformed.[11]

Precisely because of its damaging effects on the opposition's reputation, the series of coups of 2002 also taught the government that it pays to drive the opposition to extreme positions. From this point on, Chávez never again sought reconciliation, calculating that provoking the opposition to irrational acts can actually bolster the president's popularity, at least within one pole of the ideological spectrum.

The 2002 crisis did prompt the mediation of the international community, but to no avail. César Gaviria, secretary general of the Organization of American States (OAS), moved to Caracas for several months to promote negotiations between *chavista* and opposition forces, with representatives from the Carter Center serving as observers. Negotiations soon reached a stalemate. Chávez remained unwilling to concede his resignation and to change course on his policies, and Venezuelan society remained polarized. Under the Democratic Coordinating Unit (Coordinadora Democrática), an umbrella organization comprising political parties and civic movements, the opposition remained unwilling to accept constitutional rules mandating the opposition to wait until scheduled elections. In terms of game theory, government and opposition were locked in a game of chicken, a dangerous situation in which neither party agrees to yield even though the stalemate leads to the worst possible outcome for both parties.

As the chance of reaching some accommodation dwindled, the opposition chose a second non-electoral line of attack: a three-month strike supported by workers and managers of the state-owned oil company, Petróleos de Venezuela, S.A. (PDVSA). From the time the oil industry was nationalized in 1974, PDVSA had been managed as a fairly autonomous entity, often referred to as "a state within the state" (see chapter 4 for a detailed discussion of the oil industry). Following the April 2002 failed coup, PDVSA's leadership feared for its autonomy. Indeed, the government blamed top PDVSA management personnel for abetting and participating in the political uprising of early 2002, and Chávez made it clear he wanted to have both political and operational control over the oil industry. To protect itself, PDVSA's top management organized a quasi-union, named Gente del Petróleo (Oil People), that recruited a sizable group of members from middle- and top-management positions. This group soon decided to strengthen its relationship with the Democratic Coordinating Unit, which it tried to pressure in favor of abandoning negotiations and launching a national strike. By late November 2002 Gente del Petróleo prevailed, convincing politicians and the National Labor Confederation (Confederación de Trabajadores de Venezuela, or CTV) to launch a strike. The Democratic Coordinating Unit called for a national strike on December 2, 2002.

Although public services, the media, banks, and leading food producers and supermarkets continued operating, many companies and almost the entire oil industry closed for the better part of three months. Venezuela's oil production came to a standstill. In just a matter of weeks, the country plunged into an economic depression.

Again, rather than negotiate, Chávez responded by punishing. He arbitrarily fired nearly 60 percent of the PDVSA personnel, including most managers, and assigned control of the oil industry to the military. Gasoline distribution collapsed. In large urban centers, certain foodstuffs and other convenience goods were in short supply or simply unavailable. Chávez persuaded the military and the international community that PDVSA had been used for subversive purposes and that the national interest required direct state control of the industry. The military gladly accepted its new responsibilities, and with the support of *chavista* militants and low-ranking PDVSA managers, production was slowly restored.

Once again, extremism hurt the opposition more than the government. Because of the economic recession that ensued, leading to a 17.6 percent contraction of GDP in the first quarter of 2003, public opinion turned against strikers, and the strikers began to give in. By early March, the oil strike, which *chavistas* had labeled an "oil coup," had been politically defeated.

Following the oil strike, the opposition chose a third angle of attack: a recall referendum. For the first time, the opposition posed a truly electoral and unambiguous constitutional challenge to Chávez, in part because previously no such constitutional mechanisms were available (the constitution stated that recall referenda could be scheduled only three years into a presidential term). The problem was that the constitution set high thresholds for this kind of challenge. To initiate the referendum, proponents were required to collect valid signatures from 20 percent of registered voters. Furthermore, to remove Chávez from office, the referendum needed to produce more votes against Chávez than the number obtained by the president in the previous election—that of August 2000, when he was reelected by a massive landslide. But in 2003 all polls suggested that the opposition would have no trouble generating these signatures and votes. Chávez's approval ratings were at their lowest historical point (see figure 2-1).

In response, the administration came up with several legal and administrative barriers to discourage the collection of signatures, another example of the use of institutional manipulation to confront electoral pressures. First, the CNE declared null and void the process whereby the opposition had initially gathered the required signatures with support from local civic associations specializing in electoral affairs. Instead, the CNE crafted

FIGURE 2-1. Growth of Real Public Spending and Chávez's Popularity Ratings, August 2001 to July 2009

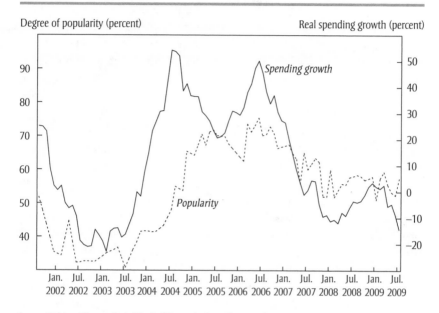

Source: Ministry of Finance, Central Bank of Venezuela, *Datanalysis Omnibus National Polls 2001–2009.*

strict rules for signature gathering and announced that it would directly supervise the process. Even under these strict procedures, the opposition again managed to collect the required number of signatures.

Second, the CNE declared void a large number of signatures, despite the opposition's compliance with CNE procedures. CNE forced the opposition to validate these signatures one more time, which required the opposition to mobilize signers yet again. At the end of March 2004, CNE finally agreed that the opposition had indeed collected more than enough valid signatures to hold a referendum, and preparations began to schedule it for August 2004.

Early in 2004 the opposition was leading in the polls; this was the administration's weakest moment ever. It was thus not surprising that the administration agreed to comply with the law in response to opposition pressures. But the government remained tough; it did not respond to the referendum movement by softening exclusionary policies. Instead, the state introduced an old tool in Latin American politics to deal with threats from below: vintage clientelism.

Act III: Spend and Deflate

Faced with the mounting challenge of an unstoppable recall referendum, Chávez deployed his now famous *misiones* programs. Up to early 2004, Chávez had been relatively inattentive to social spending. He had dismantled most social programs inherited from the previous administrations, even dropping aid for widely used urban day-care centers. In effect, social policies were minimal, and what existed was delegated mostly to the military under Plan Bolívar 2000.

This changed in late 2003. Alarmed over the massive movement on behalf of the recall referendum, Chávez took advantage of suddenly rising oil revenue to launch a set of social programs described by him as "missions to save the people." Once the referendum was scheduled, an astounding amount in public spending, almost 4 percent of GDP, was channeled into these missions quickly.[12] The scope and depth of these programs provided a sense of social inclusion, which symbolically contrasted with the last two decades of the *puntofijista* regime and first years of *chavismo*. This spending tactic had long-lasting political consequences.

Despite the program's inefficiencies, the missions helped the government build a stronger popular base and left the opposition deprived of means to compete against a state that was spending lavishly for the poor. The spending paid off in electoral results: in the recall referendum Chávez succeeded in transforming his low 2003 approval ratings, which had been hovering at 45 percent, into a victory in which he gained 59 percent of the vote.

Dismayed, the opposition claimed fraud. After a very superficial audit, international observers (chiefly from the OAS, the Carter Center, and the United Nations Development Program) dismissed the charges of fraud. Part of the problem was that a new electronic system of voting was used, and neither the opposition nor the observers had a grasp on how to audit such a system, and the government, of course, had no interest in an exhaustive audit.

Leaving aside the question of fraud and the auditability of automated voting, there is no doubt that the expansion in public and social expenditure (see figure 2-1) boosted Chávez's popularity as election day approached. Weeks prior to the election, independent polls were revealing a rise in the president's popularity.

Stunned by the outcome of the referendum, the international support for Chávez's win, and the lack of a credible audit, the opposition fell into a prolonged coma. So great was the reversal of fortune from a mere four months earlier that the opposition's political energy simply collapsed. The state had turned into a new type of machine—in addition to a penchant for power concentration, this machine exhibited now a penchant for spending like no other since the 1970s. Even the international situation changed, with most observers now recognizing Chávez's democratic victory and showing little interest in accepting any of the opposition's complaints. The opposition became so demoralized by this new state and this new international situation that it barely mobilized for the upcoming gubernatorial and mayoralty elections held just two months later, in October 2004.

Buoyed and elated by his referendum victory, Chávez maintained unprecedented levels of public spending to support the candidacies of *chavista* gubernatorial and mayoral candidates. In a country that had undergone almost twenty-five years of economic travail, this new conditional-but-still-abundant level of resources proved enticing to large portions of the population. As a result, he succeeded in taking control of twenty-one out of twenty-three state governorships, and more than 90 percent of municipalities. In addition, the government proceeded to pack the Supreme Court with twelve additional magistrates, all of whom had passed the test of being deemed avowed "revolutionaries."

In a span of only few months, the political atmosphere in Venezuela changed from one of heightened power competition in 2003 to power asymmetry in late 2004: electoral victories and possession of control of all branches of government emboldened the government and deflated the opposition, which now felt that any strategy was simply futile.

Furthermore, the government struck back at those who had signed the recall petition by publishing on the Internet a list of voters' electoral preferences that had been compiled through sophisticated technology. Locally known as the *lista Tascón* (Tascón's list) because it was publicized by a *chavista* assembly member, Luis Tascón, the document was generated from a digital database of signatures that CNE released to Tascón for transmission to the National Assembly. The *lista* was deliberately employed to induce citizens to withdraw their signatures or else face job termination and denial of access to public contracts and social benefits.

This type of punishment of the opposition has been one of the most blatant violations in Chávez's Venezuela of democratic principles—most specifically, the right to a secret ballot and the right to vote one's conscience without fear of reprisals. It also instilled fear among opposition and ambivalent voters.

Exhausted, discouraged, and feeling hopeless about the gains from participation, the opposition failed to prepare adequately for still another upcoming election scheduled for December 2005, that for delegates to the National Assembly. Most polls reveal that opposition voters were going to abstain, and so at the last minute the leadership of the top five opposition parties opted to boycott the elections, claiming that the government never addressed their most serious complaints about the unfairness of the electoral system. The boycott proved to be a foolhardy choice: Chávez ended up with total control over the legislature.

In retrospect, the decision to boycott the 2005 election turned out to be the opposition's most serious mistake in dealing with Chávez. Essentially, the opposition handed total control over the legislative branch of government to the executive branch. The reason the opposition decided to boycott was twofold. First, the opposition knew it was going to lose ground in the National Assembly anyway. Second, the opposition hoped that the boycott would pressure the international community finally to listen and compel Chávez to yield to demands from the opposition. But the international community did not respond as the opposition had hoped. There was no international call for Chávez to postpone and negotiate, so Chávez neither postponed nor negotiated.

By early 2006 the opposition had virtually collapsed. Every effort to counter the move toward hybridity had failed, from mobilizing vast public demonstrations, to plotting with military factions, to shutting down the oil industry by means of a national strike, to holding a recall referendum, to boycotting one election, to denouncing corruption and power grabs. Nothing worked. The opposition got little support from the international community. Each successive election further weakened its power and was followed by fewer concessions by the government. In Venezuela, as in any oil-producing country where the state runs the industry, the government controls the "oxygen tank"—the money that flows from oil—and most of the oxygen went to Chávez's supporters. Deprived of oxygen, the opposition virtually stopped breathing. In 2006, in contrast to 2003, everything looked bleak for the opposition.

Act IV: The 2006 Presidential Election and the Opposition's Dilemmas

Heading toward the 2006 election, the opposition was faced with a series of dilemmas. For starters, it was playing on an uneven playing field, a result of unfavorable rules and biased state spending. An even bigger challenge was to find a unified approach to the rise of a hybrid regime that offered some democratic channels while curtailing many others. The opposition essentially split into three schools of thought—those who believed in a belligerent strategy toward the government; those who preferred to abstain electorally; and those who preferred to follow constitutional rules, despite the flimsy guarantees of fairness.

The first camp argued that the best course of action was to "delegitimize" and pressure the regime by protesting. The second camp argued that abstaining was the only rational choice, since the game was stacked irremediably in favor of the government. The third camp argued that promoting protests and electoral abstention only favored Chávez.

In addition there was internal division within the third camp (those who intended to participate in the flawed electoral system) arising from different ideological orientations and political styles. At the start of the 2006 presidential race, three reputable opposition candidates from different ideological backgrounds faced off: Teodoro Petkoff, a former guerilla leader in the 1960s who had been planning minister under Caldera in the 1990s and editor of the respected daily *Tal Cual* under Chávez; Julio Borges, the leader of Justice First, a new party whose members included some well-regarded mayors in a few municipalities; and Manuel Rosales, then the governor of the western oil-producing state of Zulia. For a time it seemed as though an accord to select one unity candidate would be impossible.

To everyone's surprise, the three contenders reached an amicable pact to select a candidate by means of an opinion poll that pointed toward Manuel Rosales as the voters' favorite. The remaining candidates opted to endorse his campaign. This solved the problem of unity at the leadership level.

The other two problems for those in the third camp—fighting the potential voters' tendencies in the first and second camps to protest and to abstain from voting—were harder to solve. As late as mid-2006 many in the opposition, acutely aware of their lack of political strength vis-à-vis the regime, were still undecided as to whether they should even vote. Conditions for fair and transparent elections remained very much in doubt. Specifically, members of the opposition pointed to the following problems:

—CNE was not independent of the regime.

—The electronic voting system was susceptible to manipulation.

—The voter rolls had been inflated by indiscriminate issuance of a record number of voter registrations, some of them questionable.[13]

—Access to the media was uneven and overwhelmingly favored the incumbent.[14]

—The state was greatly exceeding spending limits on political campaigning.

The Government's Partial Reforms

In the months leading up to the 2006 presidential election the government addressed *some* of these issues, but not others. This partial response complicated the chances of unifying the opposition, since its members heatedly debated whether the reforms were satisfactory or not. It is important to understand this process of partial reforms since it seems to be a favorite instrument of hybrid regimes. The reason the incumbent finds it appealing is that it keeps the opposition in constant disagreement.

Regarding voter rolls, for instance, CNE allowed CAPEL (Center for Elections Promotion and Assistance), an electoral organization affiliated with the Inter-American System of Human Rights, to audit the electoral registration system. CNE also authorized a group of national universities to audit voter registration. However, the country's three most prestigious universities—Simón Bolívar University, Central University of Venezuela, and Catholic University Andrés Bello—declined, as they considered the statistical methodology proposed by CNE to be invalid. Neither CAPEL nor the study undertaken by other institutions found evidence of rigged voter registration, but they did confirm that the system did not fully protect against voting by unregistered voters.

Reforms were also partial on issues concerning the electronic fingerprint machines installed at polling stations. In the 2005 election for delegates to the National Assembly, opposition analysts had discovered that under certain conditions these machines could be sequenced with touchscreen voting machines in a way that allowed government officials to identify who voted how. The opposition asked for a manual vote, but CNE dismissed the request, arguing that the electoral law required automated voting, prompting the famous boycott. For the 2006 presidential elections, the OAS provided CNE with technical assistance to reduce the possibility of tracing voting records through fingerprints, but the opposition pressed for more changes. The government agreed to remove fingerprint machines from certain polling stations, but retained them in densely populated, poorer communities. The opposition claimed that by keeping fingerprint machines in these key polls, the government was deviously playing a "psychological" game: encouraging people to question the secrecy of the vote, which would boost abstention rates among opposition voters.

CNE addressed the problem of skewed campaign finance, but it focused only on regulation, not on enforcement. Because this was the first general election under Chávez in the context of an oil boom, the issue of inequitable state spending was uppermost in the opposition's mind. In response, CNE agreed to ban public officials from using official acts and events for electoral purposes and to limit each candidate's daily television advertising time—but it failed to follow through. The best example of a failure of enforcement was captured on camera. In November 2006 Rafael Ramírez, the president of PDVSA, called forcefully on PDVSA employees convened in assembly to vote for Chávez because the state-owned company was "red, very red" (*roja, rojita*), a reference to the color of the ruling party. Rather than fire the minister for breaking the law, Chávez congratulated him and urged other ministers and public officials to repeat the message. This time even the international community criticized the administration.

All told, some voting conditions improved for the December 2006 presidential elections when compared to the December 2005 legislative elections and the August 2004 recall referendum. But campaign finance conditions actually deteriorated, because nothing was done to restrain the unaccountable political spending machine set up by Chávez in 2003 and 2004. Even in terms of access to the media, the opposition stood at a disadvantage: the regime invested more than $40 million in upgrading the state-owned TV channel and the state news agency; established three other TV stations; acquired as many as 145 local radio stations and 75 community newspapers; and launched up to 66 pro-government websites. The opposition had no access to any of this communications infrastructure.

Partial (rather than full) reform of the electoral system placed the opposition in a dilemma. Had the opposition stayed quiet, a good many opposition voters would still have felt betrayed by its leaders. But if the opposition had rejected the reforms on the grounds of insufficiency, it would have hardened its image of recalcitrance and disloyalty, which in the past cost the opposition electorally and internationally.

As it happened, the opposition's leadership took a gamble in favor of the former option—accepting partial reforms, competing for office, and accepting the results. But accepting partial reform did come with a cost. The opposition had to lure to the ballot box not one, but two large electoral blocs: voters who were ambivalent about whom to support (the so-called *ni-nis*) and the pro-abstention anti-*chavistas*.

Ultimately, Rosales can be said to have run a successful campaign, even though he lost the election. Proclaiming unity among the different candidates and deciding to compete despite partial reforms opened the way for the opposition to return to the electoral arena, a shift that would pay off in 2007 and 2008, when opposition forces succeeded in beating Chávez's effort to overhaul the constitution and in winning several mayoralties and governorships. But first, the opposition had to deal with a new round of restrictions.

Act V: Misreading the 2006 Presidential Election

Venezuela's December 2006 presidential election result reflected the incumbent's post-2003 political renaissance and the opposition's demoralized mood. President Chávez won reelection for a six-year term with 62.9 percent of the vote, compared to the opposition's 36.9 percent. Chávez won with the widest margin and highest voter turnout in Venezuelan history, despite voter abstention levels of at least 25 percent. He obtained at least 50 percent of the vote in all Venezuelan states, including Zulia, the home state of the opposition candidate, Manuel Rosales. This time the opposition did not claim fraud. The CNE approved a manual audit of votes that confirmed the official tally, according to international observers such as the European Union and a local nongovernmental organization, Ojo Electoral (Electoral Eye). Although there were a number of irregularities in the electoral registry (for example, an unprecedented 31 percent rise of registered voters between 2003 and 2006), everyone agreed that these did not surpass the government's margin of victory in 2006.

This decisive 2006 reelection victory gave the president added momentum. Chávez had widened his margin with every major election since 2000; this time he increased his share of votes in the rural states of Amazonas, Apure, Cojedes, Delta Amacuro, Guárico, and Sucre. Only in urban centers did the opposition candidate, Rosales, prove competitive. In Petare, for instance, a district of Caracas that is home to the capital's largest concentration of poor voters, Rosales trailed by only 19,000 votes. However, voter support for Chávez was strong in the oil-producing states of Anzoátegui, Falcón, Monagas, and Zulia. Chávez's political party, Movement of the Fifth Republic (Movimiento Quinta República, or MVR), took an overwhelming share of the votes. Other parties supporting Chávez—Podemos (We Can), Patria Para Todos (Fatherland for All), and the Venezuelan Communist Party (Partido Comunista de Venezuela, or PCV)—took 14.6 percent of the vote.

The one glimmer of hope for the opposition may have been that the tendency for opposition voters to turn away from political parties—strong since 1992—began to ease. Party dealignment had caused political fragmentation, which weakened society's bargaining leverage vis-à-vis the state and, under Chávez, benefited the incumbent.[15] In 2006 fragmentation of the opposition lessened: most of the opposition votes were concentrated in two nontraditional parties, Un Nuevo Tiempo (A New Time) and Primero Justicia (Justice First).

Despite this moment of glory for the government, one could argue that Chávez misread the meaning of the 2006 electoral results. The vast majority of Venezuelans who voted for Chávez in 2006, except for the most radical supporters, viewed his reelection as an expression of approval of the status quo rather than as a call for more radical changes. The incumbent was being rewarded for delivering a formidable spending boom, after almost twenty-five years of economic contraction, and for restoring political peace following three years of intense instability.[16] Instead, Chávez saw his reelection as a mandate for further radicalization, and soon he announced how far he was willing to go.

Act VI: The Government Radicalizes while the Opposition Moderates

During the period from 2002 to 2004, one could have argued that the government's political radicalization was a response to the opposition's rising extremism. Although we don't quite accept that causal argument, we recognize that it is impossible to refute because both government radicalization and opposition radicalization were occurring simultaneously. For the period since the 2006 election campaign, however, that same causal argument is easier to refute. The government became ever more radical while the opposition actually moved toward greater moderation.

For instance, the opposition's discourse became less extreme: instead of calling for Chávez's ouster or boycotts, the opposition stressed campaigning on behalf of opposition candidates. Instead of taking to the streets, the opposition focused on finding a basis of unity and mobilizing the vote for legal electoral contests. But despite the opposition's return to more institutionalized forms of discourse and behavior, the state responded by increasing its counterattacks.

Chávez celebrated his 2006 presidential victory by proclaiming that "nothing can stop the revolution!" Full of self-confidence, in a famous Christmas speech following the election he announced plans to hold a constitutional referendum expressly aimed at advancing a socialist agenda. This constitutional reform was part of a more radical phase of the revolution that involved five new "axles" (*ejes*): The first axle was using a new enabling law to change more than sixty pieces of legislation. The second axle was changing the constitution by means of a presidential committee (with no members from the opposition) that would offer proposals to be voted on in a referendum, including no term limits for the president and more stringent conditions for recall referenda. The third axle was redrawing the administrative political map at the regional and local levels to curtail the influence of governors and mayors. The fourth axle was expanding ideological guidelines for hiring and training public school teachers. The fifth axle was the creation by Chávez of still-unspecified centers of power at the submunicipal level, the so-called communal assemblies, to challenge the authority of mayors and other local officials. Chávez's new vice president, Jorge Rodríguez, who had served as CNE president when the recall referendum was initiated, labeled this new phase of the revolution a "dictatorship of true democracy."[17]

Chávez's speech also contained some rather audacious policy decisions. First, Chávez announced the decision not to renew the license of the oldest and most popular television channel in Venezuela, privately owned RCTV. The license was about to expire, as were those of several other privately owned TV stations. Despite international and domestic protest, Chávez went ahead with this decision in May 2007, becoming the first popularly elected government in Latin America since the 1980s to blatantly ban a media company from operating. The only reason given for not renewing the license was that the channel acted as a *golpista* (a coup "generator"). No court had ever ruled on this accusation, so shutting down RCTV was clear evidence of the regime's political bias in managing economic affairs, its contempt for basic civil liberties, and its low regard for due process. Chávez also announced the nationalization of the telecommunications and electricity sectors, as well as increased state involvement in other areas of the economy such as agribusiness and banking.

Response to this round of power grabs came from a new quarter: students at public and private universities. They organized protests against closing RCTV as well as Chávez's plans to advance a constitutional reform that many legal experts claimed would have required calling for a new Constituent Assembly. Chávez dismissed the student movement as "elitist" and encouraged *chavista* supporters to counterprotest, leading to a few violent clashes.

In the end the government proceeded to revoke RCTV's license, despite much protest from multiple international NGOs such as the OAS, the Inter-American Press Association, and Human Rights Watch. Yet the importance of this moment of protest should not be underestimated. For the first time in years, students in Venezuela managed to organize a national movement, with contrasting views, but united by their vision of the need to constrain the *chavista* revolution. An impressive campaign was launched to mobilize against the announced constitutional reform, especially against eliminating term limits for the presidency and diluting the concept of private property by introducing concepts such as "social" and "communal" property into the constitutional text.

Gradually, the movement against constitutional reform expanded to include key former *chavistas*. Two months prior to the December 2007 constitutional referendum, General Raúl Isaías Baduel, a former minister of defense noted for having helped Chávez return to power following the April 2002 coups, publicly read a statement against constitutional reform. In his statement Baduel informed the public of rising discontent among military officers toward the idea of reforming the constitution and eliminating term limits for the presidency, and he recommended that the public vote "No." *Chavista* governors and mayors also felt uncomfortable with the reform. They disliked the fact that banning term limits was a presidential prerogative only and not extended to regional and local authorities. This time state and municipal *chavista* politicians were unwilling to mobilize voters.

Chávez lost the constitutional reform referendum by a slim margin—his first electoral defeat ever. According to unofficial results shown on the CNE website in the early-morning hours following the referendum, the margin between the No and Yes vote was a slim 1.4 percent, but official results were never published. There are rumors that Chávez accepted defeat as a result of military pressure, although Chávez denies this, claiming that he is not "pressurable." OAS Secretary General José Miguel

Insulza praised Chávez, arguing that Venezuela does have a "democracy that works." Thereafter, students continued to be intimidated, close to 800 military officers were let go, and Baduel was sentenced in April 2009 on charges of corruption.[18]

Leading up to the next election—the 2008 election for governors and local governments—the regime came up with new means for humiliating and undermining the opposition's leadership: the comptroller general, Clodosvaldo Russián, produced a list of citizens banned from running for office because they were under suspicion of corruption. More than 400 politicians (subsequently reduced to 270) were banned, of whom more than 200 were opposition candidates.

Despite all these barriers, in the 2008 elections the opposition carried some of the most urban or populous states in the country, including Carabobo, Miranda, Nueva Esparta, Táchira, Zulia, and the Capital District (while losing in more rural and poorer states). A noteworthy exception was the triumph by Justice First in Sucre, one of Greater Caracas's poorest municipalities. This is not to say that government forces fared badly. Chávez's new United Socialist Party of Venezuela (Partido Socialista Unido de Venezuela, PSUV) won in seventeen states, defeating all dissidents and even winning in states the opposition originally expected to carry—Falcón, Anzoátegui, and Mérida—proving once again that it was a potent force in Venezuela.

Despite these wins, the 2008 election revealed a major shift in *chavismo* demographics. Before the 2008 elections the government could claim that its core constituency consisted of the entire "have-not" population in Venezuela. But in 2008 growing numbers of the very poor in urban and industrial areas sided with the opposition. Chávez's core constituency became confined to voters in rural and nonindustrial regions. Thus, the opposition's decision to return to the electoral arena after 2005 yielded fruit, increasing its standing in the polls and leading to victories in some significant contests that were bastions of *chavismo*.

Nevertheless, the opposition still had to overcome the limitations imposed by biased institutions, daily insults from the president and the ever-expanding official press, and a slanted playing field. This situation continued to place major barriers on the opposition's electoral viability.

In 2009 political persecution reached a new high point when the government began to target *elected* officials. Manuel Rosales, the former presidential candidate and governor and, after 2008, elected mayor of Maracaibo, was accused of corruption and had to abandon office and seek exile in Peru. Chávez publicly threatened other governors with similar charges. And in 2009 the National Assembly stripped the recently elected mayor of Greater Caracas, Antonio Ledezma, of his administrative responsibilities, leaving him in office but exercising only meaningless prerogatives. Furthermore, in 2009 the government enacted a new electoral law that essentially gerrymandered districts self-servingly, without any supervision or input from any in the opposition. Studies using 2008 electoral results revealed that the new law would produce fewer seats in Congress than would have been the case before the law.

Act VII: The End of Term Limits

Following Chávez's reelection in 2006, perhaps the most important game changer on Venezuela's path toward a hybrid regime was the end of term limits in 2009. By ending term limits, Chávez essentially did away with one of the few remaining potential checks on presidential powers still available, as well as challenges originating within his own movement.

Shortly after the 2008 elections, Chávez announced plans to hold another referendum, this one exclusively to seek approval for "indefinite reelection." In making this decision to rush into yet another referendum, Chávez was responding to two political necessities. First, he had always been interested in indefinite reelection and concluded in late 2008 that his popularity was in decline and he needed to act quickly to obtain this most important goal. The 1999 constitution both extended the term of office and introduced consecutive reelection for one term. The defeated 2007 constitutional reform included a clause ending term limits for the president. Most observers argued that this was the clause that Chávez cherished the most. That ending term limits had been defeated electorally in 2007 led many observers to conclude that calling for a new referendum on this question was unconstitutional since the constitution banned resubmitting to referenda any item that had already been defeated within one presidential term. Chávez's twisted response to this legal argument was that since the item to be voted on was a modified version of the defeated item—term limits of *all* elected officers, not just the presidency—the constitutional prohibition was inapplicable.

Second, Chávez was also responding to a problem that became quite serious in the 2008 elections: internal divisions within his party that came to the fore in the PSUV's primary contests to select candidates for mayors and governors. Factions within the party were challenging many of Chávez's chosen candidates, and this discord led to major defections and caused *chavismo* to run disunited (that is, offering more than one candidate for governor) in eleven states (the opposition ran disunited in only five states). Chávez's insecurity deepened following the December 2008 elections: two of Chávez's closest allies were defeated—Diosdado Cabello, who ran for the governorship of the largely urban state of Miranda, and Aristóbulo Istúriz, who ran for mayor of the Greater Caracas Metropolitan District.

Both the primaries and the election convinced Chávez of the urgent need to restore and safeguard his uncontested command of the party. For the first time since 2003, there was talk in Venezuela of *chavismo* without Chávez—an open discussion about a potential successor to Chávez, or even the rise of a reformed, leftist, and Bolivarian movement that would rival the PSUV.

Proposing the end of term limits right after the 2008 election was Chávez's ingenious solution to this new threat. Ending term limits for president essentially promised to end internal disputes in the PSUV by making the issue of succession a moot point. And, as noted, to get party leaders to welcome this change to the constitution, Chávez came up with the even brighter idea of proposing indefinite reelection for all office holders, not just the president. The trick worked: the party leadership, especially those in elected office, immediately welcomed this modification, and the PSUV campaigned united, in contrast to the disarray that characterized the PSUV's campaign in 2008.

Heading into the February 2009 referendum, the PSUV enjoyed once again virtually unlimited access to public funds and, of course, the biased support of the CNE. Tibisay Lucena, president of CNE, agreed to organize the referendum even before it was formally approved by the legislature. The goal was to shorten the time required to prepare the plebiscite and overcome potentially adverse consequences for the popularity of President Chávez stemming from the fall in oil prices and the global financial crisis that erupted in the fall of 2008. The change to the constitution was approved by 55 percent of voters.

With the end of term limits, Venezuela has essentially done away with a major tenet of Latin American democratic thought dating back to Argentina in the mid-nineteenth century. Then, Argentine democrats came up with the concept of term limits as a mechanism to protect the country from a strongman such as Juan Manuel de Rosas, who used his initial popular support to prolong his tenure in office and become a dictator. The principle of no reelection was also the initial slogan of the Mexican Revolution of the 1910s, against the dictator Porfirio Díaz. In societies where checks and balances are feeble, as in much of Latin America, term limits are indispensable to protect political systems from popular leaders locking themselves into office. If judicial, party, economic, and educational systems are weak, terms limits offer an extra check against clientelism. When terms limits were done away with in Venezuela in 2009, this check on presidential power disappeared. Chávez argued that Venezuela's institutions of checks and balances (all under control of his party) and the electoral system (also biased) were all that the country needed to contain the expansion of presidential powers.

In addition, the end of term limits changed the way that leaders within the PSUV interact with the president and one another. When succession is possible, the party is bound to have more open debates and internal competition for the top post. Term limits encourage the party's leadership to break into factions, each hoping to become the succeeding team, as was beginning to happen in 2008. Now that party leaders know that Chávez will always be able to run, few leaders will dare waste their time engaging in succession battles. Instead, they will spend their time on the best way to promote their own careers within the movement, that is, demonstrating their loyalty to Chávez. Competition will continue within the PSUV, but it will be directed less toward the president, at least for as long as the president remains electorally competitive. As a result, the end of term limits boosted internal party discipline to support the president, lessened the chances of fissures within the party, and thus reduced challenges to the president's policy preferences.

By winning the constitutional amendment to eliminate term limits for all elective offices, Chávez succeeded in converting Venezuela into the most hyperpresidential hybrid political system in the region. The 1999 constitution already guaranteed the longest term in office of any Latin American president (two six-year terms). No other constitution in a Latin American presidentialist democracy allows for indefinite reelection. In fact, because term limits exist in the overwhelming majority of presidential democracies, term limits have become today one of the "defining features of democracy."[19]

In sum, this process of regime transformation, we have argued here, occurred in different stages and through different means, beginning with the 1999 constitution. Although the acts differed, all followed a similar plot line. Majorities were used to conquer and manipulate institutions.

In each act a few institutions were targeted while others were left alone. This strategy of regime transformation by means of attacking one set of institutions at a time proved effective. Power grabs in one act facilitated further power grabs in a subsequent act.

This story raises a few theoretical propositions about the way in which hybrid regimes come into being and consolidate power. We now discuss a few of those propositions.

How Electoral Support and the Erosion of Checks and Balances Reinforce Each Other

In the years between 1989, when decentralization reform was introduced by allowing state governors and municipal mayors to be elected by popular vote, and 1998, when Chávez was first elected, Venezuelan voters repeatedly turned against efforts by presidents to concentrate power in the executive branch.[20] How did Chávez manage to prevent this electoral sentiment, so strong in the 1990s, from unseating him in the years that followed?

At first, Chávez was aided by the pervasive anti-party, anti–status quo feeling prevailing in Venezuela. After 2004 Chávez was aided by oil money. To understand Chávez's electoral fortunes since 2004, it helps to clarify the symbiotic relationship between political clientelist spending and declining checks and balances institutions. As the effectiveness of these institutions declines in an improving economy, the incumbent enters the enviable position of being able to increase spending while making it more discretionary. This expands opportunities for clientelism, and thus for gaining more votes, while simultaneously eroding institutions of accountability.[21]

For the sake of discussion, we propose four types of social spending: underfunding, cronyism, clientelism, and pro-poor. *Underfunding* refers to situations where governments fail to provide sufficient funds for a given social program. *Cronyism* refers to social outlays that are, in fact, concealed direct subsidies to elites, mostly "friends" and "family," in both literal and figurative senses. *Clientelism* refers to spending that, unlike cronyism, is directed toward non-elites, but is nonetheless still offered conditionally: the state expects some kind of political favor back from the grantee. Last, *pro-poor* spending occurs when aid is offered on the basis of genuine economic need with no strings attached—without political expectations of the grantee.[22]

All democracies engage in all four types of spending, although proportions vary from program to program or from democracy to democracy. The key question is whether a newly elected administration manages to change the inherited proportions. We suggest the answer depends on the presence of two conditions: the extent of political competition and the strength of institutions that provide checks and balances.

Political competition refers to the distance between the incumbent and the opposition as a political force. If the opposition is small in terms of votes, has reduced access to state office, or has no immediate opportunity to challenge the government electorally, then we can say that the opposition is weak relative to incumbents. The other democratic variable is institutional accountability. When presidents face constraints from the legislature, the opposition is better able to oversee the administration, target social funds, and contain the incumbent's temptation to use social policy self-servingly. All this favors pro-poor spending over vote-buying through politically targeted social spending.

Different values for these two variations in degrees of democracy (high or low institutional constraints, high or low political competition) can yield varied results in terms of changes in social spending tendencies (see figure 2-2). The worst situation, for the poor at least, is low political competition. If there is little political pressure because the opposition is weak, incumbents have little or no incentive to cultivate votes and to expand spending. Social spending will remain sparse or easily diverted toward cronyism if institutions of accountability are also weak. If, on the other hand, there is heightened competition, the incumbent feels a strong incentive to cultivate votes and thus spend among a larger group of potential voters. Still, this incentive offers no guarantee that spending will be pro-poor rather than clientelist. The best safeguard against clientelism comes from the other key variable: checks on arbitrary actions by state officials. In short, pro-poor spending occurs only when two conditions are met: high political competition and strong institutional constraints.

These propositions help to explain Venezuela's social policy under Hugo Chávez. The first stage (1999–2003) represented the political shift, following the approval of the new constitution in December 1999, from high accountability to low accountability. Not surprisingly, underfunding of social spending prevailed. The second stage, 2003–08, corresponds to a move from a situation of low to heightened political competition as a result of the opposition's new focus on the 2004 recall referendum. The

FIGURE 2-2. How Political Competition and Institutional Accountability Influence Social Spending

	Constrained by institutions	*Not constrained by institutions*
Low political competition	Underfunding	Cronyism (friends and family)
High political competition	Pro-poor spending	Clientelism

Source: Javier Corrales and Michael Penfold, "Venezuela: Crowding out the Opposition," *Journal of Democracy* 18, no. 2 (April 2007).

rise in political competition prompted the executive branch to spend, and declining accountability allowed it to spend opportunistically.

No precise measures of the magnitude of social spending under Chávez are available. One indicator that can be used is the accumulated fiscal deficit for 2006, which reached 2.3 percent of GDP despite a fivefold expansion in oil prices during the previous three years.[23] As discussed in the next chapter, the government established a special nontransparent fund believed to hold more than $15 billion from the oil windfall. There was no legislative oversight; this slush fund was placed under the control of the executive branch through the Ministry of Finance rather than through the Central Bank. Direct presidential control over PDVSA also allowed the state to massively and discretionally fund social programs (discussed in detail in chapter 4).

With regard to the four types of social spending described earlier, Chávez appears to have distributed resources following different political criteria depending on the type of program, but clientelism figures heavily in most of them.[24] Although some programs were influenced by poverty considerations, most programs were used to buy votes at the municipal level. As a consequence, clientelism and poverty spending interacted closely. In fact, in the act of distributing cash, the Chávez regime was able to simultaneously "buy votes" while distributing oil income to the very poor. In other programs (Barrio Adentro and Mercal), spending followed demographic considerations *and* political criteria, namely, whether the governor or mayor was pro-regime. In these particular cases, poverty variables had no influence in determining the distribution of resources at the state and municipal levels.

The key point is that the combination of opportunistic social spending and declining accountability has decisive political effects: on the one hand, it fosters clientelism; on the other, it perhaps leads to an administration that is virtually impossible to defeat electorally. The opposition can never match the level of resources deployed by the state. In short, state spending is a product of democratic practices (heightened political competition), but after a certain threshold of irregularity, it begins to undermine democratic practices by creating an uneven playing field between the incumbent and opponents. Spending has given the Chávez regime an advantage in competing for votes: his government competes with words and money; the opposition, with words only.

Dealing with Ambivalent Groups: It's More than Just Oil Money

Clientelist spending has been crucial for Chávez to win elections and tame the opposition since 2004, but spending was not the only tool at his disposal. The *chavista* regime also relied on a less tangible but equally powerful strategy to sustain its electoral coalition: offering supporters impunity to engage in corruption and job discrimination. These two levers are not that different from the famous "inducements and constraints" typical of traditional Latin American populist corporatism.[25] The difference is that in classic corporatism, inducements and constraints were applied largely to organized labor; under Chávez and other neo-populists (see chapter 6), these tools came to be applied mostly to amorphous groups that were not necessarily organized formally.[26] In Venezuela, a key component of these groups is largely made up of nonideologized voters, that is, those who have not sided with either Chávez or the opposition, and conceivably could go either way, as noted above, the *ni-nis* (neither-nors).

Early polling has identified a significant presence of *ni-nis*. By July 2001, for instance, one reputable pollster began to classify some voters as "repented *chavistas*"; this group had swelled to 32.8 percent of voters by December 2001.[27] Some of these lukewarm *chavistas* became "lite" opponents of the regime, and others "lite" supporters—that is, their support was not blind, intense, or fixed. In 2006 as many as 30 percent of voters still were either in "slight" agreement or "slight" disagreement with regime policies. This suggests that radical leftist governments in a polarized electorate also need to develop strategies other than spending to deal with this sort of ambivalent constituency. Chávez's response was twofold: impunity for corrupt activities and job discrimination.

Impunity differs from clientelism in that benefits distributed pass from strong actors (in this case, the state) to locally powerful actors (the military, business groups). As with clientelism, opportunity for corrupt practices may serve as a strategy designed to attract nonideologized groups. To the extent that powerful actors can act as major veto groups vis-à-vis policy issues or even the regime's own survival, it is important for governments in polarized political settings to deploy significant resources to deal with these actors.[28] Moreover, in radicalized settings, the opposition becomes so galvanized that it may be vital to have at hand a mechanism for co-opting elites (military and business groups) as a potential shield against possible coups. In Venezuela, this might explain why competitive bidding was not an option for most government contracts and why few individuals close to the government were prosecuted for corrupt practices.

Job discrimination has also been a hallmark of *chavismo*. Chávez himself repeatedly boasted that the largest benefits of his administration—government jobs, state contracts, subsidies—were earmarked exclusively for his supporters. This practice is targeted mostly toward undecided groups. Ideological supporters of *chavismo* do not need job preferences to retain their loyalties, and ideological enemies do not change their minds as a result of job opportunities.

To practice job discrimination, it was therefore necessary to have knowledge of voters' preference. The best-known examples of government access to voting behavior concerned the *lista Tascón*, described earlier, which was used to blackmail voters before the recall referendum and punish them afterward. The public dissemination of voter data was bad enough, but some months later the government topped even this. In order to enhance the common belief that the government had ready access to voter behavior, the regime also published information that it could correlate *lista Tascón* data with voter registration and identity card numbers of citizens participating in *misiones*, the *chavista* aid programs, through the use of a special software program call Maisanta. This created the impression that "Big Brother" was indeed watching, and gave the regime a sophisticated tool for job discrimination in the public sector and for vote buying.

Thus, the Chávez regime actually publicized, rather than disguised, its image as a watchful government. This is an ironic reversal of roles in a democracy, where it is the citizenry and the institutions that ought to watch the state, not the other way around. For Chávez, conveying this image of a watchful government was necessary to suggest that there were significant gains to be made from remaining loyal to the regime, and large losses from dissenting. An analysis of household surveys and the government-created list of petition signers revealed that voters who were identified as Chávez opponents experienced a 5 percent drop in earnings and a 1.5 percentage point drop in employment rates after the voter list was released.[29] This strategy of favoring supporters and hurting detractors worked among nonideologized and nonpolarized groups, which after 2004 could reasonably expect personal economic losses if they were discovered to be in the opposition.

Chávez's social spending and his offers of impunity and job discrimination led to a transformation of his initial support base. Back in 1998, the movement offered a progressive ideology that promised to free Venezuela from the stranglehold of stagnated political parties and repeated economic breakdowns. This agenda was pro-change but not radical, and attracted a vast majority of Venezuela's voters. Soon, however, the agenda turned radical. This move played well with the extreme left, but at the expense of polarization and alienation of a large segment of undecided voters unhappy with both extremes. Lavish use of strategies allowing for corruption, impunity, and job discrimination kept ambivalent groups from defecting and enabled the regime to increase voter support beyond what radical groups on the left provided on their own.

Reflections

By 2006 Chávez's socialism of the twenty-first century was looking more like Latin America's "hard corporatism" of the mid-twentieth century, sans the widespread repression.[30] In this context, the opposition has fewer and fewer mechanisms, or even incentives, to undertake the cost of halting authoritarian leaps. The problem goes beyond mere internal divisions within the opposition and the presence of disloyal groups within its ranks, crippling as they might be. At the core, the opposition faces a fundamental inequality in the distribution of political resources. Its only source of financing is private contributions, but even this source is jeopardized by the state's offer of impunity and contract favoritism to cooperating business elites.

A familiar notion in politics is that *unlimited* campaign finance harms democracy. Our take on this argument is that *uneven* campaign finance is a worse curse. In Venezuela, this unevenness was not simply the result of the state's enjoying more abundant resources, it was the outcome of deploying more resources and practices in the context of eroding institutional constraints. These practices have even come to include political persecution of elected officeholders and the banning of potentially successful candidates from running for office. This erosion of institutional constraints, in our view, is what generated the governability crisis experienced from 2002 to 2004, rather than the other way around. The Chávez regime was able to overcome this crisis by deploying such policies as polarization, selective impunity, and job discrimination.

To put it bluntly, for the 2006 election Chávez put together a coalition of radicalized ideologues and economic winners. Some of these winners were clearly low-income groups, but others, paradoxically, were old-time elites who did not look all that different from winners in the Punto Fijo era—military officials, government and state enterprise employees, and state contractors. There is no doubt that this was a majority coalition, but it was not mobilized for democratic gains, an outcome that became more evident as checks and balances such as term limits were removed. In other words, social spending launched in the context of deficient democratic institutions can neutralize their assigned role and turn them into tools of the regime.

3

Economic Policy and the Oil Honey Pot

Venezuela's regime transformation took place in the context of a distinct economic background—the most spectacular oil boom in the country's history, between late 2003 and mid-2008. Chávez's economic policy responded swiftly to the surge in oil revenue. When he took office in 1999, his administration was fiscally conservative and even friendly toward foreign investment. But when oil prices began to rise to unprecedented levels, the regime deployed expansionary fiscal and monetary policies, coupled with a series of nationalizations and other antibusiness measures that smothered private investment.

Accounts of Venezuela's economic policy often fail to report these changes in economic policy; their authors attempt either to label Chávez a radical antimarket reformer from the beginning of his tenure or to offer a sympathetic view of his state-oriented policies, drawing almost exclusively on a few social indicators. All of the indicators on which these analysts rely are inflated by the size of the oil windfall, and many social programs are politically biased. And yet these authors pay little attention to distortions generated by oil or downplay the administration's political biases in spending.[1]

Our account takes a different perspective. Chávez's economic policy *became* radical—heavily antimarket and distributive—only when the removal of institutional constraints *and* the rise in oil revenues allowed him to seize the opportunity and tighten political competition, as we argued in the previous chapter. A state that depends so heavily on one sector faces diminished incentives to stimulate the growth of other sectors when the main sector is booming. To some extent such states can afford to move toward antimarket regulations because they don't depend on taxes from business as much as states governing broader-based economies. Not all petro-states adopt antibusiness policies—in fact, ideology is a better explanation for this attitude than reliance on any one particular commodity—but oil unquestionably allows states interested in antibusiness policies to implement those policies more easily.

Beyond an expansionary fiscal and monetary policy, Chávez implemented nationalizations, exchange and price controls, lavish state contracts, and massive social handouts earmarked mostly for his supporters. Until 2009, none of this represented a *major* departure from pre-1990s practice. His economic model fits nicely into what has traditionally been called the macroeconomics of classic statism and populism in Latin America.[2]

In this traditional model, the state seeks to create an electorally broad coalition through an economic approach that focuses on fiscal stimulus, expansion of state-owned enterprises, and income redistribution to support constituents; in so doing it underestimates or discounts inflationary risks, external shocks, and negative reactions from the investment community to aggressive interventionist policies.[3] Such a mix of policies tends to be anchored in artificially fixed exchange rates. Eventually, these rates generate price distortions, capital flight, and economic pressure on the balance of payments. As pressure mounts, governments fearful of political backlash spurn currency devaluation, send the economy into disarray, and introduce further controls on the private sector and even more nationalizations, which creates even deeper economic distortions. More statism is thus used to try to allay the distortions created by an initial round of discretionary statism. Venezuela under Chávez followed this well-known economic script, with the distinctive additional feature that oil revenues allowed the state to sustain these policies for a longer period of time.

One obvious reason why this mix of policies can be sustained for a longer period of time in oil-based economies is that oil revenue encourages imports, and this inflow of imports softens inflationary pressures. This is an aspect of the so-called "Dutch disease"—the theory that an increase in revenues from natural resources (or inflows of foreign aid) will deindustrialize a nation's economy by raising the real exchange rate, which makes the manufacturing sector less competitive and entangles public services with business interests. These conditions are discussed further in chapter 4. Also, access to capital facilitated by rising oil revenue enables the government to employ "market mechanisms" to buy out parts of the private sector, rather than engage in expropriation without fair compensation. Under a fiscally expansive model in an oil economy, as the investment climate deteriorates, the private sector courts the state as a potential buyer, investor, or banker of last resort; the state tends to have enough accumulated hard currency in sovereign funds and is willing to overpay for assets in exchange for a "silent" exit from the country. But in Venezuela by 2009, as one profitable company after another was nationalized, firms became more fearful of Chávez's politics and microeconomics than of his macroeconomic policies.

Companies that remained operating in Venezuela were expected to keep a low political profile, even as many engaged in rent extractions by manipulating administrative procedures, bribing officials to obtain foreign exchange, or undertaking currency arbitrage in the unofficial exchange market. Thanks to a fixed and controlled exchange rate, financial intermediation became the preferred game in town; as a result, a growing coalition of private agents colluded with public officials, which increased the stakes for prolonging these controls, even though the economic and social consequences of this mix of policies became increasingly onerous.

Living with this arrangement was easy enough for the public at large. Oil revenues provided subsidies for any number of consumer goods and services, from cheap fuel and foodstuffs to electricity and telecoms, plus a wide variety of underpriced imports. To be sure, economic doomsayers predicted this carnival could not last. A downturn in world oil prices, in fact, created a need to devalue the currency in order to fix the balance of payments and, just as important from a political standpoint, to quickly expand fiscal revenue to sustain populist spending by generating more bolívars for each dollar of oil exported. At that point, higher inflation rates kicked in and helped to undermine voter confidence.

In short, Chávez's economic model from 2003 and 2009, in contrast to his political model, represented more continuity than originality for Venezuela. Privileging state control over the economy and relying on oil, the model resembled the high point of import-substitution industrialization (ISI) as practiced in the 1970s, also a time when Venezuela experienced a spectacular oil boom. What changed this time around was the magnitude of the windfall in terms of the price of oil. But as in the past, statism did not attain the main goal of limiting imports. On the contrary, imports increased, capital flight expanded, and industrial diversification lessened, almost exactly conforming to the classic definition of the Dutch disease. This combination of new politics (concentration of power in the executive branch and constraints on the opposition) with old economics (statist controls and oil dependence) aggravated, rather than corrected, some of Venezuela's worst historical economic maladies.

Political Polarization and Moderate Economic Policies

Despite his current reputation as a rabid anti-capitalist, Chávez's rise to the presidency owed more to his political campaign against the *punto-fijista* political regime than to his critique of the economy. Initially his political goals were more radical than his economic plans. Although the team that drafted his first economic program during the 1998 electoral campaign was made up of left-wing economists, all faculty members at the Central University of Venezuela (Adina Bastidas, Jorge Giordani, Francisco Mieres, J. J. Montilla, and Jorge Pérez), Chávez's initial economic program was vague and plans were seen as contingent on the makeup of a new National Constituent Assembly.[4] Chávez's economic project at the time, as he described it, was to reinforce state intervention and promote redistributive measures without dismantling market economic reforms; he even compared these ideas with Tony Blair's Third Way in the United Kingdom. In Chávez's words:

> This vision entails three basic factors: first, the state, the need of an effective state that regulates, promotes, pushes, etc., economic development; second, the need of the market, a fair market, where the laws of supply and demand are able to exist, not a monopolized or an oligopolistic market; and finally, the individual, the human being. That is why we have talked about a "humanistic" project.[5]

In 1998, prior to Chávez's electoral victory, Rafael Caldera's government was struggling to push for market economic stabilization and microeconomic reforms. Oil prices were at their lowest point in years, close to $8 per barrel, which was generating fiscal strain and capital flight. Teodoro Petkoff, then minister of planning, attempted to appease markets already affected by the Asian and Russian crises by obtaining support from multilateral organizations, including the International Monetary Fund (IMF). In 1996, Venezuela had signed with the IMF an adjustment program aimed at reducing inflation, alleviating poverty and restoring economic growth, in an effort to complete the aborted market-oriented reforms of 1989–1992. The Caldera administration made an effort to behave responsibly by curbing public expenditure, fixing the exchange rate, and protecting social outlays. Also, with support from the Inter-American Development Bank and the World Bank, the Caldera government had put in place targeted social policies, including cash transfers to poor families with children, with the aim of increasing school attendance.

Despite the economic woes, the investment community in 1998 had a positive medium-term outlook for Venezuela, given PDVSA's success in attracting foreign investment for oil exploration and development. But in the short term, financial markets feared a possible default on foreign debt, especially after Chávez claimed that Venezuela had given up its sovereign rights when it signed oil contracts with foreign companies. Yet Chávez also publicly remarked that he was committed to maintaining the adjustment program agreed with the International Monetary Fund.

To further appease markets, as soon as he became president, Chávez reappointed Caldera's finance minister, Maritza Izaguirre.[6] Of the original campaign team's left-wing economists, only Jorge Giordani was appointed to the cabinet, as minister of planning. Early government efforts focused mainly on the fiscal adjustment process, and included some dismantling of existing social policies.[7] Funding was allocated instead to more ample safety networks such as the Social Security system and a new Social Fund, called Plan Bolívar 2000, to be managed directly by the armed forces. Oil contracts with foreign companies were respected, and PDVSA continued to honor investment commitments for new projects undertaken with foreign partners in the Orinoco Tar Belt. Chávez went so far as to approve a decree concerning investment protection and promotion that guaranteed stability of contracts and access to international arbitration in case of disputes.[8]

These and other measures suggest that Chávez sought to ensure economic continuity during his first year in office. In 2000 Chávez even opened telecommunications to foreign investment, a process undertaken within a market-friendly regulatory framework. Led by Diosdado Cabello, who has to this day remained one of Chávez's closest collaborators, this move was widely hailed by both the private sector and multilateral organizations.[9] Thus it is incorrect to claim that the political tensions

FIGURE 3-1.   **Economic Growth and Inflation, 1998–2008**

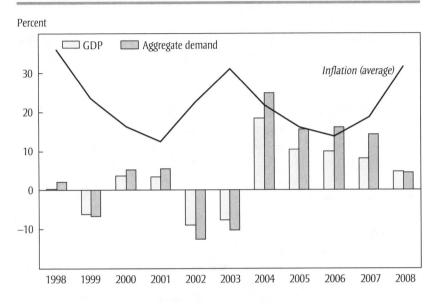

Source: Authors' calculations based on data from the Central Bank of Venezuela.

of 2001 to 2003 were the product of radical economic policies; such policies emerged later.

How did the economy fare at this early point of the Chávez administration? On the whole, the numbers were discouraging (see figure 3-1), in large measure because the international economy remained in recession, with downturns in Russia, Turkey, the United States, and most of Latin America. The drop in oil prices further devastated the economy: GDP declined by 6 percent in 1999, with public expenditure falling from 21.4 percent of GDP in 1998 to 19.8 percent in 1999. Yet despite this adjustment the central government experienced a fiscal deficit of 1.7 percent of GDP, showing structural vulnerabilities.

In a desperate move, the administration, under the leadership of Energy and Mines Minister Alí Rodríguez Araque, sought to realign Venezuela's oil quotas with those of the Organization of the Petroleum Exporting Countries (OPEC). This meant PDVSA would have to bite the bullet on two counts—not only abandon its policy of increasing output but actually cut its own production—output levels by foreign companies operating in the Orinoco Tar Belt under joint investment projects with PDVSA were shielded by contract limitations. Worse yet, public revenue was further cut because PDVSA output royalties were higher in fields with light crude (totally controlled by the state-owned company) than those for pumping heavy oil from the Tar Belt (exploited under joint ventures with foreign investors). Chávez also supported Rodríguez Araque's effort to realign Venezuela's interests with those of OPEC as a key international actor to protect oil prices. In 2000, for the first time in twenty-five years, an OPEC summit took place in Caracas, representing a milestone to underpin these international efforts and representing a new departure for Venezuela's oil diplomacy. A few months before the 2003 U.S. invasion of Iraq, Chávez traveled extensively in the Middle East, where he even challenged U.N. sanctions by making a widely publicized visit to Saddam Hussein, justified under the argument that Iraq continued to be an important OPEC member.

By late 2001, unprecedented economic growth in China and India, together with the war on global terrorism launched by the United States following 9/11, led to an almost threefold rise in oil prices. Venezuela expanded public expenditures to 25.1 percent of GDP while deciding—unwisely—to fix its nominal exchange rate to reduce inflationary pressures.[10]

At the same time that it undertook bolder public spending, the government moved ahead with its hitherto dormant political agenda. By means of an enabling law, legislation was passed that triggered institutional uncertainty and activated political polarization (described in chapter 2). Two general strikes and an appreciated currency created strong incentives for both capital flight and speculative attacks on the bolívar, eventually leading, among other political factors, to the failed April 2002 coup.

By February 2002 international reserves had declined from $21 billion to little more than $16 billion, and the government had no choice but to devalue. A further push for devaluation was experienced after the coup of April 2002. The final blow came with the oil strike in December 2002, which slowed the economy to a crawl.[11] Economic adjustments, together with political polarization, had taken a heavy toll: 2002 ended with an economic contraction of 8.9 percent of GDP, and by the end of 2003 the economy had shrunk by another 7.8 percent.

By this time Chávez had lost confidence in the possibility of a quick recovery. He decided to curtail the power of PDVSA and tighten control of the market economy. Understandably, the administration after the oil strike had few options but to introduce exchange control to deal with the collapse in exports and protect foreign reserves. But Chávez also used price controls excessively, mostly to closely monitor private firms. He outspokenly threatened to nationalize firms that engaged in what were deemed "conspiracy" activities, especially by food producers—during the oil strike, a number of food and beverage companies had shut down their operations.

The oil strike became Chávez's blessing in disguise: it allowed him to blame the opposition and PDVSA technocratic elites for what in fact was mostly gross mismanagement of Venezuela's economy from the time he took office. From 1998 to 2003, economic growth was a negative 5.6 percent of GDP. Inflation soared to an average of 24.3 percent (although this was still lower than during the second administrations of Carlos Andrés Pérez, 1988 to 1992, and Rafael Caldera, 1993 to 1998). Poverty reduction had improved by over 10 percentage points, partially as a result of the oil windfall and the real currency appreciation, which curbed the cost of tradable goods consumed by the poor. Charging the oil industry and leading business firms with sabotaging the revolution enabled the regime to promote further political polarization and control over the economy. Meanwhile, oil prices skyrocketed, allowing the administration to launch a radical populist phase.

The Scale of the Oil Boom and State Expansion

Between the years 2003 and 2008, Venezuela experienced a formidable oil boom virtually unprecedented in the history of oil production in Venezuela. Figure 3-2 shows Venezuela's oil output from 1968 to 2008, together with prices for the country's oil basket in constant dollars. Oil production fell by 50 percent from 1968 to 1985, from 3.6 to 1.8 million barrels per day (mbd), and rebounded to 3.3 mbd by 1998, the year Chávez was elected. Prices for Venezuela's oil basket rose sharply following the OPEC oil embargo in 1973, averaging in real terms close to 29 dollars a barrel from 1978 to 1982.[12] From 1985 onward oil output expanded but prices dropped, bottoming out in 1998.

From 2004 to 2008, the second five years of Chavez's presidency, the average price in constant dollars for Venezuela's oil basket was more than double the average during his first five years. The scale of the oil boom exceeded that enjoyed by Venezuela in the late seventies,

FIGURE 3-2. **Venezuela's Oil Output and Basket Prices, 1968–2008**

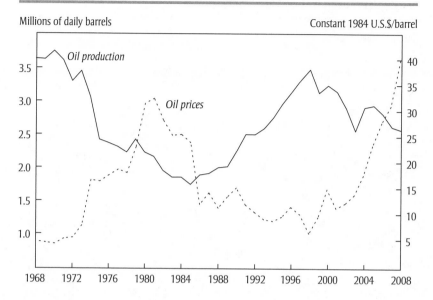

Source: Authors' calculations based on data from the Venezuela Ministry of Oil and Energy.

for output was significantly higher. In fact, Venezuela in 2008 produced 1 mbd more than average oil output from 1974 to 1982, despite a PDVSA output decline of almost 700,000 mbd during Chávez's first decade in power. In 2008, oil revenue was 155 percent higher than at the previous peak, in 1981.

Between 1981–89 and 1991–98, Venezuela experienced a profound dip in terms of oil income per capita, recovering only after 2004 with the steep surge in oil prices. From 2004 to 2008, per capita oil income in Venezuela remained impressive, despite significant population growth (figure 3-3). At the height of the 1974 OPEC oil embargo the country's per capita oil revenue peaked at $1,774 in constant terms. After dropping dramatically in the 1980s and 1990s, per capita oil income surged again in the 2000s, reaching $1,454 in constant terms by 2008.

Growth in oil revenue had an immediate and powerful impact on public finances. The price windfall allowed the administration to deploy procyclical spending to counteract economic contraction experienced in 2002–03, raising public expenditures to expand aggregate demand. In

FIGURE 3-3. Venezuela's per Capita Oil Income and per Capita Fiscal Income, 1968–2008

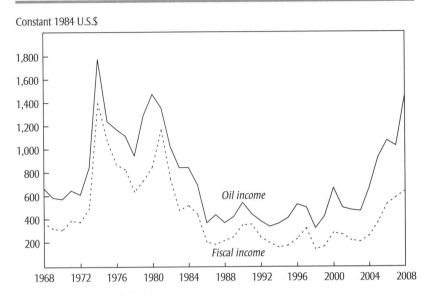

Source: Authors' calculations based on data from Central Bank of Venezuela, as well as Venezuela Ministry of Oil and Energy, Ministry of Finance, and National Institute of Statistics.

2004 public expenditures reached a robust 26 percent of GDP. Massive aggregate demand stimulus continued for the next four years. By 2006, central government expenditures surpassed 29 percent of GDP, significantly higher than the 18 percent level in effect in 1999. This new figure did not include extrabudgetary expenditures financed through the special National Development Fund (called Fonden) and PDVSA. If figures for outlays from these unaudited funding channels were available, estimated public expenditure in 2006 would have topped 35 percent of GDP.

The composition of public expenditures by the Chávez administration is a matter of considerable dispute.[13] Some specialists claim that central government social spending increased under Chávez, while others argue that in relative terms, social outlays remained about constant, except for expanded transfers to the Social Security system. According to the latter group, budget allocations for housing, health, education, and special social programs remained at the same relative level, while other sectors such as infrastructure and the military gained importance. Clarifying the

FIGURE 3-4. **Central Government Expenditures as Percentage of GDP, 1998–2008**

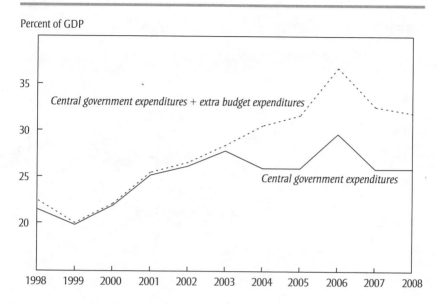

Percent of GDP

Central government expenditures + extra budget expenditures

Central government expenditures

Source: Authors' calculations based on data from Venezuela Ministry of Finance.

issue is critical to truly measure the government's real effort to redistribute income. But doing so would require taking into account huge outlays not included in budget data, beginning with support for PDVSA and other sovereign funds funneled to the *misiones* programs, plus unaccounted-for direct transfers to community councils (*consejos comunales*), social production companies (*empresas de producción social*), and cooperatives (figure 3-4).[14]

Sovereign funds such as Fonden were used to channel the regime's extrabudgetary outlays, which drew on hard-currency transfers from both international reserves and PDVSA. Fonden was managed directly by the presidency through the National Development Bank with no oversight from the National Assembly. A simple scheme was devised to maximize Fonden income: the Ministry of Finance would systematically underestimate the price of oil used in preparing the national budget in order to reduce the size of transfers that, under the Constitution, were annually allocated to states and municipalities. Undisbursed oil revenues

FIGURE 3-5. **PDVSA's Contributions to the National Development Fund (Fonden) and Other Social Investments, 2003–08**

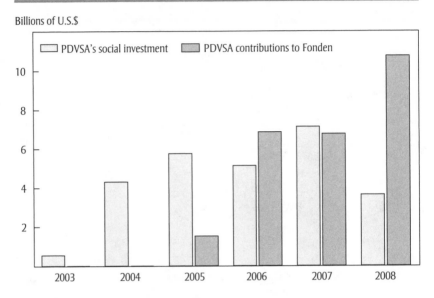

Billions of U.S.$

Source: Petróleos de Venezuela S.A. and authors' calculations.

that would normally have been assigned to either PDVSA or the Central Bank were transferred to Fonden.

The scheme for channeling funds to Fonden was facilitated by various laws passed by the National Assembly: in 2005, for example, the National Assembly approved a change in the Central Bank Law to allow transferring $6 billion from the nation's international reserves to Fonden; and in February 2006, the National Assembly approved another transfer of $4 billion. That same year, the president announced that PDVSA would transfer over $6.8 billion directly to Fonden. Given the level of support required by the *misiones* and other social causes, it is not surprising that funding by PDVSA channeled directly to Fonden for social spending became massive (see figure 3-5).

How large was the scale of unaccounted-for transfers made to sovereign funds for deployment at Chávez's discretion? Consider the following example: the 2008 budget projected revenue based on $35 per barrel of oil, but for three weeks in 2008, the Venezuelan oil basket sold for at least $116 a barrel, which was 233 percent higher than the budgeted amount.

Finance Minister Rodrigo Cabezas reportedly justified this underestimate by stating that it was a way to "minimize the risk" of an external shock; he promised to channel any surpluses for the benefit "of the people and only for the people." Such systematic underestimation generated an average revenue surplus of 20 percent each year—basically an amount that Chávez was free to use unaccountably.

This lack of transparency, at a time when oil prices were soaring, came with a hefty price tag. Public waste and graft expanded to unprecedented levels. A powerful example of public waste was the discovery in 2010 of 100,000 tons of rotting food in state-owned warehouses, all the more shocking given that Venezuela at the time was suffering from severe food shortages. The inefficiencies in the oil sector are even more serious (discussed in the next chapter). The Chávez administration is thus fraught with administrative incompetence.

Part of the explanation for this incompetence is low ministerial know-how and high ministerial turnover. Approximately 47 percent of ministers between 1999 and 2005 lacked graduate degrees in any field at the time of appointment. Between 1999 and 2008, the average minister lasted sixteen months in office.[15] A handful of ministers have lasted a long time, but the majority are transients. This is the highest turnover rate in Venezuela's democratic history, higher than the rate in the second Carlos Andrés Pérez administration (1989–2003), arguably the most unstable of all.[16] Low ministerial competence and high turnover rates combined with low checks on power wreak havoc in public administration, and this effect is magnified by the fact that the weight of the public sector has expanded under Chávez.

Corruption is another salient feature of the regime. Corruption is difficult to measure, but many examples get documented in the media. For instance, the Ministry of Finance systematically failed to comply with laws requiring competitive bids for pricing and underwriting public bonds. International banks and local financial institutions often colluded with the regime to place foreign debt in the local market, pricing it below market levels and then reselling it at above placement price on Wall Street.[17] In December 2009 a corruption scandal erupted involving a series of failing small banks, which were discovered to have had extensive dealings with the government and to have lent money to their owners and managers during the boom years. The minister of technology, Jesse Chacón, a long-time cabinet member and personal friend of the president, had to resign after his brother, Arné Chacón, the president of one of the implicated banks, was arrested on charges of corruption. A scandal involving the armed forces centered on a large sugarcane plant that was to be built in the state of Barinas—Fonden funds were disbursed for the project, but it was never built.[18]

According to the annual survey of corruption across countries by Transparency International, a Berlin-based organization that measures the degree to which corruption is perceived by analysts and investors, Venezuela in 2008 ranked 158 out of 159 countries. Corruption is defined by this index as the abuse of public office for private gain. In 2004, according to World Bank governance indicators, Venezuela was the second most corrupt country in the region, after Paraguay, which is known worldwide for having one of the most active sites of contraband in South America, Ciudad del Este. In 1996 Venezuela occupied the same position in the region, but overall perception was much better: 25 percent of the world's countries performed worse than Venezuela, as compared to just 10 percent in 2004.

Despite widespread public waste and graft, the economy grew by leaps and bounds between 2004 and 2008. In 2004 the economy grew by 18.3 percent of GDP, from the previous year's low baseline, which was due to the oil strike. Expansion continued in subsequent years, reaching over 10 percent of GDP in both 2005 and 2006, and 8.4 percent in 2007. In the second half of 2008, as world oil prices began to decline, the economy was still growing. Although the oil sector took a sharp downturn in this period (the oil economy declined by 8.1 percent of GDP), the non-oil sector surged by 12.8 percent.

Negative growth in the oil sector came about as a result not only of lower OPEC quotas to forestall the drop in oil prices but also of a decline in PDVSA production capacity. Growth in the non-oil sector was accounted for by a sharp expansion in aggregate demand, chiefly for nontradable items such as telecoms and financial services, which greatly exceeded growth in the output of goods. This gap between demand and supply was filled by higher imports and inflation.

Overall, growth was very unbalanced from 2004 to 2008 (see figure 3-6). Exports declined annually by 2.3 percent, while imports grew by 25.2 percent. Private consumption rose 14.8 percent, and public consumption by 7 percent. Foreign direct investment experienced a substantial decline, but overall investment, boosted by the public-sector infrastructure projects, expanded by 21 percent. Clearly, the government's fiscal stimulus was not affecting all sectors equally or sufficiently. The

FIGURE 3-6. Key Components of Venezuela's GDP Growth, 2004–08

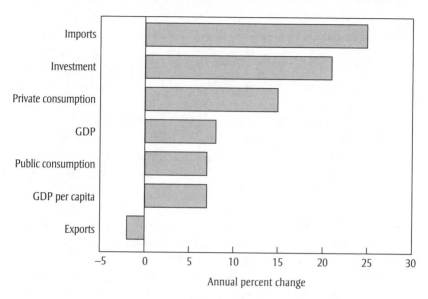

Annual percent change

Source: Authors' calculations based on Central Bank of Venezuela data.

dramatic expansion of imports and contraction of exports are evidence of an acute case of Dutch disease.

As 2008 drew to a close, currency appreciation coupled with a fixed controlled exchange rate and high inflation increased local costs, crowding out local producers and boosting imports. The balance of payments weakened, with imports rising and oil prices falling. Moreover, capital flight surpassed $20 billion. Sustaining the fixed exchange rate left the regime with a choice of only two policies: either spend international reserves to avoid price distortions driven by an unofficial parallel exchange rate almost three times the official rate, or limit access to imports at the official exchange rate to protect external accounts.

Crash Again

As in previous boom and bust cycles in Venezuela, the expansionary phase soon gave way to macroeconomic maladies: rising local debt, inflation, exchange rate distortions, declining oil production, consumer goods shortages, and capital flight. By 2008 the state had lost control of the expenditure side as liabilities surpassed revenue, creating fiscal pressure. The regime responded by tightening price, exchange, and interest rate controls, and curtailing bank liquidity, all in an effort to avoid deep austerity measures, such as severe spending cuts, massive devaluation, and higher taxes. Tightened controls led in turn to consumer goods shortages, economic slowdown, and greater capital flight. A condition of high inflation coupled with consumer goods shortages is particularly taxing on low-income groups in almost every country, even when there is economic growth, and it is one major reason why poverty alleviation in Venezuela came to a halt in 2008.

By early 2009 the Chávez administration was in a typical collapse-phase mode: withdrawing foreign reserves from sovereign funds, repurchasing international reserves from the Central Bank, curbing foreign currency available to private actors by more than 60 percent from the previous year, cutting the budget by 6 percent, raising the value added tax by 3 percentage points, and defaulting on debt owed by PDVSA to oil service and other local companies (many of them were later expropriated).[19]

Nevertheless, barring a worse downturn in the price of oil, the current collapse phase in Venezuela might prove to be less severe than those that occurred in the past. One reason previous collapses were particularly acute is that from 1981 and 2003, Venezuela experienced chronic oil revenue shortages, which precluded the state from deploying countercyclical measures to respond to economic contraction. As of this writing, macroeconomic strains in this current crisis have not been nearly as harsh as in the past, for until 2008 oil prices rose to levels never before seen in the history of Venezuela's oil industry. Oil prices fell before they stabilized in 2009, but as of summer 2010 they remained historically high.

Nonetheless, Venezuela's economy crisis from late 2008 into the fall of 2010 (when this book went to press) is one of the worst in the world, characterized by one of the highest inflation rates, despite having imposed the broadest price control system in decades; widespread consumer goods scarcities, despite massive imports; agricultural stagnation and food shortages, despite heavy agriculture subsidies; and a dearth of credit coupled with negative real interest rates, despite the expansion of state-led banking. These distortions were severe enough to fuel greater social discomfort and some political discontent. However, oil income was sufficiently high to keep the administration fiscally afloat.

Nationalization Fever

An irony of Chávez's rule is that despite being so critical of everything that came before him, his administration has closely followed economic precepts of the country's traditional parties, especially those of the 1970s, a decade when state-owned enterprises and state-connected agencies increased from approximately 148 to 268 between 1970 and 1980.[20] Venezuela under Chávez returned to a type of statism that looks like a modified form of import-substitution industrialization (ISI), the model of economic development that prevailed in most of Latin America from the 1930s to the 1980s. The government has a new term for this model of development—"endogenous development"—but in reality, it is not that different from previous episodes of inward-oriented statism. These episodes featured a vast expansion of the state into almost every domain of the economy by means of nationalizations, firm buyouts, expropriations, direct subsidies to certain corporate groups, special credits, and heavy spending, to which was added regulation antagonistic to business. As in the past, these policies have hardly delivered on their promise. Often in the past imports actually expanded and industry hardly diversified, contra economic planners' intentions. The same happened this time around.

The Heritage Foundation *Index of Economic Freedom,* which ranks countries according to their level of state intervention, shows Venezuela's descent into a more state-centric economy under Chávez: Venezuela received one of the lowest scores in 2010 and saw one of the steepest drops from 1999 to 2010 in the world.

State-owned enterprises expanded in all sectors, sometimes by heavy-handed means. New state-owned firms include the airline Conviasa and PDVSA affiliates that run social programs. Nationalizations range from CANTV, the publicly traded telecom, to AES-Electricidad de Caracas, the steelmaker SIDOR, and four foreign-owned cement companies. Expropriations include seventy-four oil-service providers and more than forty factories and companies. International oil companies operating joint ventures in the Orinoco Tar Belt were also forced to turn them over to PDVSA. Also, directly in line with ISI, the regime relied heavily on price and exchange rate controls; exchange-rate controls led to the development of two exchange rates, the official one and a "parallel" or floating unofficial one. In 2010, a third official exchange rate was announced together with currency devaluation.

Chávez often justifies the growth of state-owned enterprises as necessary to regain control over sectors deemed "strategic." But as occurred in previous ISI episodes, state expansion was deployed less for strategic than for political gains, mostly to court certain labor groups. Often the government would encourage *chavista*-connected labor organizations to disrupt work, driving a firm to bankruptcy, which the regime then used as justification for taking it over. This is what occurred with Constructora Nacional de Válvulas (a valve manufacturer for the oil industry) and Venepal (a paper products mill).[21] Another way to soften resistance to takeovers was to promise workers expanded employment and relaxed productivity standards following any given nationalization; this happened with the nationalization of the steelmaker SIDOR.

Whichever the route, the result was the same: the state became the principal economic agent in a particular region or among a group of workers, which increased the regime's co-optation capacity. Some authors have argued that this political bias made Chávez's nationalizations "qualitatively different" from previous means for strengthening state power, but this difference seems to be overstated.[22] Similar political intentions have been identified in previous episodes of statism in Latin America.[23]

A political motive behind these nationalizations was to increase the size of the workforce under state control. Between 2007 and mid-2008, when the pace of nationalizations picked up, the state brought almost 41,400 new workers onto the state payroll, a 7.2 percent increase from early 2007 and a 53.5 percent increase from the start of the Chávez administration. The total change was from 1.4 million to 2.1 million workers on the state payroll. In contrast, the private sector had expanded its payroll by only 28 percent since 1999 (from 7.3 million to 9.4 million).[24] Because private-sector job creation has lagged seriously behind the public sector, the economy has been left with an astoundingly large employment shortfall of approximately 8.7 percent of the workforce by early 2009 despite the massive fiscal stimulus of 2003–08.

Not only the motives, but also the outcomes of Venezuela's statism seemed to repeat previous patterns. The public sector became bloated with labor, while productivity plummeted. PDVSA provided the best illustration: in 2009, the minister of energy and the president of PDVSA announced that the company's payroll had increased by 266.7 percent, going from 30,000 to 80,000 employees since 1998, when Chávez took office.[25] In the meantime, the company's productivity declined, as measured in terms of barrels per day produced (see chapter 4).

Despite similarities, there are at least two major differences between classic ISI and Chávez's "endogenous development." First, the Chávez administration made little effort to restrict imports. Tariffs and import quotas did exist (for example, in auto parts), but these were not high, widespread, or rigid. In fact, the government relied on an avalanche of imports to fight inflation (by exerting downward pressure on prices) and mitigate recurring consumer goods shortages. To the extent that import limitations existed, they were implemented by means of exchange control: importers had to apply for dollars at a designated government agency, and the agency restricted the number of dollars it sold. Hence, Venezuela experienced an import boom that was inconsistent with classic ISI, although consistent with the import spree that took place during Venezuela's first oil boom, under Carlos Andrés Pérez, when imports registered an average 33.7 annual growth from 1973 to 1978.[26] In fact, during the market-reform period of the second Carlos Andrés Pérez administration (1989 to 1993), often billed as a period of trade-induced deindustrialization, imports actually declined.

An even greater departure from traditional ISI was the dearth of private investment in manufacturing and other industrial activities. This contrasts sharply with policy from 1960 to 1990, when investment in industrial activities expanded, in defiance of traditional resource-curse theories that predict export booms to produce deindustrialization.[27] The decline in private investment under Chávez was noteworthy in both oil and non-oil activities.

By neglecting private investment, the state was shifting onto the public sector the entire burden of meeting the country's investment needs. Private investment was not forthcoming, largely because the government did very little, other than offer a fiscal stimulus, to create a business-friendly environment. The World Bank's *Ease of Doing Business Index,* which ranks countries in terms of domestic investment climate, had by 2008 placed Venezuela near the bottom of the list.[28]

These economic policies—openness to imports combined with unfriendly business regulations—led, of course, to fewer private industries. From 2001 to 2006 the number of private manufacturing firms in Venezuela declined by 13 percent, while food- and beverage-related industries declined by 8.4 percent.[29] Another outcome was capital flight following 2006. This combination—decline in number of firms coupled with increased capital flight—was shocking for a country undergoing the biggest consumer goods boom in decades. But it was highly predictable in the context of a pro-imports, anti-investment economic model. The worst economic outcomes from the resource curse—oil booms leading to deindustrialization—had never transpired in Venezuela, at least until the 1980s. Under Chávez, these effects were in full swing.[30]

Like most heavy-handed statist models, the *chavista* political economy contained a built-in mechanism for generating its own demand. The regime brought on adverse business conditions for many sectors, which led to a rise in the cost of doing business (through price controls in the context of inflation, exchange rate restrictions, labor unrest, onerous taxation, and inconsistent rules). Companies responded by laying off workers or underutilizing capacity, or both. The government would then use this outcome as an excuse for taking over the sector.

In a famous critique of capitalism, Charles Lindblom argued that the private sector could hold the government hostage because it can always threaten politicians with unemployment and thus force them to adopt business-friendly policies.[31] The leaders of the *chavismo* movement discovered that a petro-state could reverse this relationship: the state can afford to corner the private sector into underperformance and thus generate demand for more state intervention.

In a non-resource-based economy this model would be unsustainable: at some point the state would run out of funds. In a petro-state enjoying an oil-price boom such as Venezuela's from 2003 to 2008, the model proved more durable because both supply and demand were feeding on each other.

One final domain where the regime's political economy exacerbated pre-Chávez political vices was cronyism—state economic favors for the privileged. Almost invariably, state contracts awarded to the domestic private sector were undertaken without any form of bidding. In addition, mergers and acquisitions flourished in the five-year boom from 2004 to 2008, during which a good many buyers were individuals and firms politically linked to the government. Some of these mergers and acquisitions took place in the financial sector. In mid-2009, for instance, a leading insurance company, La Previsora, was acquired by Baninvest, an investment firm headed by Arné Chacón, the brother of Jesse Chacón, the minister of science, technology, and intermediate industries.[32] The transfer of state and private assets to private hands that were closely linked to the government—locally known as *boliburgueses* (a play on the words "Bolivarian" and "bourgeoisie")—led press reports to refer to Chávez's *robolución* (a play on the words for "theft" and "revolution").

The Exchange Control and Electricity Crises:
More Scarcity and Darkness

By the end of 2008, the expected failures of Chávez's misguided macro-economic policies had surfaced. Freezing the exchange rate, expanding aggregate demand by means of unsustainable fiscal spending, and anti-business regulations fueled capital flight and high inflation. As already mentioned, an overvalued bolívar promoted a level of imports the Central Bank was unable to fully accommodate. This became clear when oil prices turned downward and revenue began to decline, creating further pressures on the balance of payments. Soon the authorities had no choice but to allow the private sector to buy dollars in the parallel exchange market to pay for imports, which generated enormous inflationary pressures and sent the unofficial exchange rate through the roof. Venezuela's spectacular consumption boom came to an abrupt end. By 2009 the economy had shrunk by 3.3 percent of GDP.

The regime was also facing a fiscal crisis that could only be handled through a massive devaluation. Expenditures spiraled as a result of costs ranging from the rise in the public-sector payroll and benefits to payments for successive nationalizations and expropriations, support for *misiones* and other social outlays, and coverage for the loss-making and badly managed state-owned enterprises. Equally important, for PDVSA a frozen exchange rate combined with high inflation implied a huge increase in local currency operational costs, which reduced the oil company's capacity to make fiscal contributions. By the final quarter of 2009, the projected fiscal deficit reached 5.7 percent of GDP, and the prospect for funding the deficit by issuing additional external debt was limited by uncertainty in world financial markets.

Further fiscal pressures evolved as the year came to a close, resulting from inadequate regulatory controls over the financial sector. Cronies closely linked to the regime managed to use deposits available in several small banks to finance the acquisition of institutions. Soon the government intervened to stop the banks from handling these money transfers, but according to informal accounts, the government had to replace several billion dollars in private and public funds on deposit at these banks.[33] The banking crisis that ensued triggered a conflict among *chavista* factions, forcing President Chávez to crack down on some of the *boliburgueses*: both Arné Chacón (brother of long-time minister Jesse Chacón) and Ricardo Fernández Barrueco (a leading agribusiness figure closely linked to the armed forces and Mercal) were arrested.[34] In the aftermath of the banking crisis, several brokerage houses were closed, and their owners charged with fraud and arrested.

By early 2010, the much-anticipated mega-devaluation finally arrived: the official exchange rate (until then fixed at Bs. 2.15 to the dollar) was devalued to a new dual rate, an official rate of Bs. 2.60 and a second official rate at Bs. 4.30, plus a floating unofficial rate, which the government promised to keep down—with no success.[35] Although devaluation was expected, economic agents were forced to further adjust prices. Strict measures against price rises by retailers were announced. The military was called in to monitor the pricing behavior of retailers, and the government proceeded to expropriate a large chain of supermarkets owned by the French multinational Casino. Such takeovers at the retail level were unprecedented, with the exception of the recent expropriation of a shopping mall owned by a leading construction firm, Grupo Cohen.

Overall, Chávez has responded to the economic crash by accelerating nationalizations, which increased from seventeen cases in 2007 to 174 cases by mid-2010. Previously, in the mid-2000s, Chávez's nationalizations focused mostly on "unproductive" lands, but after 2007 the focus shifted mostly to industrial firms in the energy and food processing and retailing sectors. The Confederación Venezolana de Industriales (Venzuelan Confederation of Industries, known as Conindustria) estimates that the total bill for nationalizations amounts to 11 points of the gross domestic product.[36] The outcome of this statist stampede has been a deteriorated investment climate, with all large firms now worried that they too could become government targets.

In tandem with the 2010 devaluation, Chávez announced the need to ration electricity. A dearth of public investment in thermal generation, together with a drought brought about by the weather phenomenon El Niño that affected installed hydroelectric capacity, threatened the country's ability to meet existing demand for power and light. As electricity outages increased, even offices and shopping facilities shut down. Further damage was inflicted on existing industry and the economy at large, dampening Chávez's support in polls. As a desperate measure to save electricity, the government declared all of Easter week 2010 a national holiday for nonessential workers in the public and private sectors. During the first half of 2010, analysts were fixated on the water level at Venezuela's Guri Dam and its hydroelectric plant; the level of the lake behind the dam was dropping to the dangerous level of 240 meters (about 260 yards) above sea level, the point at which the bulk of the dam's turbines would have to be shut down, depriving Venezuela of its primary power source. Venezuela's thermoelectric sector went into a crisis as well, as just one unit of the four at Planta Centro, the country's main thermoelectric plant, was operational, and the plant was experiencing technical failures, causing additional strain on the country's other plants.

Weather explains much of Venezuela's electricity crisis, but three hall-marks of Chávez's political economy—neglect of investment, incompetence, and tolerance for corruption among its ranks—played a role as well. Despite early warnings, the government did not start to worry about the state of disrepair of the electricity sector until too late, an example of the tendency of the government to neglect infrastructure investments. Furthermore, corruption impaired the repair operations. Many of the invoices for electricity equipment are believed to be for highly inflated costs, which allows officials placing the orders to siphon a substantial portion of the payments into their pockets. Officials apparently place purchase orders without consulting engineers, resulting in the acquisition of equipment that is unusable but leading to huge economic gains to the actors involved.[37] Thus, energy-rich Venezuela went into the dark in 2010 because of the weather and the government's political priorities of favoring consumption over investment, and applying the law mostly to enemies and seldom to friends.

Reflections

The word "revolution" has two meanings: radical change or repeating cycles. Chávez's "Bolivarian revolution" encompasses both meanings, but in different realms. In politics, Chávez has introduced radical change—greater restrictions on and obstacles for the opposition, less transparency in governance, and heightened power concentration. In the economic realm, on the other hand, he has repeated old vices—dependence on oil for state revenues, the exercise of state power for political goals, verging on classic ISI, and so-called "ax-relax-collapse" economic policy cycles.[38]

On the issue of sustainability, some consider that because the Chávez regime is repeating economic mistakes of the past, the system is likely to crumble, much like the political regime that unraveled in the 1990s, a victim of economic mismanagement. This time, however, the regime may prove more resilient, for at least two reasons. First, oil prices by 2010 remained relatively high. And second, research has shown that economic downturns do not jeopardize the survival of autocracies as much as they jeopardize the survival of democracies.[39] *Chavismo* is of course not an autocracy, but rather a hybrid regime. An economic downturn no doubt would hurt the regime's competitiveness, but the regime has acquired enough autocratic features so that it could very well survive the crisis, although with some cracks in its political structure.

In this sense, the Chávez regime owes its consolidation partly to high dependence on oil flows, yet its duration in office may not depend as much on oil as could be expected. An oil bust, or an economic downturn, will certainly lead to cracks in the system and even spawn political opportunities for opponents, but will not necessarily mean that *chavismo*, at least in the short term, will collapse. During an oil boom, economic agents in this type of setting are tempted to bandwagon with the administration, for siding with the opposition offers no payoffs. During a collapse phase, the regime, with its large repertoire of powers, can repress the cost bearers (if they protest), blame exogenous actors for economic misfortune, and continue to offer cronies and ideologues much of what they like—assets both tangible (some side payments and government transfers) and intangible (impunity from accountability and radical ideology). This is one reason that the regime, after 2008, has become more economically radical toward the domestic private sector, expanding nationalizations, imposing more stringent exchange rate controls, restricting credit, and constantly attacking the business sector. These steps could lead to regime stress, further economic decay, and even heightened political discontent, but not necessarily to regime demise. The connection between oil, economic development, and the resilience of hybrid regimes is a complicated question, and it is the topic of the next chapter.

4

Institutional Resource Curse: Seizing Political Control of PDVSA

Historically, oil has played an overarching role in shaping Venezuela's political economy, and its importance did not wane under Chávez.[1] The scale and length of the oil boom following 2003 are too obvious to overlook. Thomas Friedman, in an effort to capture the link between oil and democracy across countries worldwide, argued famously that the price of oil and the degree of freedom invariably move in opposite directions.[2] He calls this the "first law of petropolitics" and even invokes the case of Venezuela under Chávez as a perfect example. Nonetheless, positing a causal, unmediated relationship between oil and (erosion of) political freedoms is an oversimplification, especially when one looks at Venezuelan politics from both a historical and an institutional perspective.

There is no question that oil has come to be seen as an obvious example of a "resource curse" for both economic and political development. The resource curse refers to the idea that economies dependent on natural resources such as oil are prone to suffer chronic distortions that hinder long-term growth, diversification, and efficiency. This curse manifests itself in numerous ways: exchange rate appreciation, deindustrialization, high levels of indebtedness, overspecialized production, institutional dysfunction, and widespread corruption.[3] Public policies aimed at correcting this curse are equally diverse and, largely for political reasons, difficult to implement. Among these policies are macroeconomic stabilization funds, fiscal responsibility rules, transparency in oil contracts, and programs to strengthen institutions.[4] Oil dependence not only prevents finding political solutions to economic problems but also causes politics to become more contentious than would otherwise be the case, because oil increases the stakes of officeholding.

From this simple resource-curse perspective, Chávez's spectacular electoral rise and consolidation of power might appear relatively straightforward to explain: oil provided both preconditions and opportunities for Chávez to concentrate power in the presidency, including the ability to finance an expansive fiscal policy that in another type of economy would prove unsustainable.

However, the story is never that simple. The impact of oil on economics and politics often depends on institutional factors. This is true of Venezuela under Chávez, and for this reason in this chapter we revisit the simple resource-curse perspective. We show that the role of oil, at least on political development, is influenced by multiple variables, many of them institutional, making for outcomes that are not necessarily the same for all countries, or even for a given country at different points in time. We propose therefore the notion of an "institutional resource curse" in contrast to the simple resource-curse perspective. According to our view, preexisting institutional conditions shape the effect of oil, in boom times and at other times.

We present this institutional resource curse argument in three parts. First, we examine the role of institutional change prior to the oil boom. Between 1999 and 2003, Chávez enacted a series of measures that undermined the autonomy, not just of the other branches of government (as argued in the previous chapters) but also of Venezuela's oil sector. Before Chávez, Petróleos de Venezuela, S.A. (PDVSA) enjoyed considerable autonomy, from a corporate governance standpoint. Following the 2002–03 oil strike, Chávez dismantled the company's managerial capacity and took full control of the entire industry's operations. These institutional changes, at the level of the political system and inside the oil industry, occurred prior to the oil boom. Without them Chávez would not have been able to use the oil windfall to rearrange the relationship between the state and society after 2004 in the manner that he did and enable his hybrid regime to consolidate power between 2004 and 2008.

Second, we discuss how the politicization of PDVSA ended up hurting its performance and, in the end, the regime's ability to meet many of its socialist goals. Chávez's zeal to end checks and balances within the sector, to extract as many resources from the company to fund his political campaigns, and to jeopardize relations between PDVSA and private investors took a heavy toll on PDVSA's productivity. By 2009 Venezuela came to suffer not one but two types of oil busts: the one stemming from the sudden drop in the international oil in price in 2008, and the self-inflicted shock of having brought PDVSA close to operational and financial ruin.

Finally, we discuss the question of oil and regime sustainability. We agree that oil (with institutions) helped Chávez consolidate power. The question is whether an oil bust—whether externally or internally induced—has the capacity to undermine hybrid regimes such as Chávez's. Our answer is: not necessarily. Again, the impact of an oil bust depends on institutions, and more precisely, on regime type. In democracies, an oil collapse no doubt imperils incumbents, maybe even the entire regime. However, in a setting with strong concentration of powers, an oil collapse may not imperil incumbents or the regime nearly as much, although it can create opportunities for the opposition. We thus conclude with a series of arguments on behalf of the proposition that oil cycles have different impacts depending on regime features.

Oil, Institutions, and Governance

A broad and rich range of arguments can be found in the literature on the relation between oil and political regimes. Empirical evidence shows that the lineal relation between level of oil revenue and level of democratization is generally negative.[5] Considerable debate surrounds the issue of how to measure the importance of oil in an economy, but robust statistical results emerge when one uses the same data to determine oil's impact on democracy in different countries. Other empirical evidence also suggests that oil negatively affects the quality of economic and political institutions in general.[6]

Nonetheless, certain recent econometric studies questioned this correlation on the grounds of specification problems, finding it spurious, especially because oil's effect should be measured in long historical time series within countries, not only among them.[7] Other studies have tried to highlight the contingency of this relationship and the conditions under which oil can produce an authoritarian or democratic outcome.[8]

Apart from this debate over methodology, oil can, theoretically at least, undermine the functioning of a democracy while strengthening the hybrid features of a regime via multiple potential mechanisms. One often-mentioned mechanism is that in oil-dependent economies, by definition, the state does not require raising fiscal revenue domestically that much, but turns instead to international oil markets, a condition that ends up divorcing public institutions from citizens' watch. The state in this type of economic system can subsist without approval and control by the citizenry and economic agents, which increases the authoritarian or unaccountable features of states and weakens public institutions.[9]

Another potential mechanism by which oil can affect regime quality is through increases in public spending, especially clientelist spending, which swells during boom periods but becomes difficult to roll back when revenue falls. Rent capturing on the part of public and private agents also significantly expands corruption and ends up weakening institutional quality.[10] In general terms, oil dependence grants ample opportunities for incumbents to engage in clientelism and corruption for the purpose of building either winning coalitions or repressive capacity.

Clearly, state control of oil rents raises the power stakes among incumbents vis-à-vis the opposition.[11] Political conflict in oil-dependent economies becomes centered mainly on access to rents, which in turn is mediated by existing institutional arrangements. In authoritarian countries such access is mostly monopolistic, reinforcing the power of the incumbent, whereas in a democracy access is more open and, theoretically at least, subject to oversight by the legislature and other public institutions, although it can always be cartelized by a group of parties.[12] The importance of oil rents in defining how to compete in the political and electoral arena means that control of state institutions makes the opposition feel even more threatened than is the case in non-petro-states. Unless the state takes steps to be more inclusive, the opposition is likely to feel far more left out than opposition forces feel in non-petro-democracies.

Yet it is not entirely clear under what combination of circumstances oil will lead to hard-core authoritarianism, hybrid political systems, dysfunctional democracy, or stable, pro-poor democracy. Recent studies indicate that the relationship between oil and authoritarianism is complex and conditioned by both socioeconomic factors (such as inequality) and institutional factors (such as party configuration).[13] The relationship is not necessarily lineal. This type of argument is fairly consistent with studies of Venezuela, where existing institutional arrangements made the democratic or authoritarian effect of oil become manifest in one or another direction.[14] For instance, oil has been invoked time and again to explain virtually every type of political configuration in Venezuela's history, from the type of regime in place (democratic or authoritarian) to the nature of the party system (uni-, bi-, or multiparty). No matter what the political outcome, the explanations all place oil at center stage. This is further proof that oil can be linked to a wide variety of regimes. Furthermore, petro-states in general differ in their political economy, with some—Kuwait, Qatar, and Saudi Arabia, for example—moving toward greater market orientation in the 2000s, and others—Venezuela, Iran, Nigeria, and Ecuador—moving in the opposite direction. Thus, imputing too much significance to oil alone strikes us as faulty and excessively deterministic reasoning.

In contrast to simple resource-curse arguments, the best qualitative studies of Venezuelan democracy have shown that oil interacts with a variety of institutional configurations, leading to different outcomes across time. In *The Paradox of Plenty: Oil Booms and Petro States,* for instance, Terry Lynn Karl notes that the structure of the Venezuelan state at the time of the 1970s oil boom was a key factor in explaining the country's political excesses of the 1970s and the subsequent weakening of the country's institutional capacities.[15] Juan Carlos Rey and Daniel Levine found that oil facilitated a democratic transition in 1958 only because established political parties of similar power were able to reach a pact that favored democracy, after a conflictive historical process.[16] Moisés Naím and Ramón Piñango view oil income as an instrument controlled by political parties to create "an illusion of harmony," disguising the fact that parties had created a cartel for the distribution of rents mostly among themselves.[17] In short, the best works on Venezuela have always insisted that oil has explanatory capacity only when institutional variables are taken into account, and these variables are often shaped by non-oil-related political factors such as the incumbent's ideology or partisan powers, lobbying pressures, and electoral incentives.

Following this tradition, we suggest that existing institutions exercise a decisive effect on whether or not the resource curse materializes.[18] The interaction between institutional arrangements and oil rents becomes a central aspect when we examine the dynamics of political power concentration or lack of it. An existing institutional configuration is generally the outcome of historical and political conflict, independent of oil, whereas oil revenue hinges on international markets and fiscal arrangements agreed to by the state and participating oil companies. The two aspects must be examined separately.

When institutional arrangements ensure concentration of power by the executive, incumbents are able to employ oil rents (available from favorable market conditions) as a mechanism to remain in power by both patronage and autocratic means. Where institutional arrangements create a level political playing field, oil may not necessarily promote such an outcome, although of course it can still lead to corruption, rent seeking, and the decline in the quality of state institutions, which is what happened in Venezuela in the 1970s.

Governing PDVSA

In chapter 2 we discussed how Chávez gained political control in the different branches of government. Here we focus on how he gained political control over the oil industry. Gaining this control was made possible by changes in PDVSA's corporate structure that occurred in the 1990s and changes that Chávez introduced in his first few years in office.

Changes prior to Chávez

In the early 2000s, PDVSA's governing corporate structure no longer resembled that put in place right after nationalization in the mid-1970s. That initial structure was intended to prevent politicians from meddling with the oil industry. But over time, such an institutional configuration—the rules for controlling the oil industry—had greatly changed.[19] Little attention has been paid to this change, yet it is the underlying precondition that allowed Chávez to bar political opponents from sharing Venezuela's oil rents. This transformation in PDVSA's corporate governance took place before Chávez's rise to power and thus of course also before the oil boom.

Venezuela nationalized the oil industry in 1976, when political power was largely in the hands of two traditional political parties, Acción Democrática and COPEI. Party leaders sought to safeguard the valuable industry from political manipulation: they wanted to subordinate PDVSA to the state, yet ensure professional management of company operations. To achieve this autonomy, operational control was decentralized among competing national companies while supervision of the industry was granted to the board of directors, headed by a president directly appointed by the executive branch. A new charter was written for the state company. The PDVSA board of directors was in charge of supervising overall performance of the industry while politicians delegated operational control to professional managers for each competing national enterprise. Access to oil rents was managed politically by means of the budgetary process more than by direct party control or presidential control over the company's operations.[20]

A novel arrangement for the newly chartered PDVSA was worked out with major international oil companies. Managers of Exxon, Shell, and Gulf Oil stayed on for one year, working side by side with newly designated Venezuelan counterparts at Lagoven, Maraven, and Meneven oil fields. Each subsidiary had its own board of directors drawn from top management. The functioning of these operating firms was shielded from political meddling and control of the industry as a whole. This corporate governing structure led to competition among operating companies and fostered innovation and effective professional management, without sacrificing political control of the state over the oil industry.

All of this changed in the 1990s. A new governing structure for PDVSA was introduced following the opening of the oil industry to foreign investment. The company president, Luis Giusti, argued that PDVSA was competing both in Venezuela and abroad with international companies, and so the affiliated operating companies should be merged to make for a single, large, lean, efficient, and market-oriented oil giant. Independent units were set up to replace the subsidiaries: services, finance, procurement, gas, production, exploration, and so forth. Following this change, the PDVSA board of directors assumed a much greater role in the functioning and control of the industry, including former subsidiaries. Similarly, the president of PDVSA, who previously served as chairman of a holding company, now became in practice both chairman and CEO. This change, justified for technocratic reasons, perhaps unintentionally left the industry without adequate space to protect itself politically—a takeover of the top management would deliver control over the entire corporate structure.

Changes under Chávez

From the start of his electoral campaign in 1998 and later, when he became president, Chávez and his oil advisers championed a nationalist view of the oil industry under closer alignment with the executive branch.[21] Not surprisingly, this led to a less than cordial relationship with PDVSA's corporate structure early on. A series of confrontations occurred between Chávez and PDVSA management over the appointment of the company's president. During the 1970s and 1980s, the process of appointing PDVSA's president had invariably led to some discomfort for top management. But this had not reached the threat level, for professional managers would still be appointed to run the various affiliates autonomously. Following the corporate change of the 1990s, control of the board of directors implied decisive control of the company's affiliates and thus, the entire industry. This meant that the country's executive branch could end up controlling the entire industry through the top echelons of PDVSA.

Chávez's appointments of successive PDVSA presidents in his early years—Héctor Ciavaldini, Alí Rodríguez Araque, Guaicaipuro Lameda, Gastón Parra Luzardo, and Rafael Ramírez—generated considerable uncertainty and tension between management and the state. By and large, most board members appointed by Chávez had little business management experience, and shared ideological views incompatible with those of industry-groomed top management. Conflict was thus inevitable.

The 2003 oil strike handed Chávez a historic opportunity. Back then, Chávez was a president in jeopardy. With a recall referendum coming up, declining approval ratings, and ongoing street protests, Chávez had only one goal in mind: fighting for survival. Controlling PDVSA would mean controlling a large checkbook for political campaigning. Gaining political control of PDVSA would require displacing not just the president but the entire management and large parts of the staff. The move was risky, but it offered Chávez the promise of unrestricted access to oil revenues. The political benefits were thus too obvious. And so Chávez made the decision to take over. From a technical point of view, this move turned out to be costly, because PDVSA began to suffer a productivity crisis that continues to this day. But from a political-electoral standpoint, the benefits of taking control of PDVSA for Chávez were greater than the costs in the short and medium term, even if not the long term. Asuming operational control of PDVSA could very well be considered one of Chávez's most rewarding strategic moves during the early part of his administration.

Political Control in "The New PDVSA"

To achieve full operational control of PDVSA, Chávez undertook a series of moves. First, he named loyal followers to the board of directors and merged the Ministry of Energy and PDVSA under one single leadership. Second, he fired some 18,000 employees, including most of the top and middle management. Third, he altered the financial arrangements between PDVSA and the Central Bank. Fourth, he expanded the range of activities that PDVSA could engage in beyond the oil industry and energy sector.

FIGURE 4-1. Percentage of PDVSA Staff Expelled from the Company Following the 2003 Oil Strike, by Department

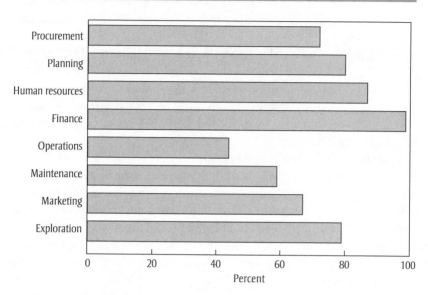

Source: Gente del Petróleo Civil Association 2003.

The staffing changes that Chávez introduced perhaps did the most damage to PDVSA's operations. PDVSA was considered one of the world's leading energy companies, a rare example of a state-owned company that was also internationally competitive and a major actor in both the wholesale and retail oil business in the United States. Chávez fired close to four out of five of the successful company's exploration and well engineers; about an equal share of staff was sacked from the human resources and planning departments, and an even higher share was fired from the finance department (see figure 4-1). Lesser but nonetheless significant firings occurred in the maintenance, marketing, procurement, and operations departments. The loss of human capital, far and away the best trained and most experienced staff of any oil company in a developing country, was devastating for PDVSA's operations.

Staffing changes were significant, but equally important and even less discussed were the changes in the way PDVSA interacted with the other branches of government. Before the oil strike, PDVSA had been set up under the supervision of four separate entities: the Ministry of Oil, the

Central Bank, an internal comptroller general, and the Securities and Exchange Commission (SEC) of the United States.[22] Each entity had a specific objective relative to the interests of PDVSA's board of managers, so as to ensure proper separation of powers and checks and balances. For instance, the Oil Ministry supervised budgets; the comptroller prepared audits that were released to the general public; the SEC ensured the creditworthiness of PDVSA's bonds; and the Central Bank ensured that PDVSA would sell all of its dollars from oil exports and maintain foreign hard-currency assets of up to $800 million in a revolving fund, for the purpose of paying its debts and the bills for contractual services outside Venezuela.

Gradually Chávez ended this system of checks and balances. The board of managers and the comptroller general became mere appendices of the presidential cabinet. In April 2004 the Central Bank changed the terms of its covenant: PDVSA was now allowed to expand its hard-currency fund to several billion dollars, and could finance social, agricultural, and infrastructure projects both locally and abroad. And in 2006, PDVSA paid off its debt in the United States with the explicit intention of no longer being required to disclose information to the SEC.

In terms of expanding PDVSA's activities, the most important change was to convert PDVSA into the state's most important welfare agency. Shortly after the strike, PDVSA set up the Social Development Fund (Fondespa), distinct from Fonden (the National Development Fund). Directly run by the president of PDVSA (thus, a presidential cabinet member), Fondespa had authority to finance special social programs (*misiones*) in Venezuela and foreign aid projects elsewhere. Under these administrative reforms PDVSA could now disburse funds locally and internationally without reporting to the Central Bank or the National Assembly and bypassing local elected officials. The upshot of the move was that PDVSA suddenly became a key source of direct, unaccountable spending for the central government.

Prior to these moves Chávez had pushed for legislation that tightened state control of the industry beyond provisions already included in the 1999 constitution. The constitution already precluded privatization by establishing that the oil industry, because of its strategic importance to the state, must remain the property of the state. But strategic associations between PDVSA and private-sector companies were accepted along with other types of contracts that dated from the opening of the oil industry to foreign investment in the late 1990s. The phrasing of the constitution was flexible enough to allow continuation of the oil industry's opening to foreign investment. To change this, the government enacted the 2001 Hydrocarbons Law. This law restricted further the role of private-sector oil-industry companies. The law stated that any future projects developed by PDVSA required at least 51 percent state ownership and would not be subject to international arbitration. A single legal instrument for developing the oil industry was established. The text did not explicitly regulate already existing projects, but left the door open to do so in the future. The 2001 law also increased royalties from 16.66 to 30 percent for all projects. Previous legislation had established that under special circumstances (such as developing costly projects in the Orinoco Tar Belt), royalties paid to the state could be substantially reduced to facilitate financing. The new law contained no such provision. Income tax for oil companies, including PDVSA, was reduced from 60 to 50 percent, taking into account the increase in royalties.

When Chávez took over full control of the oil industry and expanded the role of PDVSA as a spending arm of the central government, no specific reference was made to existing contracts with foreign oil companies. Given the sweeping nature of the reforms, legal and fiscal uncertainties came to dominate the sector. Because no provision was announced for existing contracts and no conditions were specified for foreign investment in the oil sector, owners and managers of private foreign companies in the energy sector wondered whether the new rules contained in the 2001 law could be applied retroactively. These private firms had committed billions of dollars to developing and extracting oil from the Orinoco Tar Belt and operated gas refineries or other facilities as well as service stations across the country.

Political Control of the New Private Oil Sector

Once the internal structure of the state-owned energy sector was overhauled, Chávez accelerated his overhaul of the privately owned energy sector. The oil price boom at the end of 2003 offered yet another opportunity to change oil contracts in the direction of greater state control over private operators. As foreign companies had feared, Chávez abruptly raised royalties paid by foreign companies operating in the Orinoco Tar Belt that had entered into "strategic associations" with PDVSA, including ExxonMobil, Conoco, Total, and Chevron. The stated reason was that high and sustained oil prices had substantially altered market conditions.

At the time of this change, heavy oil extracted by foreign companies in the Tar Belt had already reached almost 20 percent of Venezuela's total oil output. Even though royalties were jacked up and conditions changed without previous consultation with the foreign companies, the government's move was made skillfully: the new royalty was fixed at the same rate as that established by the 1943 Hydrocarbons Law, under which fiscal conditions were originally granted. Royalties for all heavy oil projects were raised from 1 to 16.66 percent.

Other changes were introduced as well. On the grounds that these companies were producing more oil than the amount foreseen in the original contracts, the state demanded payment of fiscal revenue retroactively. All the companies except ExxonMobil accepted the new conditions.

The state's next move stunned the world oil industry. In mid-2007, as high oil prices persisted, the government announced the nationalization of all Orinoco Tar Belt projects. Foreign companies operating in the Tar Belt were required to join mixed enterprises to be set up under state control. All fiscal conditions were now adapted to the 2001 Hydrocarbons Law. This second round of changes prompted Conoco and ExxonMobil to exit the country and seek international arbitration to secure just compensation. Total and Chevron, in contrast, voluntarily accepted the new rules of the game.

Also in 2007, the regime scrapped service contracts between thirty-two private firms and PDVSA, claiming that these were contractual arrangements not previously approved by the legislature. PDVSA believed it had the authority to cancel these other contracts and asked foreign companies to voluntarily merge to a new scheme controlled by PDVSA. All of the foreign companies, with the exception of ExxonMobil and ENI, accepted the new scheme. Rather than challenge this new property arrangement in international courts, ExxonMobil was pressured by the regime to sell its share of the project. ENI opted to explore the possibility of negotiating an amicable settlement rather than challenging Venezuela in an arbitration process (the settlement amounts of these deals were never disclosed).

It is important to emphasize that Chávez has not ended international participation in Venezuela's oil sector. In 2008 there were eighteen countries actively participating in Venezuela's oil business, according to Venezuela's ambassador to the United States, Bernardo Álvarez. What Chávez changed is the preponderance of privately owned transnational firms: they have been replaced with state-owned corporations, many of which are based in non-democracies (China, Iran, and Russia). This shift from a system in which PDVSA interacted with privately owned companies (accountable to shareholders) in democracies (accountable to citizens and courts) to a system of interaction with mostly state-owned companies from non-democracies (accountable only to state leaders) also diminished the level of transparency of the oil business in Venezuela. Under Venezuela's new international oil regime, secret negotiations between the state and transnational companies have a greater chance of remaining secret.

A Socialist PDVSA

Remaking PDVSA entailed turning the company into the government's chief mechanism for distributing rents, an entity that privileged social investment over and above that required for oil output productivity. Its new motto became "PDVSA now belongs to all of us," intended to broadcast the government's plan to channel resources to social ventures in Venezuela and abroad. In practice, PDVSA displaced traditional ministries in charge of social spending. During the *puntofijista* era PDVSA had been censured for being a "state within the state"; it could now be said the company had turned into a parallel state.

The scale of social effort undertaken by PDVSA meant that the company's management changed focus. Its key business initiatives were no longer concerned exclusively with finding, extracting, refining, and marketing oil but rather running innumerable social initiatives, even outside Venezuela. PDVSA also began to serve as employer of last resort, mostly for *chavistas*. Nationwide activities directly managed by PDVSA included the aforementioned Misión Ribas and Misión Vuelvan Caras, which financed start-up community-level cooperatives to provide primary health care, road construction, or office-cleaning services, or to produce foodstuffs and simple manufactured goods. PDVSA also undertook to assist Misión Mercal, a retail chain selling food at subsidized prices, by setting up PDVAL, a food-purchasing, production, and wholesale distribution firm. PDVSA also directly financed construction of Barrio Adentro I and II, preventive health-care centers housed in more elaborate facilities than those for primary health care, and directly managed relations with Cuba to ensure the availability of Cuban medical equipment, supplies, and physicians for these centers.

From 2003 to 2008, PDVSA spent more than $23 billion in social programs. Certainly the scale of spending gave rise to a feeling of social inclusion and empowerment that Venezuela had not experienced in

FIGURE 4-2. Percentage of Total Households in Poverty, 1998–2009

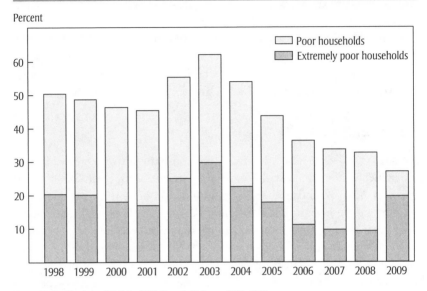

Source: National Institute of Statistics (INE), Household Surveys 1998–2009.

decades. And of course the transfer of such vast resources to the poor constituted a significant form of income distribution.

The massive deployment of public resources for social programs—made possible by the size of the oil windfall—brought about an improvement in basic social indicators. According to Venezuela's National Institute of Statistics (Instituto Nacional de Estadísticas, INE), overall and extreme poverty declined drastically over a short period of time (see figure 4-2). The proportion of households living in poverty fell from over 49 percent in 1998 to 29 percent in 2009. Extreme poverty in households was also reduced from 20 percent in 1998 to close to 9 percent in 2008, rapidly rising since then. In little more than a decade, over 3.5 million people rose above the poverty line, of which almost 3 million overcame extreme poverty. The increase in oil wealth had certainly helped augment the income of poor households, and the retooling of PDVSA to social uses secured the transfer of oil revenues to low-income groups.

But not all social outcomes were crystal-clear. Clientelism governed the targeting of many disbursements, and poverty criteria did not always prevail in deciding who got aid.[23] Programs were conceived as short-term assistance, not as components of a structural vision for reducing poverty by improving both access and quality of social services.[24] For instance, the quality of continuing education offered by Misión Ribas, which provided students with a high school degree, was questioned by different NGOs and academic institutions.[25] Barrio Adentro's primary health-care posts often ended up being abandoned. PDVAL, in charge of distributing food, was involved in numerous corruption scandals that significantly weakened the effectiveness of Misión Mercal. Misión Vuelvan Caras handed funds to thousands of cooperatives organized for the express purpose of gaining access to "soft" loans that were in fact outright donations. The vast majority of these co-ops were unsustainable, and the funds granted to them were wasted and left unaccounted for. In sum, investment-return ratios for these social disbursement were substantially less positive than official sources claimed. Even poverty reduction has been more the result of a vast increase in oil wealth and short-term transfers than of a structural change in poverty's underlying conditions.[26] In fact, some analysts have concluded that given the size of the oil windfall in Venezuela, poverty rates should have been reduced more than they have been.[27]

The Operational Costs of Socializing PDVSA

Politicizing PDVSA, using its revenues to fuel electoral coalitions, and giving it a central welfare role has led to a monumental decline in oil-sector investments and company productivity. During the strike, oil output shrank to just 500,000 barrels per day. Soon after, production recovered to 2,800,000 barrels per day. But from this point on, PDVSA experienced a steady decline in daily output. Several years after the end of the stoppage, many oil refineries were still not operating at full capacity, owing to a shortage of technical capacity and sufficient gas pressure. High technical competence is needed to extract oil from mature and geologically complex fields, such as those under Lake Maracaibo, and to inject associated and non-associated gas into fields that require gas to boost output. PDVSA's technical shortages forced the company to close numerous oil wells. Many fields that were reopened failed to reach previous output levels. Some reserves recorded for these wells were probably lost in the extraction process as a result of management limitations.

Another casualty was PDVSA's information technology (IT) infrastructure. On the grounds that technical staff had joined the strike, PDVSA suspended commercial relations with INTESA, its IT outsourcing company, a joint venture with US SAIC. Only about 5 percent of IT staff was rehired. Because of the damage inflicted by strikers to the information system and the lack of managerial competence of the new PDVSA to restore it, it became virtually impossible to account for the vast losses and multiple transactions made by the company during the oil strike. Sales and shipments were recorded by hand, without needed approvals. Trade and brokerage instructions were issued manually to traders not directly controlled by PDVSA. The military shipped gasoline from refineries and delivered it to service stations but without issuing invoices, and tankers left ports without proper authorizations. The lack of accurate information and backup records, along with opaque administrative procedures, made auditing the company well nigh impossible.

The auditing issue became acute and came to light when PDVSA failed to provide financial statements to the SEC. PDVSA was required to disclose information in order to provide bondholders with company financial data as per SEC regulations. In April 2003 the SEC reminded PDVSA to submit its financial statements, and the company requested a one-month extension, until May. In May, PDVSA asked for an additional thirty-day extension. There were penalties for failure to comply with SEC requirements. Unable or unwilling to disclose information, PDVSA opted to buy back the entire $2.7 billion in outstanding foreign debt, thus sidestepping the SEC's requirement. The buy-back decision was strategically leaked to the market, which allowed a number of investors to profit before the announcement was made public.

Nonetheless, PDVSA had provided additional collateral and financial guarantees for projects not directly controlled by the company, mainly in the Orinoco Tar Belt. Hence the company was still required to provide critical financial and operational information to foreign investors. By 2005, PDVSA had not finished auditing financial and operational statements for 2003 and 2004. Early in 2006, PDVSA submitted to the SEC financial statements for 2004, audited by KPMG, an international auditing company.

The lack of records was not the only problem. PDVSA was reluctant to reveal information on disbursements made on behalf of its social programs. Chávez routinely ordered Fondespa to directly fund and even manage certain social programs, including Misión Ribas, a distance-learning continuing education program for secondary studies, and Misión Vuelvan Caras, offering training for the unemployed and funding for newly launched cooperatives. The Misión Ribas program was directly

FIGURE 4-3. PDVSA Operating Costs and Total Costs plus Social Expenditure, 2001–08

Costs by barrel (U.S.$)

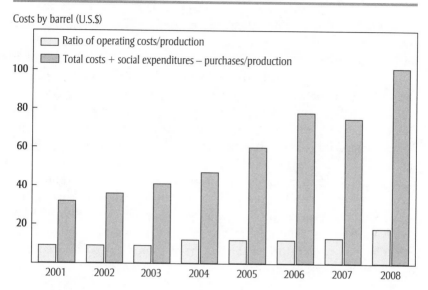

Source: PDVSA, auditing reports, 2001–08.

managed by PDVSA, not placed under the Ministry of Education—an example of PDVSA's new role in implementing social policies in Venezuela. By 2004, when the recall referendum for President Chávez took place, PDVSA had invested more than $4 billion in social programs, an amount that continued to grow in subsequent years. To this day these funds have never been independently audited.

All of this squeezed PDVSA financially; its contribution to fiscal revenue surpassed $175 billion from 2004 to 2008 but during this period the company's cost structure deteriorated, investment projects were delayed, and maintenance spending declined (see figure 4-3). In 2001 operational costs had been nine dollars per barrel; by 2008 these costs had doubled. Total costs for each barrel (excluding social expenditures and transfers to Fonden) had climbed from $13 per barrel in 2001 to $29 in 2008. Total costs including social spending and transfers to Fonden jumped from $32 to $101 per barrel during that period. Currency appreciation exacerbated financial pressures on the company.

The burden imposed by the gasoline subsidy for the domestic market also increased substantially. For years, gasoline prices in the domestic market had remained nominally constant, despite high inflation. By 2008 domestic gasoline prices in real terms had fallen by more than 70 percent from 2002, further raising the financial cost of this direct subsidy for PDVSA.[28] In the meantime, domestic consumption of gasoline grew steadily, driven by expansion in economic activity and soaring vehicle imports. According to some estimates, Venezuela consumed more than 800,000 barrels a day by 2007.[29] Because PDVSA lacked idle capacity, the only way to meet domestic demand was to cut crude oil exports.

By the end of 2008, as the global financial crisis erupted, PDVSA's financial and operational shortcomings and operational handicaps became impossible to ignore. Oil prices sank below $60 a barrel, affecting the company's cash flow. Despite financial constraints, PDVSA's president, Rafael Ramírez, favored transfers to Fonden and Fondespa to protect social spending and payments to bondholders over payments to local and foreign creditors. In the second quarter of 2009, PDVSA owed its suppliers almost $9 billion, which put its entire operation at risk. These payment priorities showed the true impact of political control on the oil industry, even to the extent of threatening the financial and managerial viability of PDVSA.

Cash-flow restrictions in 2009 were so severe that the National Assembly passed a law in May allowing the regime to take over oil-service contractors, including small oil-service firms operating in Lake Maracaibo such as providers of transportation for workers from shore to wells or maintenance services for underwater equipment. Some of these companies were foreign-owned. Presumably, compensation eventually to be paid to former owners of these firms will offset almost one year of overdue payment for services rendered.

In short, socializing PDVSA led to a worrisome decline in PDVSA's operational performance, which ended up hurting the government's own socialist goals of helping the poor. Figure 4-4 shows the contraction of Venezuela's oil sector GDP following 1998 as well as the decline in number of drills employed to extract oil. Both variables are fairly good indicators of oil industry activity and investment. Admittedly, part of this contraction is attributable to cutbacks mandated by OPEC. However, the extent of contraction is significantly greater than the mandated cutbacks, and shows a systematic decline in Venezuela's real production capacity. For PDVSA to continue serving as the country's chief source of fiscal revenue, the company must soon expand investment in oil production.

FIGURE 4-4. **Oil GDP and Oil Drills, 1998–2009**

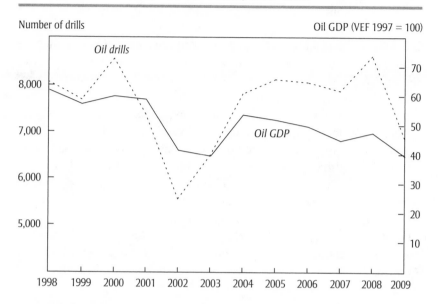

Source: Central Bank of Venezuela; Bloomberg.

The problem is that PDVSA no longer possesses the managerial, technological, and financial capacity to expand oil production. It takes billions of dollars and skilled know-how to turn tar into refinable heavy oil, and that's the only kind of oil output that Venezuela can readily expand. This makes the company increasingly dependent on foreign investment to rebuild the oil industry.

The one glimmer of hope is that Chávez's 2001 Hydrocarbon Law does not forbid foreign investment; it only establishes that majority control of joint ventures in the oil sector must remain in state hands. But greater collaboration between PDVSA and private foreign companies may not materialize if restrictions such as high royalties, scarce fiscal benefits, and lack of access to arbitration remain in place. Moreover, the political risk of expropriation faced by foreign-owned firms in Venezuela makes overcoming these issues more difficult, especially for the types of capital-intensive projects that are required for developing heavy oil deposits in the Orinoco Tar Belt.

By the end of 2009, despite the recovery of the price of oil, conditions within PDVSA were so dismal that the government was forced to soften its nationalist rhetoric. In an effort to re-attract foreign investment, the government announced a bidding process to grant exploration licenses in the Tar Belt. A delegation visited Washington in the spring of 2010 to lure potential oil investors. For the so-called Carabobo Project, a number of conditions established by law were eased to increase the appeal of the project to international investors. These included early output concessions, recourse to arbitration for project financial flows although not for property, and the possibility of granting certain fiscal benefits such as temporary lowering of income taxes. In February 2010 Chevron and Repsol, among other international oil companies, showed willingness to consider investing in the project. A factor favoring Venezuela's heavy oil industry is that extracting tar from the Orinoco Tar Belt to produce heavy oil does not arouse world environmental concerns, as does development of Canada's Athabasca shale deposits.

The scale of Venezuela's oil reserves as certified by the U.S. Geological Survey has reached almost 513 billion barrels, most of it heavy oil in the Orinoco Tar Belt alone. The size of these reserves means the country will always be able to attract investment to its oil sector. But restoring PDVSA as a leading company in global energy will prove much more challenging. Only a few years ago PDVSA overshadowed the management and technological capacities of state-owned Petrobras in Brazil and even Ecopetrol in Colombia, but today these two other state-owned Latin American oil companies are better positioned than PDVSA in global markets.

In short, it was not the price of oil alone that helped the regime consolidate power; it was the institutional changes that were made prior to the oil boom together with the oil boom that did the trick. Likewise, it was not just the decline in the price of oil after 2008 that led to an economic crisis (and, more recently, a softening of the government's resource nationalism), as the literature on the resource curse would predict—the price of oil recovered to historically high levels by 2010. Instead, it was the decline of PDVSA's productive capacity that landed the country in one of its worst economic crises.

Economic Sustainability and Regime Survival

We now turn our attention to the theoretical implications of oil dependence for regime type. Chávez has been able to build his economic model thanks to oil. Nobody disputes this point.[30] The key question is whether a severe oil downturn and continued economic crisis puts the Chávez regime, or any hybrid regime, for that matter, in jeopardy. Our answer is: "not necessarily."

An oil bust will not necessarily bring about the rapid demise of Venezuela's current political model. This is because, we argue, the impact of oil-flow fluctuations on economic and political sustainability differs depending on the kind of regime in place. Under a democratic regime, an oil boom may or may not strengthen the regime. This is hard to predict in advance. However, under autocracy, an oil boom most certainly helps the regime consolidate power. Conversely, an oil bust hurts both democracy and autocracies, yet it is likely to be more devastating for democracies than for authoritarian regimes.[31] Because the Chávez regime has both democratic and autocratic elements, it is unclear how an oil bust will impact the regime. To help us understand these different impacts, it helps to consider the effects of both oil booms and oil busts along three regime dimensions: economic policy, checks on the executive branch, and societal response. Consider oil booms first.

Oil Booms

Oil booms provide incumbents with plenty of resources, but also pose enormous challenges.

Economic policy. Under both democracies and autocracies, oil booms have an inebriating effect on heads of state (as both Terry Karl and Fernando Coronil have clearly noted).[32] Oil booms drive state leaders to overspend, typically on "mega-infrastructure" projects, often in utter disregard of macroeconomic and financial viability. One key difference is that in a democracy, hyperactive state spending is channeled through (or takes place under the scrutiny of) political parties and a legislative body, whereas under a regime with concentration of powers there is no mediating institution between the executive branch and economic agents receiving public funds. Oil booms can therefore promote party competition in democracies, at least initially, since large parties, not just the ruling party, can benefit from state largesse.[33] This is one way that oil booms help democracy, and the literature on Venezuela often points to the period between the 1950s and the 1960s as a demonstration of this point that oil can strengthen party-based democratic competition. In a regime with concentration of powers, on the other hand, because the incumbent has a virtual monopoly on state spending and its accompanying policies of clientelism and cronyism, the chances of rival forces capturing oil resources to challenge the incumbent are minimal.

Despite the mitigation of incumbent monopoly power in a democracy by means of opposition parties, oil booms in a democracy may eventually result in political party collusion as traditional parties begin to cooperate with each other in sharing the spoils of office.[34] To compete, parties overemphasize patronage to the detriment of sound capital investments, which is especially unfortunate for development, may impede economic adjustment, and can lead to antiparty and anti–status quo sentiment across the electorate.[35] The literature on Venezuela points to politics in the 1970s as an example of this argument about the corrosive effects of oil on party-based competition.

Checks on the executive branch. Higher spending expands the capacity of incumbents to co-opt political actors (especially in the context of weak institutions). During oil booms incumbents thus become harder to defeat electorally or to restrain. Their enhanced power to spend inadvertently leads to declines in key democratic features, such as notions of limited government, transparency in fiscal affairs, fair treatment of the dissenting parties, and balanced competition between incumbents and the opposition. The key point is that these trends are detrimental to democracies but not necessarily to other types of regimes. Strengthening the incumbent vis-à-vis the opposition may not necessarily be good for democratic development and alternation in power, but it is always good news for incumbents in an autocracy.

Societal response. In many petro-states, a consistent economic response to oil booms by societal actors is that they become addicted to rents.[36] To extract oil-based rents, economic agents focus their energies on searching for them. Because the state controls the oil sector, this societal response translates into demand for greater state involvement in economic affairs. In democracies, the rising demand for oil-derived rents does not necessarily erase political competition: political parties will compete for votes in their quest for state power, with each party advocating its own view of what constitutes the fairer or better way to distribute rents. But ideological competition among parties does decline: all parties end up defending one version or another of a strong state.

Some analysts have openly complained that in the *puntofijista* Venezuela there was no one (no political party, no media group, no politician) openly defending any economic ideology other than statism.[37] In a democracy, where both incumbents and opposition forces share rent revenues, rent seekers can indulge their appetite for rents by capturing both incumbent and opposition forces. In a setting with no checks and balances, by contrast, there is only one way to satisfy the appetite for rents—to bandwagon with incumbents. Because the opposition, if at all active, has almost zero chance of winning, there are weak incentives for rent seekers to side with the opposition, which appears to be a hopeless and possibly dangerous gamble. Thus, in an hybrid regime where the opposition has fewer chances of prevailing, an oil boom expands the tendency of actors to bandwagon with incumbents, and this too bolsters autocratic features.

In sum, oil booms risk weakening democratic regimes, if not right away, then down the road, but they can strengthen both autocracies and hybrid regimes. Booms lower checks on the executive branch and increase society's demand for rents. Political party competition for electoral office in a democracy may still endure, but collusion expands, and ideological competition wanes. Consequently, over time oil booms also risk weakening political party competition and provoke voter disaffection, as citizens turn increasingly against all parties. In political frameworks with greater concentration of powers, on the other hand, these same effects combine to strengthen the regime, since executive power by definition thrives in contexts of societal demand for state controls, and uneven distribution of resources between incumbents and the opposition. Moreover, oil booms allow these regimes to embrace a greater degree of clientelism and cronyism, which expands the number of regime supporters and fosters greater hegemony over the distribution of rent benefits. This compounds the bandwagon effect, thereby increasing the ruler's capacity to co-opt others and thus become an even more dominant actor.

Oil Busts

By the same token, collapses in oil revenue can jeopardize democracies far more than other type of regime.

Economic policy. Because petro-states have few sources of public revenue other than oil, they are particularly susceptible to oil busts. Oil busts tend to produce severe fiscal crises and recessions, which force the executive branch to implement spending cutbacks, with serious costs for incumbents' popularity. For democracies, economic adjustment measures are especially potentially destabilizing because most reforms (reducing spending, raising taxes, privatizing, deregulating, and, at the worst, devaluation or default) require adherence to the law.[38] For most of these reforms the executive branch must seek legislative approval, which in turn requires support from political parties and their constituents, all of whom are highly addicted to oil rents and are thus averse to reform. By contrast, in a context where the executive branch has no institutional checks, it can more easily get away with ruling by decree, or at least writing off certain constituencies. This provides these types of regimes with a greater likelihood of surviving oil busts and may be one reason why some studies find that autocracies survive economic crises more often than do democracies.[39]

Checks on the executive branch. Faced with the urgency of addressing a severe fiscal crisis but hindered by a congress or society that is unwilling to accept the cost of adjustment, presidents in democratic petro-states will feel tempted to carry out profound reforms by fiat, often circumventing existing democratic channels, by governing through decrees or bypassing consultations with parties.[40] To the extent that the executive branch is pressured to accrue more power and consult less, oil shocks hold the potential to weaken democracy.

Often in democracies, societal demand for greater concentration of power in the hands of the executive branch can increase during economic downturns. For instance, a public opinion survey of Venezuelans taken in 1995 and 1998 (a period of poor economic performance coupled with political instability) shows that the percentage of respondents who supported "government intervention in the economy" skyrocketed across all income groups, from 29 to 80 percent among upper-income Venezuelans and from 68 to 86 percent among lower-income strata.[41] The share of respondents supporting "radical political changes" expanded as well, most remarkably among upper-income respondents, from 8 to 17 percent.[42]

In non-democratic political contexts, oil busts hinder the capacity of the administration to be generous (to spend heavily on clientelism) but do not technically make the executive less powerful, since the starting point was not a competitive political regime. Demand for radical change across the population may very well increase, especially among those who most bear the cost of economic reforms, but the disaffected groups will lack institutional avenues to channel their discontent or will fear the costs of protesting.

Societal response. In democracies, economic adjustment has the potential to generate political conflict in two areas. One area of conflict arises between the state and the cost bearers, the societal actors who bear the brunt of economic adjustment.[43] The second area of conflict emerges between the executive branch and the political organizations that resist the administration's efforts to concentrate more power.[44] A severe clash between society's democratic forces and the state may occur in situations where powers are delegated to the president, or "party-neglecting" policies are deployed by the executive branch. In settings in which the president monopolizes power, adjustment will mainly engender conflict with cost bearers. Conflict with political organizations is less significant. Either it antedates the oil shock or has already been resolved, assuming the regime's power has stabilized.

For a democratic regime, the most likely impact of an oil bust is thus greater risk of regime decay (inability to govern), concentration of power (delegative democracy), or instability. All institutions come under strain, as indeed occurred in Venezuelan politics between 1989 and 2002. Economic adjustment in the 1980s and 1990s generated policy paralysis and muddling through. State-society conflict brought citizens, especially among the urban poor, into the streets to protest top-down efforts to reform the economy. Traditional political parties suffered voter defection, driven by rising voter discontent with professional politicians. Because the economic crisis was prolonged (from 1979 to 2001), resentment over the status quo and against politicians became especially acute. No body politic likes austerity measures any more than it likes politicians who appear to be immobile in the face of a crisis. From almost every angle, the politics of adjustment in democratic petro-states risks jeopardizing the quality and institutional foundations of democracy.

In a setting that lacks division of powers, on the other hand, an oil bust can lead to either of two outcomes. The executive branch may survive in office, perhaps becoming even stronger. This can occur if the regime intensifies authoritarian features, for example, by repressing protests of cost bearers and preventing cronies from defecting. The other possible outcome is for the executive not to survive in office. This occurs if cost bearers become too hard to repress or cronies abandon the regime.

This book has argued that Venezuela under Chávez has moved toward a regime of greater concentration of power. In the event of a prolonged oil bust, which of the two outcomes we described is Venezuela likely to suffer? Many analysts contend that an oil bust will promptly put an end to the regime's populist spending, thereby disarming Chávez. But a number of points suggest this may not happen anytime soon. First, even if austerity provokes protests by cost bearers, it could very well be that Chávez will find himself with a stronger capacity to repress, given the regime's enormous spending on weapons and on measures taken to increase loyalty within the armed forces and other potentially armed groups. Second, the regime controls important institutions that—fearing a backlash were political conditions to change—would not likely court the opposition. Third, the regime's support is not exclusively linked to clientelism; it also relies on cronies, who need to extract rents, and on other supporters, usually radical partisans who receive intangible rewards through ideological commitments. Thus an oil bust will not necessarily undermine the regime's capacity to provide these other forms of rewards, although it can certainly provide a wedge for new groups to exert pressure in favor of economic and political change. Oil busts can undermine the hegemony of the incumbent and could well do so for Chávez's regime, but not necessarily ensure its sudden collapse.

Reflections

The 2003–08 oil windfall played an important role in Venezuela's transition toward a hybrid regime in the 2000s, even as it helped improve living conditions for the poor and made possible a sense of social inclusion among a large sector of the population. Yet Chávez's ability to manipulate the oil windfall at will depended on political and institutional changes that occurred prior to the oil windfall: party collapse in the early 1990s, the internal centralization of PDVSA in the late 1990s, the concentration of power in the executive branch in the 1999 constitution, the undermining of the autonomy of the different branches of government between 1999 and 2003, the 2001 Hydrocarbon Law, and the restaffing and restructuring of PDVSA in 2003. Political control over the oil industry and the freedom to allocate oil revenue enabled the Chávez regime to build strong popular support. However, the cost of this political strategy has been a steady decline in the productivity of the nation's oil company. In a matter of four to five years, PDVSA was brought to a state of financial and operational disarray not seen in years—paradoxically, at the time that saw unprecedented profitability for the oil business worldwide.

At first glance, the Venezuelan story appears to confirm some simple resource-curse theories that posit a clear inverse relationship between oil and political freedoms. However, our analysis differs somewhat. We tried to show that this relationship is nuanced and mediated by existing institutional configurations—what we call the institutional resource curse. Institutional changes, both prior to Chávez and in the first years of the Chávez administration, allowed Chávez to seize control over the political system and the oil industry. The subsequent oil windfall allowed him to save his government and consolidate his control. The effect of oil on economic outcome and regime type thus depends on the preexisting institutional setting.

The combination of institutional change with oil windfall facilitated regime change, but it was the government's ideological zeal and political excesses that produced the worst self-inflicted wounds. Chávez's massive social investments initially excited Venezuela's masses after decades of widespread despair, and brought about unprecedented electoral dividends for the government. The "new PDVSA," now under the complete control of the president and deprived of institutional checks and balances, played a central role in ensuring this political outcome. Yet Chávez's pursuit of political and electoral gain, to the neglect of almost everything else, came at a huge price: an astounding decline in PDVSA's productivity. What used to be a topnotch transnational was reduced to financial and operational ruin by 2009. The government likes to blame domestic actors (the so-called oligarchy) and external forces (capitalism, free trade, the White House) for its economic travails. But ultimately, it was Chávez's own approach to the oil sector—his disdain for checks and balances all around him—that did most of the damage. Ironically, this damage was concentrated precisely in the regime's most cherished treasure—the oil business.

Oil may have fueled the dragon's fire, but in the end, the dragon himself ended up getting burned by its own flame. The burn might not be lethal for this type of hybrid dragon, but the wound will not heal easily.

5

Venezuela's New Foreign Policy: Soft-Balancing and Social-Power Diplomacy

Chavismo has entailed a fundamental revamp not only of Venezuela's political regime and oil industry but also of its foreign policy. The latter is mostly a result of the former. Regime change and an oil windfall allowed Chávez to transform Venezuela's historical partnership with the United States into a relationship characterized by suspicion and antagonism. By the mid-2000s, Chávez's fire-breathing anti-Americanism had become legendary worldwide, especially after his famous speech at the United Nations in 2006 declaring that he smelled sulfur following a presentation by "the devil" George W. Bush. This acerbic anti-Americanism has made Chávez today one of the Latin American political leaders with the most name recognition across the globe.

Despite Chávez's international fame, his foreign policy is not always fully understood. For some, especially sympathizers, Chávez's foreign policy is mostly an uncomplicated, even desirable, effort to challenge unipolarity and promote alternative forms of democracy across the planet. Staunch critics, on the other hand, say that Venezuela has become nothing less than a rogue state, interested in threatening the security of the region for the sake of an ideological war on behalf of outdated, radical causes.

Heuristically, neither vision is fully helpful. Chávez is neither the altruistic and selfless champion of peace and development of the first image, nor the irrational actor oblivious to international constraints of the second. In this chapter we provide a more textured analysis of Venezuela's foreign policy, highlighting the way that regime factors and international politics, especially the exigencies of the oil market, interact with each other to shape it.

Chávez's objectives at the international level seem to be oriented toward expanding his global influence by leveraging the country's oil windfall and balancing any regional attempt to challenge his control of power domestically, particularly from the United States. To achieve this, Venezuela has developed two key policy tools: "soft-balancing" and what we call "social-power diplomacy."

Soft-balancing is conventionally defined as an effort by a state to contain and frustrate—rather than merely negotiate with—the foreign policy of a more powerful state, in this case the United States. Social-power diplomacy refers to efforts by the state (in this case a petro-state) to spend abroad purportedly for social development, but in reality, as we explain in this chapter, with aims in mind that have little to do with development. This chapter discusses the extent to which Venezuela's new foreign policy can be analyzed in terms of both soft-balancing and social-power diplomacy. In some areas, Venezuela's foreign policy fits nicely with these concepts; in other areas, different concepts are required to capture Venezuela's foreign policy aims.

Taking a staunch anti-U.S. stand and distributing oil rents abroad as a form of international aid has been risky and often costly for Chávez, both at home and abroad. This chapter also considers some of these risks and costs. Domestically, soft-balancing and social-power diplomacy have been hugely unpopular across the electorate; internationally they have also created unnecessary conflict in the region, with very few countries following Venezuela's radical stance. These foreign policy tools have not rallied the nation behind Chávez, nor have they inspired a powerful anti-American coalition in Latin America.

Despite these costs and setbacks, soft-balancing and social-power diplomacy have not gone unrewarded. Perhaps the most important political gain has been the enlistment of support from radicals, both at home and abroad. In addition, soft-balancing appeals to the anti-American sentiment of large sectors of the Latin American public, and soft-power diplomacy appeals to many Latin American elected leaders, who see opportunities to use those cash transfers and subsidies as blank checks for their own electoral purposes. These tools have thus helped Chávez to constrain international critics, inhibit potential regional political coalitions, and weaken existing multilateral institutions that could potentially be the sources of criticism of Chávez's domestic politics. We show why these gains, however minimalist compared to the larger goal of containing the United States or mounting a regional Bolivarian crusade against imperialism, are nonetheless rewarding enough to sustain Chávez's costly foreign policy.

We also discuss reasons why the United States has not reacted as aggressively as it could have—such as by imposing trade sanctions on Venezuela. This entails addressing the role of oil in foreign policy. One obvious element holding the United States back is that it has no interest in losing Venezuelan oil, which under Chávez continues to flow uninterruptedly into the United States. Venezuela is the fifth largest supplier of oil to the United States, and this oil dependence explains a certain passiveness in Washington toward Caracas's excesses. In Caracas, on the other hand, dependence on U.S. markets actually generates considerable nervousness. Chávez complains that the United States wants full possession of its oil reserves. However, the real fear in Caracas is that the United States might one day stop buying Venezuelan oil to punish the regime.

Since 2003 Venezuela has been actively interested in ending this financial dependence to protect itself, but for complicated reasons has not managed to do so. Entrenched commodity and market dependence, together with declining production, has locked Venezuela in a situation of more rather than less dependence on the United States than a decade ago. This is both an embarrassment and a restraining factor for a regime that claims to be interested in asserting its independence from the United States and capitalism.

Unable to break its dependence on the United States, Venezuela turned to a foreign policy preference for maximizing the price of oil in world markets. This in turn led, as we explain in this chapter, to closer ties with Iran and Russia. Opting for price maximization has also entailed costs: it has placed Venezuela at odds with Saudi Arabia and, to a much lesser extent, China. This alone poses a problem for Venezuela: it contradicts the country's stated objectives of strengthening the Organization of the Petroleum Exporting Countries (OPEC), which is Saudi-dominated, and of strengthening ties with China, which, contrary to Venezuela, wants low oil prices. Few analysts give evidence of understanding this internal contradiction in Venezuela's foreign policy.

Our goal in this chapter is to discuss not only the origins but also the consequences of and contradictions inherent in Venezuela's foreign policy. Like any foreign policy leader with a grand-scale global strategy,

Chávez tries to juggle multiple goals simultaneously. Our ultimate conclusion is that Chávez has taken advantage of opportunities afforded by international factors (rising anti-Americanism under Bush and rising demands for new forms of participatory development worldwide), the type of regime at home (high concentration of powers in the executive), and rising oil demand worldwide—yet he is trapped by the contradictions inherent in trying to be an oil supplier to the very same country that he seeks to undermine.

The Rise of Soft-Balancing

Venezuela's foreign policy under Chávez underwent a tectonic change. Historically, Venezuela's foreign policy aimed to promote democratic movements in countries run by dictatorships, and to support governments that pursued reconciliation rather than confrontation with opposition forces.[1] Venezuelan presidents placed a high value on collaboration with the United States, especially in democracy-promotion projects in the Americas. Prior to Chávez, Venezuela saw itself as a "good conscience" partner, willing to offer advice to U.S. presidents on how to deal constructively with social-democratic forces in the region, and discourage them from behaving too "cold war"–like or "pro-capitalist" in the region. Venezuela did not adhere to a policy of unconditional alignment with the United States nor to a policy of working exclusively with democracies—even though Rómulo Betancourt, one of the founding leaders of Venezuela's democracy (he was president from 1945 to 1948 and again from 1959 to 1964), had at one time hoped for this.[2] There were moments of tension and ingenious attempts to display diplomatic independence, but before Chávez, Venezuela never entertained seriously the idea of perpetuating a policy of noncooperation with the United States.

Under Chávez, Venezuela changed direction. Vis-à-vis the United States, Venezuela became the most uncooperative country in the region after Cuba and a strident critic of almost every U.S. foreign policy initiative. Vis-à-vis other Latin American countries, Caracas started to emphasize close ties with social movements and political leaders seeking "revolutionary" change, rather than political conciliation and gradual reforms (the relatively moderate Lula, in Brazil, is an exception).

This is not to say that every aspect of Chávez's foreign policy represents a departure from the past. Between the 1930s and 1980s, Venezuela pursued a fairly active foreign policy. Under Chávez, Venezuela's activism in foreign policy changed only in degree, and mostly in relation to the 1990s, when the main focus was to ensure mere democratic survival.[3] Moreover, Venezuela had always exhibited a nationalist agenda, looking for opportunities to foster South–South ties and supporting alternative international forums. Accordingly, Venezuela cultivated good relations with all powers of various political stripes, even if they were at odds with the United States. For example, Venezuela was a founding member of OPEC, quickly made peace with Cuba in the 1970s following years of animosity, and hosted a number of third world conferences. This nationalist orientation did not change under Chávez, except perhaps in the degree of radicalism. In the economic realm, even less change has occurred: Venezuela has remained as dependent as ever on oil revenue, chiefly paid for by the United States. If anything, this dependence actually increased during Chávez's regime.

Nevertheless, the level of tension and the decline of cooperation in U.S.-Venezuela relations are without precedent, and so is the degree to which Venezuela chooses to take the opposite side on any debate in which the United States expresses a foreign policy preference. One term that can be invoked to characterize Venezuela's new foreign policy toward the United States is "soft-balancing." This is a relatively new term in international relations. It refers to efforts by nations to *frustrate* the foreign policy objectives of other, presumably more powerful nations, but stopping short of military action.[4] Soft-balancing is a variation of traditional balancing behavior. Where hard-balancing involves efforts, typically military in nature, to reconfigure the international system (such as ending the predominance of a great power), soft-balancing reflects less ambitious goals centered primarily on raising the costs of action for the more powerful state.[5] Precisely because its goals are less ambitious, soft-balancing can become a particularly appealing foreign policy tool for second-tier nations that disagree fundamentally with more powerful nations.

Soft-balancing should also be distinguished from more conventional diplomatic bargaining. Under traditional bargaining, neither party eschews cooperation systematically. Instead, nations select lists of items to negotiate, maybe even disagree on, while still finding many other items on the agenda to cooperate on. Brazil's policy toward the United States during Lula's second term constitutes a clear example of this type of traditional bargaining. Lula decided to challenge some vital U.S. policies, including free-trade in the Americas, agricultural subsidies, hardline policies toward Iran, and relations with Honduras after the 2009 coup, but he found many other areas of far-reaching cooperation, such as investment, research on ethanol, and military and security affairs. Under soft-balancing, in contrast, there is a consistent refusal by at least one of the parties to negotiate, let alone cooperate, on a great number of political and security issues.

Scholars debate the causes of soft-balancing and whether it ever works, whether it is all that new, and whether it is all that common.[6] Specialists in U.S.-Venezuela relations might contend that the concept does not adequately describe relations between the two countries, and in some ways, we agree. At times, for instance, Venezuela's foreign policy toward the United States is too soft to be considered "balancing"—there is more rhetoric than concrete action. In other areas—Venezuela's arms purchases and alleged secret ties with nuclear or terrorism-sponsoring states and movements—Chávez's foreign policy has become too "hard" to count as "soft." Furthermore, soft-balancing is not always at the center of Chavez's foreign policy; he often resorts to alternative foreign policy objectives, as we discuss later in this chapter.

Nevertheless, Venezuela under Chávez has displayed the usual signs of soft-balancing:[7]

—Systematically eschewing cooperation, for example, on drug interdiction and security

—Building alliances with other like-minded nations, such as Iraq prior to the U.S. invasion, Iran, Libya, Cuba, Syria, Byelorussia, and Zimbabwe

—Creating obstacles in international forums, for example, organizing an anti-U.S. parallel Summit of the Americas in 2005

—Promoting counterproposals such as launching in 2006 the "Bolivarian alternative" to Free Trade in the Americas (ALBA), a trade agreement that opposes trade liberalization and privatization

—Generating diplomatic entanglements, such as discussing with Russia the installation of military bases and deployment of missiles in either Cuba or Venezuela; intruding in negotiations between Bogotá and the FARC

—Openly accusing the United States of posing an economic and military national threat to the revolution; or of planning to assassinate Chávez or invade the country from Colombia, Aruba, or Costa Rica; and ordering the military to prepare for an "asymmetrical war" against imperialism

No other Latin American country other than Cuba under Fidel Castro has targeted the United States as explicitly and insistently as has Venezuela under Chávez.

Social-Power Diplomacy

Chávez has employed a number of foreign policy tools to render soft-balancing effective. Perhaps the most distinctive is what we dub "social-power diplomacy."[8] This means deploying substantial investments abroad, putatively to promote development and alleviate poverty but in fact to further a different agenda. From 2004 to 2009, Chávez offered investments, aid, and subsidies to a large number of countries, especially through oil discounts and direct social investments. Venezuela has invested directly in social projects in countries such as Nicaragua, Cuba, Argentina, Ecuador, Honduras, and Bolivia, often by means of binational sovereign funds. It has also invested via indirect means in México, Peru, Colombia, and El Salvador, countries where Caracas sought to influence local conditions to make them more hospitable for emerging opponents of the political establishment. Chávez went so far as to deploy focused social investments in developed countries, such as the United States and Great Britain, to boost global attention to his efforts to "soft-balance" first world leaders such as George W. Bush and Tony Blair, who at the time were targets of harsh domestic criticism.

Venezuela under Chávez has become a world champion of foreign aid. According to a recent estimate of South-South development assistance outside of multilateral organizations (by non-OECD countries), Venezuela has come to occupy one of the top positions, if not the ranking one, in development aid as a percentage of the country's national income (see table 5-1).[9] Some estimates have suggested that the total outlay of Chávez's offerings or promises of aid to other countries is as large in real terms as the Marshall Plan, the U.S. program to rebuild Europe following the Second World War.[10] PetroCaribe alone, which represented an annual subsidy of $1.7 billions' worth of oil discounts to Caribbean and Central American countries, placed Venezuelan aid on a par with that of the OECD countries Austria, Belgium, Denmark, Norway, Portugal, Spain, and Switzerland, respectively.[11] However, it should be clarified that calculating an exact figure for Venezuela's spending abroad is difficult, as the amount is kept secret and commitments do not always materialize.

Not just Venezuela's aid, but also foreign direct investment has peaked under Chávez. According to the United Nations Conference on Trade and Development (UNCTAD), Venezuela's foreign direct investment (FDI) in 2006 totaled 8 percent of its fixed capital, far above the country's 3 percent average from 1990 to 2000.[12] This figure is notably greater than

TABLE 5-1. **South–South Aid Disbursements, Selected Countries**

Country	Amount (millions of U.S.$)	GNI (percent)[a]	Total South-South aid (percent)
Saudi Arabia[b]	5,564	1.5	40.0
China[c]	1,500–2,000	0.06–0.08	14.4
Venezuela[c]	1,116–2,500	0.71–1.52	18.0
Turkey[c]	780	0.11	5.6
South Korea[b]	802	0.09	5.8
India[d]	586.6	0.05	4.1
Taiwan[b]	435	0.11	3.1
Brazil[c]	356	0.04	2.6
Kuwait[b]	283	...	2.0
South Africa[c]	194	0.07	1.4
Thailand[b]	178	...	1.3
Israel[b]	138	0.07	1.0
United Arab Emirates[b]	88	...	0.6
Malaysia[c]	16	0.01	0.1
Argentina[c]	5.1–10	0.0025–0.005	0.07
Chile[c]	3–3.3	0.0026–0.0029	0.02
Total	12,076.6–13,915.9		

Source: Reality of Aid, "South–South Development Cooperation: A Challenge to the Aid System?" 2010 report (www.reality ofaid.org/aideffectiveness).

a. GNI data used is for 2007.

b. Organization for Economic Cooperation and Development/Development Assistance Committee, *2010 Development Cooperation Report,* table 33 (statistical appendix).

c. United Nations Economic and Social Council (ECOSOC), *Background Study for the Development Cooperation Forum: Trends in South-South and Triangular Development Cooperation* (April 2008), table 2 (www.un.org/en/ecosoc/docs/pdfs/south-south_cooperation.pdf).

d. Indian Ministry of External Affairs, *Annual Report 2008–2009,* Appendix VII.

the 2 percent average among comparable petro-states, and reflects the combined activism abroad of both the government and Petróleos de Venezuela, S.A. (PDVSA).[13] Venezuela's international investment has been carried out mainly by the state, not by privately owned companies, which is one reason that the budget allocated for foreign travel by Venezuelan government officials grew by 50 percent from 2006 to mid-2008, from $30 million to $46 million. By mid-2008 Chávez himself had undertaken 225 visits abroad since he took office, averaging 22 per year.[14]

Some estimates note that Chávez made a total of $43 billion in "commitments" abroad between 1999 and 2007, including direct investments, indirect investments, subsidies, loans, and sundry grants. Of this total, we estimate that $17 billion (40.1 percent) could be classified as social investment.[15] Whether or not Venezuela fulfilled these commitments is another matter, but even if only one third of the offers made materialized, the sum of money involved was vast.

Venezuela's spending abroad encompassed a wide portfolio of projects: oil subsidies allocated to Cuba and oil price discounts to several Caribbean countries; the acquisition of Argentine commercial paper to preempt the need for Argentina to make payments to the International Monetary Fund; cash handouts to Bolivia; medical equipment donations to Nicaragua; heating oil subsidies given to more than 1 million U.S. consumers; $20 million channeled to Haiti for investments in education, health care, and housing; and multi-million-dollar investment deals with China and Iran made through special binational funds set up to promote development or create "development banks."

Sometimes the aid was offered to multiple governments, as occurred with PetroCaribe, an oil alliance of Caribbean nations with Venezuela, launched in June 2005. PetroCaribe is a Venezuelan initiative to provide small Caribbean and Central American countries with up to 200,000 barrels a day of oil and petroleum products on preferential payment terms, via these countries' state-run enterprises. Aid was also offered directly to citizens from other countries. In 2003, when Chávez learned that a Brazilian plastics factory had been shut down because the owners were in debt, he offered displaced workers subsidized raw materials in exchange for technology to produce plastic homes in Venezuela.[16] In rural Peru, according to President Alan García, Venezuela funded approximately two hundred Casas del ALBA, which were associations run from beneficiaries' homes, supposedly to provide literacy and health services. They were often staffed with Cuban doctors.[17] Peruvian authorities claimed they actually served as "indoctrination" units that spread radical leftist ideology and incited political protests.

None of this has been done discreetly. In fact, Chávez has gone out of his way to flaunt his largesse. CITGO, a U.S. company owned by the Venezuelan state, placed in U.S. outlets television and full-page newspaper advertisements proclaiming that 228,000 households in the United States had received subsidized heating oil as a "gift from the people of Venezuela." When Haiti experienced food riots in early 2008, Chávez dispatched a fleet of aircraft carrying 364 tons of food, while Brazil offered only 18 tons. At OPEC meetings, Venezuela rebuked Saudi Arabia for "not doing enough" to help the poor. Chávez often trumpeted that ALBA (Alianza Bolivariana para los Pueblos de Nuestra América—Bolivarian Alliance for the Peoples of Our America) is a "socially oriented" trade bloc bent on eradicating poverty. In Bolivia, the government disbursed Venezuelan aid by distributing checks payable to local mayors and citizens, issued by the Venezuelan embassy. In 2006, Iran and Venezuela established a joint development bank with start-up capital of $1.2 billion; the announcement was a move to undermine U.S. efforts to strengthen global financial sanctions against Iran for its alleged plans to produce nuclear weapons.

Projecting social power as a diplomatic tool is not a Venezuelan innovation. Leading powers have long deployed it, as have other petro-states in the Middle East and small powers such as Cuba. Previous Venezuelan administrations, including those of Rafael Caldera and Carlos Andrés Pérez in the 1970s, used it as well. The Chávez innovation was to make social power the cornerstone of Venezuela's foreign policy, to assign it so large a budget, and to offer it with so few conditionalities.

Few other countries compare with Venezuela in deploying social power. Cuba's foreign policy during the cold war featured a strong social policy component in its foreign policy toolkit: exporting physicians and sports trainers.[18] However, its most prominent export was guerrillas, weapons, and insurgency training.[19] During the cold war, more than 350,000 Cuban military and civilian personnel were sent abroad to assist existing insurgency movements, support socialist dictatorships, or undertake actual combat on behalf of those dictators. If Cuba's foreign policy goal during much of the cold war was to create "two, three, many Vietnams," as Guevara proclaimed, one could argue that Venezuela's adaptation of Cuba's foreign policy model is to create two, three, many . . . clinics.[20]

On the face of it, Venezuela's social power diplomacy is a type of foreign policy that few people would want to censure. In many ways, this is Venezuela's answer to the "soft power" of the United States—the set of liberal political and economic values that the United States defends worldwide and that many people find appealing about the United States' foreign policy. By flaunting social spending, Venezuela has developed a type of soft power—an image of a regime that deep-down is essentially committed to development. This image attracts international good feelings, even admiration.

In reality, however, Venezuela's social-power diplomacy has little to do with social development. Foreign governments or politicians that are recipients of Venezuelan aid have been free to employ the funds as they saw fit. Thus, from their point of view, Venezuelan aid competes favorably with the alternative channel: obtaining aid from multilateral institutions. The latter typically comes with strict conditionalities and audits. In contrast, Venezuelan aid comes with neither, rendering it as a type of blank check for any type of domestic spending—and the funds did not always end up benefiting the poor.

Chávez has in a sense developed a new type of export model: social discourse coupled with the possibility of formal and informal expansion of presidential powers for beneficiary presidents. Oil resources deployed abroad helped social movements and governments achieve political support for a more protectionist, state-oriented strategy of development. These funds also have allowed social movements and governments to promote political reforms, some as significant as constitutional reform, that often have ended up expanding the powers of the president (and lessening the powers for traditional parties and legislatures), all billed as a new form of "participatory" democracy.

Venezuelan aid also helped foster the expansion of presidential powers through corruption. Binational sovereign funds set up by Venezuela with Argentina and Nicaragua, for instance, were particularly vulnerable to widespread fraud. In addition, these funds offered an opportunity for foreign exchange arbitration in both Venezuela and the recipient countries. In principle, these sovereign funds were to be used as collateral for export loans made to the beneficiary country. But given the large gap between Venezuela's official exchange rate and the parallel unofficial market rate, openings for arbitration were readily available for public officials controlling access to hard-currency funds and potential beneficiaries in the recipient country. In Uruguay, there was a scandal when evidence emerged of overbilling for social housing and textbooks that were supposed to be exported to Venezuela. In Argentina, exports of trucks and technological support for agribusiness were subject to similar charges. In fact, the origin of the Guido Alejandro Antonini Wilson "suitcase" scandal in Argentina was closely linked to public officials from both countries who controlled access to the binational fund. (Antonini Wilson is a Venezuelan-U.S. businessman who was arrested at the airport in Buenos Aires in 2007; he carried in his suitcase $800,000 in undeclared funds, slated to be used to help finance Cristina Kirschner's campaign for president.) In 2010 a former Argentine ambassador to Venezuela, Ernesto Sadous, publicly declared before Argentine authorities that private companies paid commissions, in the range of 15 to 20 percent, to get permission to export products to Venezuela. The total value of Venezuela's imports from Argentina between 2004 and 2008 was $4.35 billion, which suggests that, if Sadous is correct, corruption levels must have been extraordinary.[21]

This possibility of expanding presidential powers formally and informally, itself the product of the low conditionality attached to this aid and business deals between the state and foreign firms, is one reason that the region has tolerated Venezuela's regime change. Venezuela has not focused on the export of guerrilla war, as Cuba did during the cold war, nor on the export of weapons, as Russia still does. Unlike OECD countries, it certainly has neither focused on the export of technological know-how, nor on the export of turnkey projects, like China. Via its aid and business deals, Venezuela has exported a particular form of corruption. Billed as investment in social services, it in fact consisted largely of unaccountable financing for political campaigns, unelected social movements, business deals, and political patronage by state officials. In times when elections are fiercely competitive almost everywhere in Latin America, this kind of aid is nothing short of irresistible.

Explanations for Venezuela's Foreign Policy Departures

What explains the rise of so much political conflict and competition in relations between the United States and Venezuela under Chávez and such a discretionary use of Venezuela's resources abroad? A single explanation doesn't suffice, but some explanations are considerably more convincing than others. To explain the rise of soft-balancing, we focus on three levels of analysis, starting with a person-based approach.

There is no doubt that an important source of Venezuela's foreign policy under Chávez is the ideology and personality of Chávez himself. As most biographers have pointed out, Chávez's anti-Americanism has an ideological component that antedates his election to office. In the early 1970s he was attracted to Marxist ideas. He also became acquainted with and enthusiastic about left-wing military regimes in the early 1970s and actually had a chance to meet personally one such leader, Peru's Juan Velasco Alvarado, during a trip there in 1974. By the late 1970s, Chávez was fully infatuated with forming left-wing armed groups, and by the early 1980s he was being labeled by his superiors as a "dangerous subversive" participating in armed groups within the military.[22] He continued participating in various courses of study offered by the military, and by the time he was working on a master's degree in political science at Simón Bolívar University in Caracas (which he attended from 1989 to 1990), Chávez exhibited all the ideological bents of Latin America's radical anti-imperialists.[23] Chávez never expressed any remorse for his failed 1992 coup, and shortly after his release from prison in 1994, he undertook a lengthy visit to Cuba.

Chávez expressed significant anti-American sentiments as soon as he became president, voicing public adulation for Fidel Castro and visiting avowed anti-U.S. regimes such as those of Iran, Iraq, and Libya.[24] He refused U.S. assistance in 2000 during the natural disaster caused by floods in the state of Vargas, even though the aid was already under way, having being requested by Venezuela's defense minister. He suspended participation in Operation Red Flag, a program of military air exercises that Venezuela had been part of since the early 1990s. A day after the September 11 terrorist attacks, Chávez declared, "The United States brought the attacks upon itself, for their arrogant imperialist foreign policy." Chávez was also one of the few leaders to harshly condemn the 2001 U.S. retaliation against the Taliban in Afghanistan.[25]

Clearly, Chávez was ideologically predisposed to lock horns with the United States and he has done so since the start of his administration. Yet ideology and personality factors cannot explain other important aspects of Venezuela's foreign policy: why Chávez's anti-Americanism never subsided, as was the case with so many other leftist Latin American leaders in the 1990s. It cannot explain either the different strategies that Chávez has adopted to implement soft-balancing. Nor can it explain how Chávez has managed to succeed in changing Venezuela's long-established foreign policy to conform so closely to what he as a leader prefers.

Another level of analysis focuses on international factors, and especially the political interactions among states. Many scholars argue that the United States is to blame for Venezuela's rapidly radicalizing foreign policy, contending that lack of cooperation between the two countries is an outcome of U.S. intolerance for the regime. Underlying this hypothesis is the idea that Chávez's regime would cooperate were it not for Washington's antagonistic attitude. Washington has never liked nationalist, independence-seeking governments, the argument goes, especially in oil-rich nations. Robert Pape has argued that the probability of (soft-)balancing increases with every bout of aggressive unilateralism on the part of the United States.[26]

Evidence in support of this argument centers largely on the role played by the United States in events leading up to and following the April 2002 coups.[27] Although the United States did not precipitate the coup against Chávez, it was quick to welcome the new de facto government led by Pedro Carmona, in contrast to most leaders in the hemisphere, who condemned this government. Moreover, the State Department publicly blamed Chávez for the whole crisis, and continued to blame him for the subsequent turmoil that culminated with the oil strike of 2002–03. Furthermore, the ongoing U.S. government discussions over Venezuela's alleged cooperation with terrorist organizations, the U.S. ban on arms sales to Venezuela, and sanctions against a few Venezuelan officials for corruption are cited as reasons for Chávez to feel threatened by the United States.

A corollary to this "United States is the aggressor" explanation is that the U.S. government sides with Chávez's domestic enemies, labeled by Chávez the "coup-plotting" opposition, and with Venezuela's regional rival, Colombia, while harboring secret intentions, as Chávez claims, to oust his government or have him assassinated. Some analysts pursue this U.S.-sides-with-Venezuela's-enemies argument by detailing how the National Endowment for Democracy (NED) increased the allocation of funds to Venezuela's opposition. Some accounts show that such aid climbed from $232,831 in 2000 to almost $10 million in 2003.[28] Chávez accused the Venezuelan NGO Súmate, which helped organize the recall referendum of 2004, of having received $53,000 from NED and $84,840 from the U.S. Agency for International Development. In 2005, when the front pages of Caracas's dailies published a now-famous photo of Súmate leader María Corina Machado meeting with President George W. Bush at the White House, Venezuela's argument that the United States was solidly behind the opposition became hard to refute.

Even so, explaining Venezuela's hostility to the United States as a reaction to U.S. hostility faces a few empirical difficulties. Venezuela's distancing from Washington began before the 2002 coup. One could even argue that Venezuela's initial anti-Americanism and uncooperative behavior explains U.S. criticisms in 2002–03, rather than the other way around. Second, aid provided by the United States to nonstate actors in Venezuela seems puny in comparison to aid allocated to other nations, and to the level of funds the Venezuelan government itself has spent abroad. These comparisons make it hard to sustain the idea that aid to the Venezuelan opposition was destabilizing. Furthermore, the U.S. government routinely provides aid to civic organizations worldwide, many of them linked to opposition forces in countries that are pro-U.S., so it is hard to think of the Venezuelan case as exceptional enough to explain Chávez's especially aggressive foreign policy toward the United States. And since 2004, U.S. aid for democracy promotion—in fact, Western aid in general for civil society—has declined or adopted a "very low profile" in Venezuela.[29]

More important, anti-Venezuelan rhetoric and policies by the United States have diminished since 2005 even as anti-U.S. rhetoric and policies from Venezuela have increased. One way to assess this is to compare U.S. rhetoric vis-à-vis Venezuela and Iran. Figure 5-1 shows the number of times per month that a high-level White House or State Department official issued a public written or oral statement against either Iran or Venezuela. Iran is included to provide a comparison between Venezuela and a country that became perceived as the most serious security threat to the United States during Bush's second term. As a measurement of U.S. hostility, the chart is admittedly imperfect. It makes no references to the tone or severity of U.S. statements and fails to detail policy, simply noting discourse. Nevertheless, the data in the chart provide evidence of declining public criticism toward Venezuela after 2006. Between January 2004 and December 2005, the United States criticized Venezuela at the same rate as Iran (0.79 and 0.75 times per month, respectively). But between January 2006 and December 2008, U.S. criticism of Venezuela decreased (to 0.59), whereas criticism of Iran increased (to 1.82). This outcome was not accidental. It was the result of a policy established by Tom Shannon, deputy secretary of state for the Western Hemisphere, designed to deliberately avoid spats with Venezuela.[30]

The rhetorical de-escalation initiated by Washington did not reduce anti-U.S. pronouncements coming from Venezuela. In fact, some of the most antagonistic policies adopted by Venezuela occurred following 2006: rapprochement with Iran and Russia, an arms spending spree, rising belligerence toward Colombia, and expulsion of the U.S. ambassador. Actions taken by the United States, together with Chávez's ideology, contributed to Venezuela's foreign policy—but again, they do not by themselves explain the increasing radicalization of Venezuela's foreign policy.

Data presented in figure 5-1 might not convince authorities in Caracas of a change in U.S. attitude, but they do raise the possibility of another hypothesis to explain Venezuela's aggressive stand toward the United States: that Venezuela pursues soft-balancing because it knows how unlikely is the possibility of U.S. retaliation such as an economic

FIGURE 5-1. **Number of Times per Month a U.S. Public Statement Was Issued against Iran and Venezuela, 2004–08**

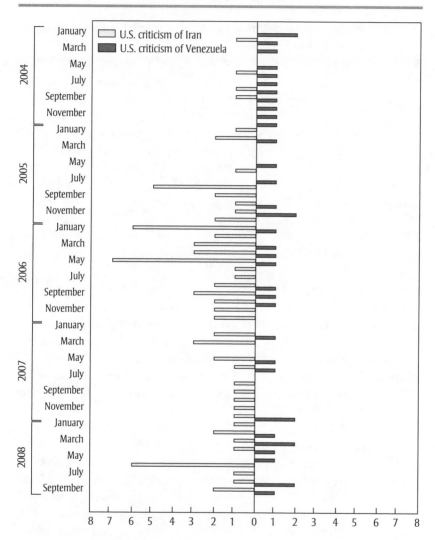

Source: Authors' calculation, based on www.timelinesdb.com.

Note: These data record the number of times that a public criticism of the Iran and Venezuela governments was issued by the White House, or a high-level State Department person or document. Each country receives a point when a government official makes a public statement or press release criticizing the foreign government (U.S.-Iran/U.S.-Venezuela). These criticisms cover a variety of themes: for Iran, nuclear and arms development, terrorism, Israel, Iraq, anti-Americanism, sanction violations, petrol production, foreign policy, economic policy, airspace, human rights; for Venezuela, they include petrol production, anti-Americanism, arms development, espionage, foreign policy, drug trafficking, airspace, human rights, economic policy. The criticisms are generated from a search engine called www.timelinesdb.com. The website compiles news from a considerable number of international news media sources. Specific search terms are entered to find relevant criticism data.

embargo or military invasion. Accordingly, Venezuela's soft-balancing occurs not so much because the United States provokes, but because the United States barely responds. Chávez wants the United States to react in order to provoke verbal confrontations. When there is no reaction, the safety of being a provocateur and the desire to keep provoking the United States both increase. We think that this perverse dynamic is one reason why Venezuela's antagonism toward the United States has escalated even as antagonism from the United States has declined.

A third level of analysis to explain Venezuela's foreign policy is domestic factors, in particular, features of the regime. A hybrid regime operating on a continent with so many democracies faces a particular foreign policy challenge: being ostracized and admonished by neighboring states. This situation compels the hybrid regime to make an effort to neutralize potential sources of criticism and even win over neighbors as allies. One way to do this is to give lavish foreign aid. Precisely because Latin America is predominantly democratic, Chávez must invest heavily in efforts to inhibit expressions of concern and to preempt rebukes coming from these countries with gifts. Moreover, to effectively buy the silence or non-censure of social progressives abroad, this foreign aid must adopt the veneer of progressive values. Hence much of Venezuela's foreign assistance is billed as development and poverty-reduction aid.

Venezuela can afford to spend abroad lavishly because of oil revenue *and* the newly created institutional setting outlined in previous chapters. Thus, a second way in which Venezuela's regime change has shaped foreign policy is by expanding the state's capacity to break with both tradition and public opinion. This is evident from surveys undertaken by both international and local pollsters that show that there is a significant mismatch between many of Chávez's foreign policy initiatives and majority views.[31] A study of attitudes toward global powers in forty-seven countries notes that 56 percent of Venezuelans in 2007 said they held "a positive image" of the United States.[32] This level of goodwill toward the United States is similar to that found among close U.S. allies in the hemisphere, including Canada, Mexico, and Chile. Moreover, Venezuela reported one of the world's highest response rates with "favorable views" of U.S. cultural exports. In short, Venezuelans might not be as overwhelmingly pro-American as, say, the citizens of certain African nations are known to be, but the majority of Venezuelans are certainly not as anti-American as their government. Further evidence of dissonance between Venezuela's foreign policy and the citizenry's views comes from local surveys. Polls consistently show that a majority of Venezuelans disapprove of many of Chávez's foreign policies, such as buying arms from Russia, subsidizing Cuba, and aiding Evo Morales in Bolivia. Venezuelans also disavow the regime's stance against cooperating with the United States in anti-narcotics operations.

Two points emerge from this discussion. First, the government's foreign policy is not exactly demand-driven—at least it is not driven by the wishes of majorities. Second, precisely because Chávez's policy diverges from public sentiment, it is clear that without the rise of the enormous concentration of power in the executive branch, it would not have been possible for Chávez to put in place such drastic departures in Venezuela's foreign policy.

Nevertheless, there is one domestic group that welcomes, and maybe even demands, more rather than less aggressive posturing toward the United States: the most ideologically radical members of the ruling party. Chávez could very well have concluded, halfway through his first administration, that displaying a radical anti-American foreign policy is a reliable instrument to unite a movement that is especially prone to internecine battles over domestic policy. As explained in chapter 1, Chávez has always had to struggle with issues of internal lack of discipline and defections. It is the *chavistas*, rather than Venezuelans at large, who are more likely to buy Chávez's argument that the government's setbacks are the result of imperialist opposition. Insofar as Chávez's anti-U.S. rhetoric and soft-balancing policy serves a domestic purpose, it is perhaps as a unifying factor and convenient excuse, crafted for consumption mostly within his own movement. This domestic-level factor is not the only explanation for Chávez's radical soft-balancing policy, but it is no doubt a potent one.

Oil as Facilitator and Constraint

Venezuela's relations with the United States tend to attract most scholarly attention, yet it is vital to bear in mind that Venezuela's foreign policy has never been exclusively about relations with the United States. Venezuela is first and foremost a petro-state, perhaps the only major one in the Western Hemisphere. As a result, it must navigate within the possibilities and constraints offered by the world oil market and Venezuela's own dependence on oil, whether it likes it or not. Most observers understand that oil is the one resource that allows Venezuela—more than any other Latin American country—to exercise social-power diplomacy and aspire to soft-balance the United States. Yet few scholars appreciate the extent to which the international political economy of oil has constrained Venezuela, even under the seemingly irrepressible Chávez.

Oil imposes on Venezuela two types of dependencies: first, dependence on a mono-commodity–oil; and second, dependence on a mono-market—the United States, which to this day remains the most important buyer of Venezuelan oil by far. This dual dependency makes Venezuela altogether vulnerable: to strangle Venezuela, all the United States needs to do is stop buying its oil.

In light of this vulnerability, Chávez has come to understand that he must lessen this dual dependence. But as discussed in the previous chapter, Chávez essentially chose to increase rather than lessen dependence on oil, leaving him one option alone: trying to relieve dependence on the United States. Yet, this effort failed as well. Market and industry rigidities simply made it hard for Venezuela to find alternative markets. Venezuela's crude oil cannot be placed easily outside the United States: heavy and impure, with a high sulfur content, it requires expressly built refineries mainly found in the United States. No other country has both the large energy needs and the refining capacity to process heavy crudes to absorb the bulk of Venezuelan oil.

The only market that conceivably could absorb the amount of oil Venezuela sells to the United States is China, but this market is unavailable, for technical, economic, and political reasons. Technically: China lacks the refineries needed to process Venezuelan crude. Economically: the cost of shipping oil from Venezuela to China would be prohibitive, requiring a journey either through the Strait of Magellan and then across the Pacific, or around Cape Horn and then into the Strait of Malacca. Either journey would require at least forty days at sea, in very large ships that are expensive to build, lease, and operate. China has access to plenty of oil in Central Asia and Africa, and the cost of transport from Venezuela seems hard to justify from the Chinese side. Politically: China has repeatedly refused to collaborate with Venezuela on its soft-balancing approach to the United States, although it has shown a commitment to invest in oil production. Were China supportive of Venezuela's foreign policy, it could perhaps buy more of its oil, at a loss, and place Venezuelan crude in third markets. But China has been reluctant to provide this type of sponsorship on the scale sought by Chávez.[33]

A comparison with Cuba helps illustrate Venezuela's predicament. In the 1960s Cuba executed a major political about-face when it severed

FIGURE 5-2. Venezuela's Oil Exports in Millions of Barrels to the United States Compared with Other Markets, 1998–2008

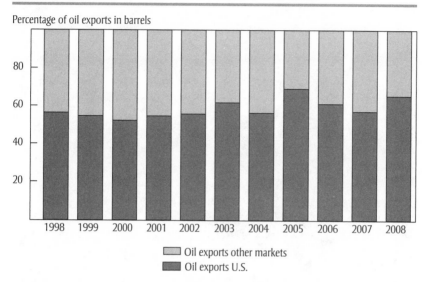

Percentage of oil exports in barrels

☐ Oil exports other markets
■ Oil exports U.S.

Source: Energy Information Administration; Ramón Espinasa, "The Performance of the Venezuelan Oil Sector 1997–2008: Official vs. International and Estimated Figures," follow-up on the paper presented at Conference on Energy Cooperation and Security in the Hemisphere Task Force, Center for Hemispheric Policy, University of Miami, October, 2008 (February 26, 2009).

long-standing ties to the United States and aligned itself with the Soviet Union. This worked because the Soviet Union was a major power willing to serve as the buyer-of-last-resort. The Soviet Union acted as Cuba's political sponsor, providing Cuba's main market for sugar and subsidies in the energy, capital, and weapons sectors. It was this sponsorship that allowed Cuba to break away from long-established trade links, and hence sever political ties, with the United States, in total disregard of economic efficiency. In the mid-2000s Chávez had high hopes that China could become Venezuela's Soviet Union, but for the aforementioned technical, economic, and political reasons, China did not come through. In 2008 Venezuela placed at most about 380,000 barrels of oil per day in China, a paltry amount compared to the 1.36 million barrels per day of crude oil and petroleum products that Venezuela sells to the United States (see figure 5-2).

This aspect of the international political economy of oil—Venezuela's dependence on the United States and China's dismissal of Venezuelan political objectives and relatively low demand for its oil—became perhaps

FIGURE 5-3. The World's Petro-States: Top Twenty-Five Oil-Producing Countries According to Proven Oil Reserves

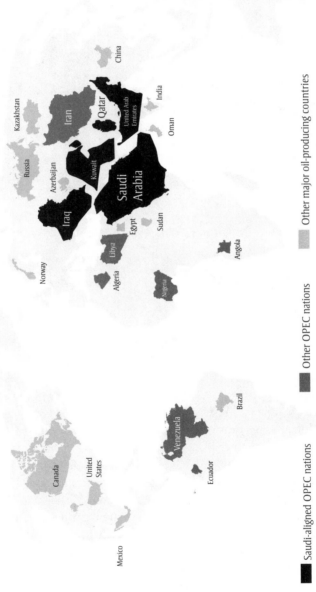

■ Saudi-aligned OPEC nations   ■ Other OPEC nations   ■ Other major oil-producing countries

Source: CIA World Factbook, estimated as of January 1, 2009, except Iran, as of January 1, 2010 (www.cia.gov/library/publications/the-world-factbook/rankorder/2178rank.html). Map designed by Andy Anderson.
Note: This isomorphic cartogram sizes countries in proportion to their proven oil reserves. It provides a visual image of the geopolitical importance of countries, measured in terms of oil reserves. The map also shows in black those OPEC nations that are aligned with Saudi Arabia; other OPEC nations are in dark gray, and non-OPEC oil producers in light gray.

one of Chávez's most serious foreign policy constraints in the mid-2000s. It forced him to endure the embarrassment of hypocrisy: being America's most ardent critic yet running one of the most lucrative businesses with the United States, the sale of oil and oil products. This paradoxical situation, together with PDVSA's declining productivity, also encouraged Venezuela to search out foreign policy tools other than soft-power diplomacy to soft-balance the United States.

Chávez's solution was to focus on maximizing the price of oil in world markets, by encouraging restrictions in the world supply of oil. But this policy of price maximization is not cost-free either. It entails entering into a conflict with Saudi Arabia, the largest petro-state in OPEC and arguably the world. Since the end of the OPEC crisis in the 1970s, Saudi Arabia's key oil policy has been to preserve a stable and affordable world oil price.[34] So to counter the Saudis within OPEC, Venezuela discovered the benefits of an alliance with Iran. Within OPEC, Iran and Venezuela are the second- and fifth-largest producers, respectively. Partnering with Iran made for a powerful bloc within OPEC that could effectively counter Saudi Arabia's efforts to keep prices stable. Thus, Iran and Venezuela have signed agreements covering trade, investments, and diplomatic coordination. Venezuela has supported Iran's dispute with the United Nations regarding Iran's nuclear program, and was the only nation to oppose the resolutions adopted by the International Atomic Energy Agency sanctioning Iran in September 2005 and February 2006. Although nuclear arms cooperation between Caracas and Teheran has not been confirmed, it has been the source of widespread speculation.[35]

One way to explain the logic of Venezuela's close alliance with Iran is to look at a map that shows country sizes according to the size of oil reserves (see figure 5-3). This map does not include the recent certification of further reserves of heavy oil in the Orinoco Tar Belt. Several important points become clear from this map. First, Saudi Arabia stands as the preeminent power among petro-states. Second, most of the large oil powers—Kuwait, Qatar, Iraq, Canada, and United Arab Emirates— are friends of the United States and Saudi Arabia. The only "large" oil power left in this map to balance Saudi Arabia's stable-price policy is Iran (and to a lesser extent Nigeria).

Venezuela's complicated relationship toward Saudi Arabia helps explain the emergence of Venezuela's "special relationship" not only with Iran but also Russia.[36] Since 2005 Venezuela and Russia have signed more than twelve arms purchase agreements worth over $4.4 billion, covered by cash payments from Venezuela and a $1 billion credit line from Russia.[37] In 2007 Venezuela became the third world's largest buyer of Russian weaponry, after China and India. In arms imports per capita, Venezuela is by far Russia's best customer: in 2007 Venezuela spent $33 per person on Russian weapons. Other arms suppliers trailed far behind—China spent just $0.96 per capita and India, just $0.79. In 2008 Venezuela ranked as the world's eighth largest arms importer, up from thirty-ninth in 1999.[38] In November 2008 Russia and Venezuela staged four-day joint tactical communication maneuvers and navy exercises, the so-called Joint Venus Operation. Two months earlier, the Russian government announced that two of its strategic bombers would be departing from a Venezuelan military base and flying over Caribbean air space.

There are a number of ways to explain Chávez's decision to become a leading buyer of Russian armaments by 2009. One could argue, as Chávez did, that it was a pre-emptive defensive response to a possible U.S. attack, although the kind of weaponry acquired would not do well in countering a hypothetical war with either the United States or Colombia. Possibly Chávez was seeking political protection, especially if international attention turned against Venezuela's weapons buildup. For us, a more compelling explanation is that Chávez sought to become one of Russia's major customers because Chávez needs Russia to cooperate with his foreign oil policy. Russia is the world's second-largest oil exporter and accounts for almost 10 percent of global oil output. If Russia were to refuse to cooperate with OPEC efforts to restrict supplies, it would automatically neutralize Venezuela's foreign policy objective of maximizing the price of oil. Thus, Chávez needs the Russians on his side, even if that means buying far more weapons than the Bolivarian revolution needs or can afford. In short, one of the primary purposes of Venezuela's ties with Iran and Russia was not just to soft-balance the United States, but to influence the world oil market, and somewhat contain Saudi Arabia.

And yet, Chávez cannot become too confrontational with Saudi Arabia, and this is the country's predicament, lest it provoke a severe crack in OPEC, thereby erasing the cartel's international bargaining leverage. Venezuela has therefore developed a dual, somewhat precarious, policy in its relations with Saudi Arabia: challenging the Saudis to cut back production but learning to live with whatever decision they make so as to preserve unity within the cartel.

The result is the rise of a set of alliances in the international oil market that is complex, tacit, and often mutually conflictive. Venezuela and Iran are compatible allies because they share similar policy goals: strengthen OPEC *and* raise oil prices. The United States and China are tacit allies in that they pursue goals that are contrary to Venezuela's and Iran's: diluting the power of OPEC and lowering the price of oil. Although China and the United States are generally seen as geopolitical rivals in the quest for declining sources of oil worldwide, both countries nonetheless share a desire to keep oil prices down and supplies plentiful.[39] Saudi Arabia is the intermediate player: it sides with Venezuela and Iran on the issue of strengthening OPEC, and is somewhat sympathetic to the United States and China on the issue of avoiding oil price hikes.[40]

This distribution of preferences across these nations suggests that the United States is not at all helpless in countering Venezuela: to the extent that the United States has kept China and Saudi Arabia on its side, an international political economy environment has prevailed in which some of Venezuela's foreign policy goals could be effectively contained.

Nonetheless, an entirely plausible confrontation between the United States and Iran might undo this balance by disrupting Iranian oil deliveries to China and so forcing China to move closer to Venezuela. China has significantly increased its oil ties with Iran in the last decade: Iran ships about 8 percent of its oil exports to China and has become its second-largest supplier of imported oil. Were a confrontation to occur between Iran and the United States that led to a disruption in Iranian oil to China, the tacit alliance between the United States and China would become strained. At the very least, China would want to find new suppliers, which would turn Venezuela into a more attractive option. This probably explains why in July 2010 China was willing to open a line of credit to PDVSA for almost 20 billion dollars for potential investments in heavy oil in the Orinoco Basin.

Why Venezuela Is Somewhat Trapped

To summarize our points thus far, it is useful to consider the internal contradictions in Venezuela's foreign policy. Venezuela's new foreign policy objective of soft-balancing the United States has uncovered a series of foreign policy needs that sometimes contradict or counteract each other. Success in reaching one goal might frustrate some other foreign policy objective sought by Venezuela. For instance, Venezuela would like to end its dependence on the U.S. oil market, but this would entail sacrificing social-power diplomacy, because Venezuela has no alternative market for its oil, no alternative source of revenue. Hence Venezuela undertook to expand oil sales to China. But a decisive Venezuelan effort to build this market would require considerable investment in refineries to process heavy crude, not to mention a way to lower shipping costs. Laying a pipeline across Colombia's Andean mountain chain to the Pacific coast would be a Herculean task, quite apart from the challenge of dealing with complex foreign policy issues with its neighbor that such a project would raise. And Venezuela's declining oil production, massive fiscal spending, and constraints in raising the world market price of oil mean that even its nationalist policy toward the foreign oil companies has had to be relaxed as well. Saddled with a very low after-tax profits ($4.5 billion in 2009), the new PDVSA is simply unable to meet its own stated goals of investing $124 billion in the next several years (or $21 billion annually) to stay competitive, and this forced Venezuela in late 2010 to reopen the oil sector just a bit: the government began to offer stakes to private companies in two oil projects in the Carabobo area of the Orinoco belt and four projects in the Junin area.

Thus, in almost every domain, even the ideologically rigid Chávez has had to face the reality of trade-offs imposed by the realities of his mismanagement of oil. The conclusion is that Chávez finds himself in a sort of foreign policy trap stemming from the inherent contradictions that arise from Venezuela's record-level dependence on oil, the U.S. oil market, and OPEC. In the context of declining productivity and declining investments, the result is that many of Chávez's foreign policy goals needed to be scaled back against Chávez's ideological wishes.

Symbolism and Realism: Cuba and Colombia

Venezuela's foreign policy under Chávez is not driven only by domestic political goals (regime-based explanations) and economic interests (oil-based explanations). There is a strong element of symbolic signaling in Chávez's foreign policy. This is of course evident in Venezuela's relations with the United States, where Venezuela seeks to project a David-and-Goliath image, and is even more salient in its relations with two smaller nations, Cuba and Colombia.

With Cuba, Venezuela pursues the closest form of collaboration imaginable, to the point where critics wonder whether Chávez is interested in a transnational merger. With Colombia, Venezuela pursues increasing levels of tension, to the point where analysts wonder about an inevitable war. Both merger with Cuba and war with Colombia seem too far-fetched for now, but there is no question that these are, by Latin American standards, extreme examples of "bandwagoning" (or partnering), in the case of Cuba, and "balancing," in the case of Colombia. Beyond the concrete political and economic issues, symbolism plays an important role in Venezuela's relations with both countries.

The Special Case of Cuba

Among Venezuela's relations with autocracies, the relationship with Cuba has been both the closest and the most symbolic. Cuba may not have brought Venezuela all the benefits the latter has gained from its relationships with China, Iran, and Russia, especially in terms of investment and weapons, but Cuba has fulfilled two objectives that no other alliance provides. The first is that Cuba has allowed Chávez to earn his credentials as a revolutionary. To this day, many Latin American radicals romanticize the Cuban Revolution as the epitome of Latin American resistance to imperialism. Playing up to Cuba serves the purpose of allowing Chávez to position himself as an heir to the island's revolutionary tradition. This is one reason why Chávez, even before being elected president, assigned high priority to Venezuela's relationship with Fidel Castro. Cuba thus offers a symbolic gain to Venezuela.

However, not everything is symbolic; Venezuela's relationship with Cuba has also fulfilled an advisory and intelligence role, especially in politics. By his own admission, Chávez has held frequent consultations with the Castro brothers on all issues bearing on both domestic and international affairs. It is believed that Fidel Castro was personally responsible for recommending and designing Chávez's *misiones,* and thus saving his government during the recall referendum in 2004. Numerous Cuban political, military, and intelligence advisers are stationed in Venezuela. And policies adopted by Chávez, not to mention rhetorical slogans, have often had close resemblance to Cuban policies and slogans (Chávez's latest slogan, "Motherland, socialism, or death . . . we will prevail," is almost a plagiarism of Cuba's famous slogan, "Motherland or death . . . we will prevail").

Because of the symbolic and informational value of the Cuban connection, Chávez has spent considerable time cultivating relations with Cuba. An analogy can be drawn between Cuba's cold war relationship with the Soviet Union and Venezuela's Cuban ties. For Cuba, Venezuela has become the Soviet Union 2.0, supplying handsome oil subsidies well in excess of the island's domestic consumption needs. PDVSA maintains a sales office in Havana, and Cuba is believed to re-export perhaps as much as 40 percent of Venezuela's oil imports, which occurred earlier with Soviet oil sent to Cuba. This Venezuelan subsidy is provided with almost no political conditionality, which beats any aid and investment Cuba might receive from almost any source. Referring to Venezuela's aid, Yoani Sánchez, Cuba's most famous blogger, aptly described Venezuela as "Cuba's Viagra."[41]

In exchange, Cuba has supplied Venezuela with a certificate of "radical" credentials, allowing Chávez to flaunt anti-imperialist tirades and score points with Latin America's most radical left-wing sectors. Cuba has also provided tangible assets such as almost 40,000 technical personnel, including physicians, nurses, teachers, and sports trainers, as well as military, security, and intelligence personnel who help run Venezuela's ports, telecommunications, police training, the issuing of identity documents, and the business registry.

Since Raúl Castro became head of Cuba's regime, there have been rumors that he was uneasy regarding Cuba's dependence on Venezuela, that he disliked Chávez personally, and that he fired Foreign Minister Felipe Pérez Roque and Vice President Carlos Lage for being too pro-Venezuelan. Nonetheless, there are reasons to expect that the special relationship between Cuba and Venezuela will endure, despite any existing reservations. The reason is that each country provides the other with resources that are cheap owing to their abundance in the sending country.[42] The oil sent to Cuba represents only a small fraction (3.5 percent in 2005) of Venezuela's oil output. Conversely, Cuban technical experts are in large supply because of the country's low productivity and surplus of trained personnel, and so little is lost, and much gained, by sending them to Venezuela. As a result, each country provides a subsidy that is inexpensive for itself but quite valuable for the other, which suggests that there are few economic reasons to end this relationship.

In fact, there is evidence that the relationship may recently have strengthened. In the Health and Agriculture ministries, Cuban advisers are said to wield more power than Venezuelan bureaucrats.[43] This situation created resentments within the government and even forced the resignation of a minister who had allegedly complained privately about this situation. It was said that Barbara Castillo, a former Cuban trade minister who had been detailed to the Venezuelan Ministry of Agriculture, was making decisions about which coffee growers' farms in Venezuela to expropriate, and how.[44] Ramiro Valdés, who ranks third in Cuba's ruling hierarchy, early in 2010 was invited by Chávez for a technical sojourn. Some members of Venezuela's opposition believed that Valdés, who is well known in Cuba for having designed and implemented policies to restrict access to the Internet, came to help Chávez ahead of a legislative election in September.[45] And in April 2010, when Cuba's president Raúl Castro concluded a visit to Caracas by stating publicly that each day Cuba and Venezuela are becoming "more and more alike," nobody in the Venezuelan government batted an eye. Whether true or not, all of this reveals the depth of Venezuela's political ties with Cuba.

Conflicts with Colombia: Escalation, De-escalation . . . Repeat

In contrast to cozy relations with Cuba, Venezuela's relations with Colombia are the most tense in South America. As of this writing, Venezuela has broken relations with Colombia four times (2005, 2008, 2009, and 2010), talked about a military response against Colombia twice (2008 and 2009), and imposed trade restrictions once (2009–10). Some analysts think that these tensions are ephemeral: the economic gains from trade, constantly growing since the late 1980s, not to mention the sizable population of Colombians long residing in Venezuela, push toward peace and cordiality between both nations. After all, in all four crises, Venezuela sought reconciliation, sooner or later. Other scholars expect tension to get worse: the security threats each nation poses to the other are seen as uncontainable. Analysts point to the 2009 trade embargo, which lasted longer than anyone expected—at a huge cost for both countries— as a sign of how far Venezuela will go to punish Colombia. Our view is that neither peace nor war is probable. Rather, a high degree of tension but with controlled limits is more likely to obtain. Venezuela has much to gain by maintaining a certain level of tension with Colombia, and as María Teresa Romero remarked, staging occasional mini-crises followed by fragile reconciliations soon after.[46]

There is no question that economic interdependence plays a major break in tensions between both countries. Economic interdependence accelerated rapidly since the late 1980s. By the early 1990s, a bilateral diplomatic agenda that was almost exclusively centered on border conflicts was intelligently extended to deal with security, trade, infrastructure, and immigration, paving the way for more trade. By 2009

Venezuela was Colombia's second largest export market. Infrastructure projects, particularly in the energy sector, became the focus of several strategic partnerships between the two countries. According to official estimates, there are more than 650,000 longtime Colombians residing in Venezuela, many having entered the country illegally.

For a while, this growing interdependence ensured a cordial relationship between the conservative, pro–United States government of President Alvaro Uribe (2002–10) and the increasingly radical Chávez. To be sure, Uribe's stepped-up, partly U.S.-financed military efforts against Colombia's guerrilla movements, an initiative known as Seguridad Democrática, and Chávez's amicable gestures toward the guerrilla movements created a serious split between the countries. Even so, relations remained stable and often cordial during most of the 2000s. A brief crisis erupted in 2005 when Colombian agents, without permission from Caracas, penetrated Venezuelan territory to capture Rodrigo Granda, the so-called "FARC foreign minister" (FARC stands for Fuerzas Armadas Revolucionarias de Colombia, the Revolutionary Armed Forces of Colombia, a guerrilla group). In response, Venezuela broke off relations with Colombia, but not for long—within a month relations returned to normal. In 2007, Uribe even invited Chávez to participate in an effort to liberate people kidnapped by the FARC guerrillas. This incident ended in an embarrassing failure, but both governments agreed to save face and not to make too much of the fiasco.[47]

This era of relative cordiality ended decisively in March 2008, when Colombian armed forces raided and destroyed a FARC guerrilla camp based in Ecuador. Venezuela instantly took the side of Ecuador—a member of ALBA—broke off relations with Colombia, and ordered the deployment of ten military battalions to the border region. Not much happened—as in 2005, relations were restored quickly—but since this incident tensions have lingered to a greater degree than in the past. Until 2008, political rivalry between Venezuela and Colombia seemed relatively innocuous. At one point the two governments actually competed in a noble cause, to see which country would succeed in liberating Ingrid Betancourt, a former presidential candidate who had been kidnapped by the FARC. But with the 2008 crisis relations took a nasty turn, with talk of war in the air for the first time in the Chávez era.

There is no question that both countries have plenty to fight about. Security and narcotics are sensitive issues for both, and the situation became acute and problematic from the start of Plan Colombia. This is a U.S.-Colombia jointly financed program aimed at countering drug trafficking and guerrilla activity. In 2005 Chávez announced his unwillingness to cooperate with the United States in counter-narcotics; U.S. Drug Enforcement Agency (DEA) staff were reduced and no further visas were issued to DEA agents. Venezuelan cooperation with Colombia suffered by extension, complicating Colombia's national security goal of containing the drug trade. During the March 2008 incursion into Ecuador, Colombia captured the computers of the FARC leader Raúl Reyes, and claimed to have discovered irrefutable evidence of Venezuelan support for the guerrilla group, a charge that Bogotá has never doubted but Caracas has consistently denied.

Likewise, Colombia's increasing reliance on the U.S. military exacerbates Venezuela's sense that its security is under threat.[48] This was the context behind the third major crisis in Venezuela and Colombia relations: in August 2009, a report was leaked indicating that Colombia had granted U.S. armed forces access to as many as seven military bases. Predictably, this leak and its poor handling by the United States and Colombia gave Chávez a pretext to publicly announce that this move by the United States was directly targeted at ousting his government. Although the agreement between the United States and Colombia did not really include an escalation of U.S. military operations, Venezuela predictably talked about becoming encircled. Chávez proceeded to break relations with Colombia and called on the army to prepare for war. This time, he went further, imposing trade restrictions on Colombia. Although nothing came of this talk of military action, the trade barriers did stick. Bilateral trade dropped from $7 billion annually to about $1 billion by 2010.

With the 2009 crisis, Venezuela conveyed clearly to Bogotá that the most effective way to punish Colombia is through trade restrictions. Colombian exporters of textiles, agribusiness products, automobiles, and other goods had been enjoying record-level sales, thanks to Venezuela's oil boom. Chávez knows that trade restrictions hurt Colombia, and he has used this tool frequently enough. First, Venezuela withdrew from the Andean Pact after Colombia began negotiating a free trade agreement with the United States; this decision increased commercial uncertainty and enabled Chávez to pursue unilateral measures to hamper trade. Second, Venezuela has restricted trade at the border by closing roads, sometimes immediately following a public exchange between the two presidents. More significant, Chávez has opted to use exchange controls to severely limit access by Colombian exporters to official-rate dollars, favoring instead Brazilian and Argentine exporters. Uribe responded by limiting gas supply to the Maracaibo area, where gas is essential for extracting oil and supplying local industrial plants.

Nevertheless, one has to be careful not to exaggerate the probability of all-out conflict, despite the serious security threats. Even though Venezuela has broken off relations with Colombia four times, four times it has reopened relations soon afterward, often in return for very soft concessions. The latest crisis is a perfect example of this escalate/de-escalate pattern. In mid-2010, Colombia provided evidence before the OAS that Venezuela was tolerating, maybe even sheltering, guerrilla activities and personnel in Venezuelan territory. Venezuela responded to Colombia's revelations by breaking relations again. But as in 2005 and 2008, the 2010 crisis was quickly resolved. As soon as Juan Manuel Santos took office as president of Colombia a few days after Colombia's revelations, Chávez sought reconciliation. Colombia hardly yielded anything, except to say that it would not intervene in Venezuela's domestic affairs; it did not pledge to abandon plans to bring charges against Venezuela in the international arena. Thus, it took little to get Venezuela to de-escalate its response.

This cycle of frequent escalation and quick de-escalation has a logic. There are huge conflicts of interest, but neither country wants an armed conflict—neither country has much to gain from it. Colombia's military has too much on its plate to be interested in a border conflict, and Venezuela's military is completely unprepared to meet one of the hemisphere's most experienced, battle-ready armed forces. In fact, Venezuela's armed forces reacted unenthusiastically to Chávez's calls for war in March 2008 and November 2009. This makes sense. Venezuelan armed forces do not share Chávez's bellicose attitude toward Colombia—or, for that matter, the United States. For one thing, the large presence of Colombian immigrants in Venezuela suggests that many ordinary Venezuelans, especially those who live in western states and serve in the military, have Colombian relatives. Furthermore, most ranking Venezuelan officers have likely benefited from American military training and don't want to be ordered to fight American troops in Colombia.

Another reason why outright war is unlikely is that Venezuela's armed forces are major beneficiaries of both licit and illicit trade with Colombia. Venezuela's boom from 2003 to 2008 formidably expanded both legal and illegal bilateral trade, and Venezuelan troops stationed along the border were among the main beneficiaries and brokers of this exchange. Even during days when the border was officially closed, street peddlers selling gasoline canisters smuggled from Venezuela were a common sight on the Colombian side of the border, where the price of gasoline is several times that in Venezuela. If there is any merit to the theory that economic interdependence acts as a force for peace, it should hold in this pair of countries whose economies and populations are highly integrated.

Notwithstanding de facto close associations, there is no question that each of the nations has discovered that it has something symbolic to gain by keeping tensions high rather than low. The issue of the military bases and the unpopularity across Latin America of the drug war provides Chávez with a new opportunity to use tensions with Colombia as a way to showcase an anti-American stance, rather than merely an anti-Bush stance. Now that the more internationally popular Barack Obama has replaced Bush, Chávez needs to deemphasize opposition to Bush in favor of opposition to U.S. imperialism and militarism. Tensions with Colombia, which are so bound up with U.S. militarism in the region, allow him to make that case.

There are symbolic gains for Colombia, too, in sustaining tensions with Chávez. Despite his frequent commentary on candidates during Colombia's 2010 presidential election campaign—which might have been expected to please some of the candidates—Chávez is a highly unpopular figure in most of Colombia. In fact, all the candidates, including one whose party has been linked to Chávez, condemned his comments as undue meddling. Criticizing Chávez for his alleged connections with the guerrillas and the drug trade allowed Uribe to rally support for his fight against these foes, and became an election issue favoring his candidate. Uribe also gained respect by appearing as the more commonsensical of the two heads of state in this otherwise belligerent bilateral relationship.

In short, there are reasons to expect the Venezuela-Colombia relationship to stay strained, but within bounds. Both countries benefit from the tension, as long as it doesn't become a trans-border war. As with relations with the United States, Chávez knows that there are benefits from maintaining a discourse of animosity as well as huge costs from disrupting actual ties. For Chávez, Colombia has become a scapegoat in his effort to transition from an anti-Bush policy to a broader self-defensive, anti-imperialist stance. For Colombia, Chávez reinforces the government's call for a stronger approach to combating the guerrillas and narco-trafficking and for forging closer collaboration with the United States. Chávez has no interest in helping the political careers of Colombian politicians who are ideological rivals—whether Uribe or

Santos—and this keeps Chávez interested in maintaining a certain level of tension (as a possible way to eclipse these rivals) short of war (so as to avoid generating a rally-around-the-flag effect in Colombia). Thus, full peace will not come despite the potential economic gains, but full war is also unlikely, despite the enormous security threat each country poses to the other.

Does the Policy Work? Maximum Failures and Secondary Achievements

We now turn to the question of payoff. Has Venezuela's new foreign policy benefited the Venezuelan government? The answer is complicated. In terms of the objectives articulated by the Chávez administration itself, the answer is no. But in terms of secondary, even unstated, goals, there is evidence of huge rewards. These rewards in secondary goals continue to provide incentives for Chávez to sustain many of his foreign policy actions, even if the administration's more grandiose goals remain elusive. Let's look at the grandiose misses and the secondary hits.

The misses are obvious. Venezuela's effort to soft-balance the United States has in no verifiable way contained the power and actions of the northern power globally or in the Western Hemisphere. It has not even produced a major realignment in world politics. Chávez failed to rally support from the United Nations General Assembly when he sought to gain a seat for Venezuela on the Security Council in 2006, despite last-minute visits to several countries, including some in Africa, where petro-dollars were reportedly offered as a reward for support. Arguably, even Brazil has moved closer to the United States in the 2000s, signing a series of development agreements with the United States in 2007 (under Bush) and security agreements in 2010 (under Obama). There is also evidence of the failure of soft-balancing pursued to deliberately provoke a confrontation with the United States, which has thus far adhered to the policy of downplaying Venezuela's aggressive rhetoric.

Likewise, social-power diplomacy has not led to a realization of Chávez's grandiose visions for a paradigm shift in Latin America. It has not given rise to a massive coalition of Latin American nations against the United States. Venezuela has not slowed the pace at which countries sign free trade agreements. Few Latin American politicians now running for office want to be openly associated with Chávez. Chávez did play some role in helping a few anti-American governments to get elected (in

Bolivia, Ecuador, and Nicaragua) and to survive (Cuba), but it is unclear that Venezuelan influence, rather than domestic issues, underlies the rise and survival of these regimes. Outside the hemisphere, Venezuela's effort to raise the price of oil by balancing Saudi Arabia within OPEC has not borne fruit either. Few OPEC members have joined a Venezuela-Iran axis against the Saudis, and the price of oil continues to be determined by supply, demand, and speculative factors more than by Venezuela-Iran geopolitical moves.

Yet despite these major misses, the rewards at the level of secondary objectives are impressive. Although soft-balancing has failed to unite the region or the country, sustaining a strong anti-imperialist foreign policy does unite the radicals, both domestically and internationally, and this is politically beneficial for Chávez. At home, this unification of radicals—who now control all the key policy institutions—gives much-needed energy to Chávez's domestic political agenda as its performance in office loses some luster and as he seeks to curb the power of regime soft-liners. Likewise, impressing radicals abroad is useful for at least two reasons. First, it provides an international constituency willing to forgive Chávez for his excesses and governance failures. There is also a second, less direct, benefit with respect to relations with other Latin American governments: most Latin American governments, whether on the left or right, do not want to find themselves in trouble with the radical sectors of their respective countries, and they all use cordial relations with Venezuela as a way to appease their own domestic radical groups.

The secondary effects of social-power diplomacy are even more impressive. Social power has served as a magnificent publicity stunt, allowing Chávez to win over two types of international allies: other states that refuse to smite Venezuela, especially if they benefit from petro-dollars via either trade or aid, and intellectuals on the left, especially in Europe and even the United States.[49] Social-power projection allowed Chávez to score points among opinion makers who would otherwise be appalled by Chávez's domestic and international failings.

A comparison of Venezuelan and American aid to other nations shows how aggressively Venezuela tried to play this competitive game with the United States. It is hard to measure the extent of Venezuelan aid, since official figures are unavailable or untrustworthy, but a World Bank report attempted to estimate Venezuelan bilateral aid in the form of subsidized oil plus concessional lending in 2006 by reviewing official signed documents. The report divides aid between a lower bound (the minimum

T A B L E   5 - 2 .   United States and Venezuelan Assistance to PetroCaribe Nations

Millions of U.S.$

Nation	Average U.S. assistance, 2005–07	Total Venezuelan aid, 2006 (upper bound)	Total Venezuelan aid, 2006 (lower bound)
Antigua and Barbuda	0.01	134.94	45.0
Bahamas	5.78	no data	no data
Belize	2.77	122.6	40.9
Cuba	14.03	2,759.4	2,621.5
Dominica	0.04	30.66	10.2
Dominican Republic	43.96	1,533	511.0
Grenada	0.47	30.66	10.2
Guyana	25.35	159.5	53.2
Haiti	224.45	143.1	143.1
Jamaica	44.26	643.9	214.6
Nicaragua	132.41	521.2	173.7
Suriname	1.29	306.6	102.2
St. Lucia	0.01	no data	no data
St. Kitts and Nevis	0.00	30.66	10.2
St. Vincent and the Grenadines	0.03	30.66	10.2
Total	494.85	6,446.88	3,946.0

Source: U.S. assistance estimated using totals from USAID, *Latin America and the Caribbean: Selected Economic and Social Data;* Venezuela's assistance from World Bank, Heavily Indebted Poor Countries Debt Strategy and Analysis Capacity Building Program (www.hipc-cbp.org/files/en/open/Guide_to_Donors/Venezuela_30_04_2008.pdf).

Notes: Upper and lower bounds were employed for both the oil subsidy and concessional loan totals for individual countries because no concrete country-specific data have been published. The upper-bound value assumes the country accepts all possible oil and concessional loans available to it under the terms of the 2005 PetroCaribe agreement. The lower-bound value is based on the assumption that countries only take up a third of their allowed quota of Venezuelan oil and concessional loans. For Cuba, the HIPC assumed that the lower bound was 95 percent of the maximum aid. Haiti was not an original member of PetroCaribe but joined in 2006. Honduras and Guatemala are excluded because they joined PetroCaribe after 2007. Oil was estimated to cost roughly $60/barrel.

that a government would receive from Venezuela) and an upper bound (the largest amount of aid possible were the recipient country to take advantage of all benefits in the agreements). Table 5-2 compares this Venezuelan aid to U.S. assistance, on the basis of annual average figures for 2005 through 2007. The comparison is staggering. Venezuelan aid to PetroCaribe nations far surpassed United States assistance, except for

U.S. aid to Haiti. Venezuelan aid to small Caribbean island nations creates formidable political leverage in the Caribbean Basin, an area historically considered an "American lake."

Social-power diplomacy thus allows Chávez to craft what could be called a coalition of the silent, even among those he annoys. There are plenty of examples of acts of annoyance, even insults, whose consequences Chávez manages to fend off relatively unscathed. For instance, Chávez has insulted Chile for not granting Bolivia access to the sea, upbraided President "Lula" da Silva of Brazil for creating an environmental threat via the development of ethanol, accused President Alan García of Peru of being an "imperialist puppy," and claimed that Colombia's administration resembles Israel's "genocidal" government. By normal diplomatic standards, these are outrageous acts, yet in most instances, the Latin American response has been tame; after a quick apology by Chávez, relations usually return to their normal state.

The famous 2007 Ibero-American summit—where Spain's King Juan Carlos said to Chávez, "Why don't you shut up?"—illustrates this deference. The king's rebuke occurred because Chávez was interrupting the Spanish prime minister, José Luis Rodríguez Zapatero, to interject insults at the previous prime minister, José María Aznar, whom Chávez was calling a fascist and lower than a snake. The king's phrase became an instant YouTube sensation and a favorite ringtone in Spain and Venezuela. What is noteworthy about this incident is not that the king admonished Chávez before the cameras, but that no one else dared utter a similar reprimand. Part of this unspoken pledge of silence is due to a long-standing tradition among Latin American presidents to avoid reproving one another on the international stage. But this "live and let live" Latin courtesy typically works only if reciprocal. What is unusual about the Chávez case is that Chávez often fails to reciprocate, and yet there is widespread diplomatic tolerance. This has much to do with his social-power diplomacy and the positive image that this diplomacy has conferred upon the regime.

Thus, Chávez's social-power foreign policy produced for Venezuela an impressive diplomatic shield that has protected Chávez against international criticism even by those who know better, and given him a reputation for humanitarianism among the less informed. This can well be considered an amazing foreign policy accomplishment.

Despite these benefits, it is absolutely essential to bear in mind that there are huge costs to many of these policies. For instance, when Chávez accused Bush of being the devil at the United Nations, he alienated so many nations that he pretty much sacrificed Venezuela's chance of gaining a seat in the Security Council. Chávez's overtures to Iran, together with the support he proffers to certain states, NGOs, and individuals involved in obscure international dealings and violence, create unnecessary nervousness even among some of his sympathizers.

Even the most seemingly successful of Chávez's policies, social-power diplomacy, has led to huge blunders. Chávez often makes no secret of the fact that he spends on some politicians and not on others, and this overt political bias generates angry responses from Latin American politicians who are not benefiting from Chávez's largesse, or who have been damaged by his moves.[50] In the 2006 Peruvian and Mexican presidential elections, when it came to light that Chávez was supposedly supporting one of the candidates, outrage spread across the political spectrum, boosting the fortunes of those Chávez had not supported. Similar resentment has sprung from other situations. In Peru, Congress launched an investigation of medical malpractice cases in Misión Milagro, a Venezuela-sponsored eye-clinic program. In Colombia, Chávez's attacks on President Alvaro Uribe, Latin America's most pro-American president, actually boosted Uribe's popularity ratings. Likewise, his attacks on the 2010 presidential candidate Juan Manuel Santos, Uribe's chosen successor, helped Santos defeat his rival by an impressive forty-one-point lead in the second round. In Argentina, the opposition and the press denounced the scandal over Venezuelan cash contributions made to support President Cristina Kirschner's electoral campaign.

Chávez's use of social-power diplomacy may have reached a turning point in Honduras. In January 2008, almost the entire political establishment in Honduras welcomed President Mel Zelaya's agreement to join PetroCaribe. Venezuela's oil subsidies would generate savings and finance a multitude of development projects, people thought. But when it became clear that President Zelaya was using Venezuelan funds illegally to build a political base and—a graver issue—to campaign for a referendum to change the constitution to permit his reelection, the entire political system turned against him. In the spring of 2009 Honduras was plunged into an acrimonious confrontation between the executive branch and all other constitutional powers and political parties. In late June, evidence was found that Zelaya had obtained from Venezuela cash to carry out a *"consulta"*—a sort of electoral referendum to ask voters if they were interested in a constituent assembly. The Supreme Court considered the *consulta* to be illegal and called on Zelaya to cancel it, to no avail. The court then ordered the military to arrest the president, who was expelled from the country. The international community vigorously condemned the coup, precipitating the worst diplomatic crisis in the Americas in years. However, while most Hondurans (58 percent of respondents) disagreed with the way Zelaya was removed from office, an even larger majority (more than 75 percent) disagreed with Zelaya's *consulta*.[51]

In Honduras, therefore, Chavez's social-power diplomacy led President Zelaya to embark on a *chavista*-like path of political reform: the use of referenda (and funds from Venezuela) to mobilize voters on behalf of a constitutional assembly, exactly as Chávez (and Evo Morales in Bolivia and Rafael Correa in Ecuador) had done. Precisely because Chávez and Zelaya had become so politically close, the non-Zelayista forces in Honduras had plenty of reason to fear that Zelaya's goal was *chavista* at heart—an expansion of presidential powers. Chávez's overtures to Honduras actually united most political actors against Zelaya, and this paved the way for the June 2009 coup.

Because of Chávez's biased intrusion into domestic political affairs—or because Chávez's aid can allow incumbents to turn reckless in their spending and treatment of checks and balances—it is no surprise that public opinion polls conducted across the region show that Chávez was considered the most "widely mistrusted" world leader, on a par with George W. Bush's ratings in 2007.[52] Despite Chávez's efforts, most countries in the region today want closer rather than colder relations with their most powerful neighbor, the United States.[53]

Reflections

It should be clear by now that Chávez, like most active international actors, pursues multiple goals in his foreign policy, and that oftentimes, the secondary objectives succeed better than the primary ones. That explains the survival of seemingly costly policies such as soft-balancing and social-power diplomacy.

But rewards are not the only factor to consider. We also highlighted contradictions in Venezuela's foreign policy goals that end up working against each other. For instance, ending the country's dependence on U.S. oil markets would significantly undermine Chávez's pursuit of wealth distribution, not to mention Venezuela's consumption boom at home and abroad, since Chávez has no alternative market for the country's oil, hence no other source of revenue. Working to develop the Chinese oil market will require making heavy investments in refineries and shipping costs, which will also undermine generous social outlays. Continuing the consumption boom via social investments has produced a huge opportunity cost: needed investments in infrastructure have not been made, which has lowered Venezuela's productivity. Pursuing high oil prices causes rifts both with China and OPEC. By preferring to work exclusively with international state-owned oil companies, rather than privately owned companies, Chávez denies Venezuela the capital and know-how required to expand its own oil output. Social-power diplomacy, when played too politically, produces disunity rather than unity in the region; seeking international confrontation with the United States polarizes the hemisphere's countries and the electorate within the countries.

Chávez's dragon-like foreign policy of spitting flames against the United States (and Colombia) and appearing, via social-power diplomacy, to be protective of some weaker actors generates huge rewards, mostly in terms of secondary, often unarticulated, goals. But along with these rewards, huge costs are also associated with many of these policies. The trade-offs are not insignificant. They help explain some of the most important checks on Chávez's radicalism—especially why he never seems to go as far in foreign policy as his fiery rhetoric might lead one to expect.

6

Conclusion: Hybrid Regimes and Populism in Venezuela and Beyond

What insights about the political economy of development can we draw from observing over a decade of *chavismo* in Venezuela? In this concluding chapter we discuss lessons learned in three broad areas. First, we summarize what we learned about the nature and actual operations of hybrid regimes—regimes that are neither fully democratic nor fully autocratic. We discuss specifically how Chávez managed to remain electorally competitive while carrying out a process of gradual political closure. Second, we focus on the issue of populism—Latin America's long-standing practice of deploying state resources to weaken institutions that mediate between the state and society, presumably in the interest of the common people. We discuss how Chávez's version of populism both emulates and modernizes the traditional Latin American model of populism. And finally, we explore the question of how replicable the *chavista* regime is: What kinds of conditions could make other societies, within the region or elsewhere, vulnerable to developing a hybrid, populist regime similar to Chávez's?

On Hybrid Regimes

Hybrid regimes—somewhat less common in the twentieth century—have proliferated worldwide in the 2000s.[1] During the cold war, the world was split largely in two camps: full-fledged democracies, mostly in the North Atlantic and a few in Asia, and autocracies, mostly in the East and the South. For a while in the 1990s, during the heyday of the so-called third wave of democracy, the balance seemed to shift in the direction of more democracies. But since early in the new century, the trend has been toward hybrid regimes. Many of these regimes—either former democracies, such as Venezuela, or former autocracies, such as Russia—have moved toward an "in-between" position, a "gray zone" in which rulers introduce autocratic practices without totally abolishing democratic institutions, particularly free elections. Using data from Freedom House, an organization that ranks countries' political rights and civil liberties, Henry Hale finds that 32 percent of all countries in 2008 could be considered hybrid and that many of them have been stable and long-lasting, which challenges the notion that democratic transitions and consolidations are inevitable.[2]

Hybrid regimes are becoming not only more numerous but also more self-confident. In its 2010 report, Freedom House stated that "not free" and "partly free" regimes are not only expanding in number, but also becoming more influential in world politics, less susceptible to Western pressure, and more effective at keeping opposition at bay. According to Freedom House we are in the midst of a "freedom recession."[3]

The Chávez regime is perhaps the most obvious and pronounced hybrid regime to emerge in Latin America, certainly since the Alberto Fujimori administration in Peru in the 1990s, or even earlier. The key feature of hybrid regimes, most scholars agree, is the use of legal and illegal mechanisms to erode checks and balances on the executive branch. Often by blunt admission of the rulers themselves, these regimes unabashedly reject the concept of "limited government." They claim that problems inherited from previous administrations are so formidable that their task as rulers is to empower government to act boldly in favor of some overall interest, such as national security and income redistribution, rather than to negotiate with special-interest groups or to waste time seeking consensus.

One key puzzle about these regimes is how they manage to obtain electoral majorities despite an obvious display of nondemocratic practices, frequently in the context of lackluster policy outcomes. Chávez's regime is a good example of this paradox. His movement has won all but one of all the elections held since he assumed power, yet many of his policy results are neither that impressive nor that different from previous administrations'. No doubt economics underlies his electoral success: the 2003–08 oil boom allowed the state to generate a formidable consumption boom and engage in target spending, all of which granted it a hard-to-match co-optation tool. That a hybrid regime became consolidated in Venezuela in the midst of an oil boom is hardly a coincidence.

Nonetheless, we have shown that together with oil economics, a number of institutional factors and policy tools played an equally decisive role. Some of these factors and tools are commonly discussed in the literature on hybrid regimes elsewhere.[4] They include:

—Packing a number of state offices (tribunals, comptroller general, electoral bodies, key government bureaucracies) with avowed loyalists

—Badmouthing the opposition as disloyal, antidemocratic, oligarchic, antipatriotic, and so forth

—Excluding the opposition systematically from policy negotiations

—Undermining the autonomy of civil society by working exclusively with loyal groups (*Círculos Bolivarianos* at the outset, and later *consejos comunales*)

—Shrinking the size of privately owned media by revoking or not renewing operating licenses; denying them advertising revenue from state-owned enterprises and other agencies; delaying approval of foreign exchange; and acquiring small radio stations in rural areas

—Invoking the law and discretionary measures to penalize opponents and offering impunity to government officials and regime-friendly business interests

—Mobilizing pro-government voters in elections and using social policy as a vote-buying mechanism (busing state employees to polling stations; threatening to terminate employment of employees who vote for the opposition; handing out cash in exchange for votes)

—Bypassing the authority of subnational officials elected by the opposition, and limiting their share of state revenue

—Designing electoral rules that are deliberately disadvantageous to the opposition: gerrymandering, making the electoral system blatantly disproportional, and banning opposition candidates from participating in electoral processes—all clear violations of political rights

—Expanding the prerogatives of the military and liberating them from the scrutiny of civilian authorities other than the executive branch

Other, less openly acknowledged, tactics employed by the Chávez regime have not received sufficient attention in the literature on hybrid regimes, or are simply more specific to a small subset of hybrid political systems, in some cases unique to *chavismo*. One such tactic was to promote massive spending in conjunction with lawlessness.[5] Unusual for these forms of government, Chávez went on a grand spending spree at home and abroad, with no controls or accountability. A lot of this aid went to the poor, especially from 2004 to 2008. This strategy produced a widespread sense of reaching out to the poor that previous administrations had never matched. The scale of social spending helped reduce poverty indicators and earned the government a favorable reputation abroad. The fact that there was a lot of waste and favoritism in managing these resources did not reduce the positive reception of the largesse.

Another *chavista* tactic, present also in other hybrid regimes, is the uneven application of the law. Although the fiscal and social stimulus caused people's earnings to rise, the uneven application of the law caused citizens to be more at risk from general lawlessness, arbitrariness, and even politically motivated job discrimination. In addition, *chavismo* coexisted with a rapidly expanding crime epidemic. Venezuela's murder rate quadrupled under Chávez, going from 4,550 homicides in 1999 to 16,047 in 2009, and making Venezuela as unsafe as the Gaza Strip under Israeli offensives in 2009.[6] The murder rate in Caracas alone is 140 per 100,000 inhabitants, making it the second least safe city in the Americas, after Ciudad Juárez, Mexico. Furthermore, there is evidence of state complicity in this lawlessness: the police are heavily implicated, few arrests are ever made, and three in four arrested suspects are released.[7]

By 2010 the accumulation of formal and informal restrictions on doing business including the growing risk of expropriation, all traits of the *chavista* type of hybrid regime, reached world-record levels. The World Bank's *Ease of Doing Business Index,* which ranks countries according to how conducive the regulatory environment is for doing business, placed Venezuela at number 177 of 183 countries ranked, the lowest position for a Latin American country and for a middle-income country.[8] Where some hybrid regimes (Armenia, Georgia, Kuwait, Russia, Singapore, Turkey) in the 2000s sought political legitimacy by attempting to provide civil order and a business-friendly environment or both, *chavismo* appeared to expand electorally while law enforcement and the country's business environment deteriorated very rapidly.

In our view, the explanation for the rise of this type of hybrid regime in Venezuela, both the conventional features and the more idiosyncratic ones, is not entirely agency-based, that is, it is not exclusively the result of the intentions and actions of the ruler. Preexisting institutional conditions, not just presidential predisposition, favored the rise of these practices. Specifically, following two decades of economic and political crises, Venezuela in 1999 was characterized by the extreme weakness of business groups, political parties, and state bureaucracies, in comparison with the relative strength of the oil sector and the military.[9] This institutional environment facilitated the rise of a president-led, oil-powered, military-based assault on business, parties, and state agencies.

Nevertheless, not all countries afflicted by uneven institutional robustness respond the way the Venezuelan ruler did in the 2000s. Some administrations, on either the left (the Labor Party in Brazil) or the right (ARENA in El Salvador) actually responded to comparable institutional weaknesses by bolstering institutional quality and liberal democracy. The rise of hybridity in Venezuela might not have been exclusively a product of Chávez, but neither was it an inevitable outcome of preexisting institutions and structures.

A second puzzling aspect about contemporary hybrid regimes is why they remain in the so-called gray zone. If these regimes are able to concentrate so much power in the executive branch, why don't they establish a full-fledged autocracy? Alternatively, if they are so successful electorally, why don't they stay democratic and refrain from imposing undue restrictions on the opposition? Chávez's Venezuela provides reinforcement for certain conventional answers to this question, but also offers reasons that are not altogether recognized in the literature.

The first conventional answer to the question is international pressure—the development since the 1980s of a powerful international norm condemning blatant forms of authoritarianism. Another source of pressure, more at the level of influence than norm, has been the growth of NGOs. Most countries have since the 1980s become populated by a gamut of NGOs, many of which draw on support from both international and powerful local actors. For states to extinguish these NGOs entirely, as conventional autocracies are prone to do, would nowadays be too costly in terms of both energy expended (there are lots of NGOs) and reputation (NGOs belong to international networks). Hybrid regimes harass NGOs, but do not extinguish them. Because NGOs survive, however battered, they offer societies mechanisms for resisting the worst excesses of state encroachment.

Yet the Chávez case shows that there is one more reason why states may prefer to remain in the gray zone: pursuing mixed practices can actually contribute to electoral victories. Mixed practices can prove to be more rewarding electorally than ordinary autocracy or outright political liberalization. Here's how: these practices polarize the political environment, which, Chávez discovered, can at times be electorally rewarding. Specifically, it can pay for the state to move to the extreme of the prevailing ideological side; and in Venezuela, during the 1990s and early 2000s, a majority of the electorate leaned toward the left. By moving to the extreme side of this larger leftist bloc, Chávez induced the other bloc to radicalize, which in turn led many in the center and center-left to either stay out of politics (the so-called *ni-nis*, neither one nor the other) or to side with Chávez, because the opposition began to appear to be too far to the right.

Some might argue that the state's radicalization was simply a state response to a disloyal opposition. Certainly from 2002 to 2004 the opposition sought to undercut the government. But after 2005, there is evidence of significant change in the behavior of the opposition, away from radical postures and more accepting of formal channels of participation. One might call this a type of political learning. In contrast, Chávez's radicalism expanded rather than retreated after 2005, suggesting that the logic of state-based radicalism has not been merely reactive.[10]

Chávez also uncovered the benefit of committing irregularities either prior to or after an election, rather than on voting day. This peculiar timing in the conduct of cheating works for several reasons. First, the international community is not well equipped to monitor, let alone sanction, pre- or postelection irregularities. Second, such irregularities divide the opposition. One side of the opposition adopts the "exit" response (as famously explained by Albert Hirschman): abstaining or boycotting the elections. Another side decides to participate, negotiate with the regime, and even vote.[11] This split in the opposition is welcome news for incumbents. The split fragments the opposition, which reduces its chances of defeating the government, while the participating opposition ends up legitimizing the electoral process.

Nevertheless, dealing with the participating faction of the opposition is not necessarily a cakewalk for the government, for this group will surely make demands, and the government must respond. In Chávez's case, the participating opposition demanded more electoral transparency. The tactical response of the state was to make minimal concessions, such as agreeing to discontinue certain irregular practices in the upcoming round, while leaving many other demands unmet.[12] This type of partial reformism tends to produce another round of divisions within the opposition, thus enabling the government to play the same divide-the-opposition game at each election. In the end, the government keeps the opposition from defecting entirely, which is necessary for maintaining a semblance of legitimacy vis-à-vis the international community, while ensuring the "improbability" (rather than "impossibility") of an opposition victory.

Chávez used the same scheme to handle Venezuela's media. A system of mixed press freedoms was put in place early on: the media were allowed to operate, but stiff regulations were imposed on content (Article 58 of the 1999 constitution; the 2004 Organic Law of Telecommunications; the Law of Social Responsibility; the 2005 reform of the penal code).[13] Moreover, the government halted the practice of placing advertisements in nonloyal media and openly excluded reporters from press conferences. These measures split the "four horses of the Apocalypse," as Chávez once described the country's largest TV stations. Two of them (Globovisión and Radio Caracas Televisión, RCTV) continued critical reporting, while the others (Televén and Venevisión) self-moderated politically charged programs.

The familiar case of RCTV is another good illustration of this mixed approach. RCTV was an independent, privately owned station that often aired broadcasts that were critical of the government. In 2007 the government opted to shut down RCTV by refusing to renew its public broadcasting license. However, other less belligerent private TV stations were allowed to continue operating, a clear sign that the government was prepared to reward self-restraint and moderation in the media.[14] Again, the outcome was divisive. A survey by the Institute of the Press and Society (Instituto de Prensa y Sociedad) revealed the extent of the split: some reporters renewed their commitment to raise hard questions following the RCTV case, but as many as 30 percent said they would reconsider what to report.[15]

In sum, the Chávez case shows that mixed practices can prove more rewarding electorally for incumbents than strict democratic practices because they divide the opposition and are less offensive to local and international audiences than strict autocratic practices. Constantly shifting the rules of the game and vilifying dissent does more than "disorient the opponents"; it also engenders a clear pro-government effect.[16] One sector of the opposition exits—it is silenced or pushed to withdraw from politics. Another sector participates, but it is weakened by internal divisions and unfavorable rules of the game. And so, hybrid regimes discover that there is a payoff to maintaining a policy mix of concessions and freedoms in some areas and harsh restrictions and unpredictable practices in others. As long as the incumbents remain electorally competitive—that is, capable of garnering enough votes—maintaining a mixed system can actually prevent the opposition from ever surpassing pro-government votes during elections.

On Populism

Chavismo also offers lessons on the adaptation of populism to modern times. "Populism" is a term that is used conspicuously but often confusedly. What many people mean by populism is a certain type of economic policy, one that promises and often delivers economic and social benefits to the populace, even when it is not affordable. But this definition of populism as making unsustainable promises to the masses can well apply to any number of politicians in a democracy, and is therefore not helpful in making distinctions between populists and everyone else. A more analytically fruitful approach is to follow Kurt Weyland and think of populism as an eminently "political" rather than economic phenomenon.[17] According to this political conception, "populism" refers to the way the state, specifically the head of state, deals politically with societal actors, especially loyalists and opponents. To summarize various sources, classic populism can thus be defined as consisting of four interrelated elements:

—The systematic effort by the state leader to undermine the role of formal institutions that mediate between the state and society, the so-called leader-mass linkage, or hyperpersonalism in politics

—The tendency to use and abuse state resources (though this is not exclusive to populists)

—Building and maintaining an electoral support base that is multiclass, with a heavy bias toward mobilizing counter-elites

—Simultaneously introducing constraints on organized groups that are either autonomous vis-à-vis the state or in the opposition[18]

These are the core elements of populism. But most scholars who study populism agree that populism has evolved with the times, prompting many to speak of a classic version of populism, prevailing from the 1930s to the 1980s, and a more contemporary version, prevailing since the 1990s.[19] Table 6-1 shows our impression of how populism has varied over the years. Although the core elements have remained constant, the individual components and manifestations of some of the elements have no doubt changed.

What is peculiar about *chavismo* is that it combines elements of both the classic *and* the contemporary versions of populism. To see this, it helps to review each of the elements in table 6-1.

T A B L E 6 - 1 . **Political Definitions of Classic and Contemporary Populism**

Features	Classic (mid-1930s to 1970s)	Contemporary (since 1980s)
Aims	Personalism (undermining institutions that mediate between the leader and the masses)	Personalism (undermining institutions that mediate between the leader and the masses)
Means	Use and abuse of state resources Privileges for loyalists	Use and abuse of state resources Privileges for loyalists
Support base	*Counter-elites:* Industrial workers Peasants	*Counter-elites:* Party orphans and defectors NGOs; social movements Informal workers The unemployed The very poor
	Middle sectors: Urban groups Middle classes Professionals	*Middle sectors:* Less important
	Elites: Armed forces Industrialists	*Elites for leftist populists:* State contractors Financial speculators Radical intellectuals
		Elites for right-wing populists: Competitive, export-oriented business leaders Libertarian intellectuals, technocrats
Political target	The oligarchy Agro-exporting sector The Church Imperialism	Political parties Autonomous NGOs Media Subnational elected officials Globalization; the IMF; free trade

Source: Authors' compilation.

We begin with populism's chief aim, to undermine mechanisms that mediate between the leader and the people. Most writers on populism begin by making this point. They emphasize that a populist movement seeks first and foremost to expand the powers of the leader, or *caudillo*, while undermining the autonomy of institutions that mediate between the state and society.[20] This is another way of saying that populism is, at its core, an effort to undermine checks and balances on the main leader. The personalization of politics that is inherent in populism implies, almost by definition, that there must be an equal process of deinstitutionalization of intermediary institutions. This deinstitutionalization translates into an erosion of checks and balances. And as we argued in chapter 1, *chavismo* is nothing if not an unambiguous example of precisely this erosion.

Populism consists of both aims and means, and here is where other components of the definition come in. One vital element is the use and abuse of state resources, which can be tangible economic assets (level of spending, or fiscal, monetary, or industrial policies), as well as intangible assets (for example, uneven application of the law, aggressive discourse against opponents, calls for some sort of privilege-free society). Few other elected Latin American governments since the 1980s have undertaken as heavy a use of state resources for electoral gain as has Chávez.[21] But to qualify as populism, the state must deploy resources selectively, favoring loyalists over opponents. As we argued, this blurring of the line separating state resources from the ruling party, so inherent in populism, has also been a hallmark of *chavismo*.

Most definitions of populism include a discussion of the support base of populism. Theoretically at least, populism seeks to become a multi-class and cross-sectoral coalition. *Chavismo* conformed to this, at first. There is no question that in 1998 *chavismo* was embraced by Venezuelans from all walks of life, almost without exception. Over time, however, *chavismo* lost support disproportionately from urban groups and the middle classes, while retaining support from some parts—not all parts—of essentially two opposite poles, elites and counter-elites. It could be argued that this transformation from a multiclass coalition to a bipolar coalition is common to many versions of populism, not just *chavismo*. Even in classic versions of populism, these two poles, elites and counter-elites, played a crucial role. The counter-elite was made up largely of newly emerging urban workers and peasants, whereas the elite group consisted of industrialists and, often, the military.

This bipolarity also exists in the contemporary version of populism that emerged in the 1990s, both Fujimori's right-wing variety and Chávez's left-wing variety. What changes somewhat is the composition of each pole. Counter-elite groups since the 1990s encompass new economic losers such as informal workers, the unemployed, slum dwellers, unskilled workers, underemployed rural dwellers (rather more than industrial workers). But it also includes a somewhat new group: political orphans, voters who came to feel unrepresented by existing political parties. Political orphans are manifestations of the "crisis of representation," which is how the literature has labeled the phenomenon that drives party de-alignment en masse.[22] In the 1990s political orphans became a huge group in many Latin American countries, with Venezuela standing as a prototypical case. Political orphans include constituents from all income categories. They often adopt an anti-establishment sentiment because they are politically disenfranchised and not necessarily or exclusively because they are economic losers. Throughout this book, we provided evidence that the *chavista* movement soon evolved into a coalition composed of mostly these two poles. Although the coalition became narrower over time, at the start it included members of all of these counter-elite groups, which explains why it came to power with such energy and in less than two years was able to produce such a drastic institutional change toward a hyperpresidential model.

We also provided evidence of the disproportionate power of elites within Chávez's coalition. Whereas a right-wing populist would mobilize elites from the technocratic class, or as some have labeled them, the "knowledge actors," as well as the export-oriented and competitive private sector, *chavismo* drew elite support from wealthy owners of firms and banks that made fortunes through special contracts or deals with the state.[23] In the literature of the 1970s, these elites would have been referred to as rent seekers; in Chávez's Venezuela they came to be known as *boliburgueses*.[24] The other elite group that Chávez has courted overtly is the military, perhaps one of the most "classic" populist elements within Chávez's support base. In the words of Venezuela's highest-ranking military official, General Henry Rangel Silva, "The Armed Forces don't have partial loyalty, rather complete loyalty to the people, a life project, and a Commander- in-Chief. We're married with this project." Reliance on the military has been central since the start of the administration and continues to expand. In 2008 as many as eight of twenty-four governorships and nine of approximately thirty cabinet positions were held by active or retired career officers.[25] The military has even been recruited to help implement fiscal policy: Chávez officially called on the military to keep an eye on businesses that raised prices following the 2010 mega-devaluation. Chávez's approach to the military followed the traditional formula of purging and splurging. The government used the period of maximum discontent, 2001 to 2004, to discharge nonloyal officers. Others were offered juicy rewards such as quick promotions and large raises. Generals were also given large budgets to administer. In the process, Chávez reduced the autonomy of the military, eliminated civilian control, and sought to reorient the ideology of officers, even imposing the slogan "*Patria, socialismo o muerte*" ("Motherland, socialism, or death"). Chávez also exhorted the military against a new domestic enemy, "the oligarchs."[26]

Thus, the Chávez case shows that in modern populism, multisectorialism is perhaps more an aspiration than an attained goal. If anything, *chavismo* shows that nowadays the support base of a populist movement in Latin America quickly morphs into a mostly bipolar rather than multisectoral coalition.

The Chávez case also shows that this bipolarity may be sufficient to sustain the government, especially during economic downturns. The elite pole supplies the government with capacity to resist potential assaults from other veto groups, and the counter-elite pole provides the votes to win elections and a justification to declare itself as the representative of the people—and by extension, to declare the opposition an enemy of the people. As long as two poles remain on board, populism can afford to lose the middle sectors and still retain power.

That modern populism requires and thus tries to cater to a bipolar coalition does not mean that each of the poles supports the populist incumbent overwhelmingly or without exceptions. In Venezuela, it did not take long for large sectors of both poles to turn against the government. The defecting elites, who were out in the streets protesting as early as 2002, have attracted more scholarly attention than the defecting poor, even though the incidence of the latter has been quite significant. For instance, support for *chavismo* among the lowest-income groups of the population dropped from 94 percent in 1999 to about 45 percent by the mid-2000s and has stayed in that vicinity since then. *Chavismo*, and populism in general, is a polarizing force—because it splits a nation internally between deserving groups and the rest—and this division is present within the same class that *chavismo* initially mobilized. So deep is the internal division within the poor in Venezuela that studies have shown that being poor is not necessarily a reliable predictor of whether a voter voted for Chávez in the 2000, 2004, and 2006 elections.[27]

In short, *chavismo* shows that populism does not need nor does it generate *overwhelming* support across *all* sectors. Rather, populism easily delivers *enough* support among counter-elites and elites to sustain electoral losses, especially stemming from defecting middle sectors. The support from these poles need not be all that massive for these gains to obtain.

Last, populism generally identifies domestic groups to attack politically, the so-called enemies of the people. Populist leaders hardly hesitate to deploy aggressive discourse and punitive policies toward them. In classic populism, typical targets were the oligarchs—for the most part, exporters of agricultural products, together with their "imperialist" allies and in some cases the Catholic Church. Of course, Chávez's populism has targeted the oligarchs, and at times, the Church, conforming with classic populism, but he has also added new groups to his list: organized sectors of civil society such as political parties and NGOs advocating democracy, and, quite conspicuously, the media. This new cohort of targets is an aspect of *chavismo* that is more in tune with contemporary versions of populism.

Some scholars of populism hold that there are irrefutable differences between right-wing and left-wing populism, pointing to Alberto Fujimori in the 1990s and Hugo Chávez as exemplars. No doubt a difference between left- and right-wing populists exists, but it is less consequential than often argued. Our view is that the difference between left- and right-wing populism depends largely on the composition of the elites in the bipolar coalition. Also, there are clear distinctions in terms of discourse. The left-wing populist typically emphasizes the need to curtail market forces, lessen inequalities, distribute wealth, fight global capitalism, and perhaps even contain the United States. Right-wing populists are more concerned with disorder, insurgency, economic chaos, immigration, even immorality, and would more likely spend fiscal resources on infrastructure than wealth distribution.

Despite these differences, judged in terms of impact on regime features, left-wing and right-wing populists have more in common than is immediately obvious. Politically, though not necessarily discursively, they are closer to each other than they each are to a left-wing or right-wing democrat, respectively. Their drive to concentrate power by way of a bipolar alliance of classes, sustained through the use and abuse of state resources, is a political project that is anathema to democrats on both the left and the right. In other words, in terms of impact on the political regime, Chávez is closer to right-wing populists such as Fujimori in Peru than he is to leftist democrats such as Tabaré Vásquez in Uruguay or Lula in Brazil. Right-wing and left-wing populists ultimately move regimes in the direction of hybridity, mobilizing majorities while courting some vital elites, and openly excluding their opponents from the policymaking process.

How Replicable Is Venezuela's Experience?

Assaults on democracy in Latin America since the 1990s have transpired mainly by way of regimes that adopt some hybrid features, instead of a return to strict autocracy. In Venezuela as in many other hybrid cases, the vehicle for this tack has been the blending of classic and contemporary strands of populism, as we just argued. It makes sense to end this book, therefore, by reflecting on conditions that are likely to foster the emergence of a radical, populist version of hybridity in other countries.

No doubt, some aspects of the Chávez experience are virtually impossible to replicate elsewhere. The most obvious is oil, or, rather, the state's monopoly over a single commodity that generates extraordinary dollar revenues for the state. That Venezuela is a petro-state means that any political project predicated on use and abuse of state resources will have abundant resources at its disposal.[28] A petro-state in boom times need not face conditionality from multilateral lenders nor fear a sudden freeze, as occurs when decentralized bond markets panic over a turn of events in emerging markets.[29] It follows that Venezuela, the only real petro-state in Latin America, under an oil boom is more susceptible to the consolidation of populism than its counterparts.[30] Most other countries in the region also draw revenue from exporting commodities—Bolivia more than any other, with its single, state-owned product, gas. Of the rest, Mexico is less and less dependent on oil, Chile's state-owned copper industry provides a declining share of export revenue, and Brazil's oil industry is neither that large in terms of total exports nor that dependent on the executive branch.

Militarism is another aspect that is almost as hard to replicate as the oil boom. In most of South America (except perhaps Peru and Colombia), there is a general culture of repudiation of military rule or military involvement in politics. Consequently, the possibility of a leftist civilian-military alliance such as that crafted by Chávez seems less likely in South America at least.

Despite these features unique to Venezuela, several of the political-economic conditions that fueled *chavismo* in Venezuela exist or might come to exist in other countries as well, making some variations of the Chávez regime conceivable. For us, the five most important conditions are inequality, instability, insecurity, intolerance, and a breakdown of the political party system.

Inequality

If the rise and consolidation of populism depend on sustaining a bipolar coalition, then it makes sense to posit that societies suffering from gross inequality are more susceptible to populist appeals. In terms of income and assets, Latin America is one of the most economically unequal regions in the world.[31] As long as Latin America remains a champion in the area of income inequality, it will continue to be vulnerable to populism. However, we feel strongly that this connection is not automatic and is often overstated.[32] Venezuela and many other Latin American societies have lived with high levels of inequality for decades while experiencing substantial regime and policy variations, making it hard to believe that inequality is the most important determinant of regime type.[33] Two of the most unequal countries in the region, Brazil and Chile, have had substantial democratic stability for almost two decades now. Although many scholars stress a strong connection between inequality and rising populism, we feel that this connection exists but it is not as powerful as other causes.

Instability

The second condition that may lead to greater demand for populism is macroeconomic instability. Populism feeds on anti-establishment sentiments, and these can grow during times of economic disarray like those experienced by Venezuela over a span of more than two decades after 1982. Venezuela was one of the few Latin American countries to have had two, not one, lost decades, and this accumulation of losses explains the demand for *chavismo*, at least initially. Remarkably, most Latin American countries have moved away from chronic economic instability. During the latest economic crisis, between 2008 and 2009, all countries except Venezuela skirted severe macroeconomic instability, no doubt a historical record. The trend toward more stable macroeconomics has lessened the vulnerability toward hybrid, populist regimes in the region. But as long as Latin America remains dependent on commodity exports and volatile financial capital, its economies will be at risk of economic instability, and this makes their political systems still somewhat susceptible to populist movements.

Insecurity and Incapacity

Populism also feeds on insecurity, which can take the form of economic insecurity or lack of personal safety due to crime or political violence. The introduction of market reforms in the 1990s, however moderate, has brought Latin Americans new economic opportunities, but also newer forms of economic insecurity, mostly stemming from erosion of job security. Advanced capitalist societies have institutions in place to help citizens cope with market-generated insecurities: they provide better education and skills to help workers adjust to change, offer welfare and unemployment compensation, feature reliable courts that protect workers from job discrimination, and so forth. Some Latin American countries have made progress, but most fall short with insecurity-abating institutions.[34] This shortage is part of the syndrome of "state deficiencies," or state incapacities, that Scott P. Mainwaring argues keeps citizens susceptible to economic insecurity. The key point is that economic insecurity coupled with state incapacity can boost demands for populism.[35]

Public insecurity is the other type of insecurity that can breed populism, though it tends to favor right-wing rather than left-wing forms of populism. When voters feel assailed by strangers, they become too eager to grant presidents blank checks to crack down on lawlessness. Public insecurity in Latin America is now mostly the result of crime, both random and organized. Almost every analyst agrees that the alarming spread of crime in the region is the most significant security threat faced by citizens and states and is showing no obvious signs of abating. This will continue to stimulate demand for populism, especially of the right-wing variety.

In Venezuela until the mid 2000s, economic insecurity probably trumped the issue of public insecurity across the bulk of the electorate, and this explains the electoral fortunes of Chávez's brand of leftist populism until 2006. Now that priorities have reversed across the electorate, with public security becoming a higher priority, it is no surprise that *chavismo*—so far quite inattentive to the issue of public security—has lost electoral competitiveness. The appeal of a left-wing populism might have eased in Venezuela, but it is not clear that the appeal of a future right-wing form of populism has eased as well.

Intolerance

Populism is typically aggressive and dismissive toward the opposition, and for this reason it has a higher chance of emerging when a general climate of intolerance prevails. Populist rulers often cultivate and foster a climate of intolerance, and Chávez was no exception. But often that climate is already present, at least incipiently, and this makes the job of the populist easier. According to public opinion surveys carried out by Americas Barometer, levels of political intolerance in Latin America are astonishingly high.[36] Responses in 2006 and 2007 surveys revealed that in all countries there is a substantial majority who hold intolerant political attitudes toward opponents, including resistance to granting them the right to protest, to appear on TV, and even to run for office. Analysis of these survey data shows that the strongest predictor of whether a person will harbor intolerant attitudes is whether he or she supports the incumbent—those who support the incumbent are more intolerant of his or her opponents.[37] Latin Americans may hold democracy in high esteem, but many individuals nonetheless show intolerance toward opponents when their favorite politicians hold office. This climate of intolerance can serve as a breeding ground for populist leaders, all of whom treat opponents intolerantly, which strikes a chord with large sectors of voters when intolerance is widespread.

Political Parties

In explaining the rise of populism, the health of political parties possibly matters more than social conditions. The four preconditions for the development of a hybrid regime just discussed—inequality, instability, insecurity and incapacity, and intolerance—can be viewed as permissive, that is, as factors that allow or even encourage populism. Political parties, by contrast, can be considered barriers to populism, institutional factors that can help prevent the rise of populism. The strength of a political party system can help frustrate the political ambitions of populist leaders. Weak parties in the opposition are, quite simply, less able to resist the institutional encroachments of populist states, as happened in Venezuela between 1998 and 2000, which came to experience one of the region's most profound cases of party system decay.

Signs of party weakness include voter de-alignment, electoral volatility, sudden party system fragmentation, lack of clear messages, giving too much power to the party's top leadership, and too-long tenure of leaders. A weak or collapsing major party, whether in power or in the opposition, offers populist leaders more room to rise to the top and dominate.

In pondering these enabling or constraining conditions, it would seem that there is little or no chance for replicating perfectly the type of regime that Venezuela developed in the 2000s. Most countries in the region do not suffer from the constellation of maladies that afflicted Venezuela by the 1990s and permitted the rise of a hybrid and populist. Nevertheless, it would be a mistake to believe that regime change in Venezuela was an outcome of idiosyncratic factors. More to the point, regime change was not the result exclusively of dependence on energy commodities in boom years, which is the one condition that separates Venezuela from most of its regional peers except Trinidad and Tobago and, to some extent, Ecuador and Bolivia. Oil did not create the Chávez regime. Instead, regime change was the result of demands made on the state by dissatisfied citizens and of policies that were possible as a result of preexisting institutional features and state-based manipulations.

It would also be a mistake to conclude that the region as a whole is completely safe from at least some versions of *chavismo*. It might be hard to find another case where all of the structural, demand-side, and institutional supply-side conditions coincide as they did in Venezuela in the 1990s and 2000s, but it would not be difficult to find cases in which at least a few of these conditions prevail. Until the five preconditions that make Latin America politically vulnerable are overcome, we cannot be certain that Venezuela's outcome as examined in this book will remain a strictly Venezuelan phenomenon.

On Political Change: Two Views

Chávez has succeeded in consolidating a fairly closed political regime in Venezuela, and his supporters have become more radical and entrenched. To what extent might Venezuela be able to escape *chavismo* in the future? We offer first a pessimistic response, followed by a more optimistic outlook.

The Pessimistic View

To be sure, regime collapse is not imminent, in part because of Chávez's social inclusion strategy and iron-clad institutional control. As with other populist phenomena in the region, especially Peronism in Argentina, the social roots of *chavismo* are deep-seated; its legacy will be more far-reaching than its opponents tend to assume.

Furthermore, Chávez is taking no chances. In 2009 he successfully introduced a constitutional amendment to allow for indefinite reelection, making Venezuela the only formally democratic Latin American country today to eliminate term limits entirely. Perhaps more than other moves by the regime, this institutional change could very well be a decisive game changer because it lessens, like few other measures, the probability of alternation in office.

The end of term limits erodes alternation in office through two mechanisms. First, it discourages the emergence of challenges to *chavismo* from within the ruling party. Knowledge that Chávez will always compete for the presidency pretty much guarantees that most *chavistas* will focus not on challenging him but on competing for lower-level political office, and this increases "verticalism," or top-down discipline, within his movement. Factions within the movement will continue to arise, but these are unlikely to bill themselves as alternatives to Chávez, since the notion of Chávez not running for office is out of the question. Instead, they will compete for positions within the movement by presenting themselves as "Chávez's most favorite or loyal" faction. The end of term limits will thus make internal factions more likely to court than to challenge Chávez's authority.

Second, the end of term limits allows the president to acquire institutional advantages that can be used to neutralize political rivals outside the ruling party as well. To see this, we must briefly review the debate about the merits and perils of reelection.

Reelection is a controversial issue in Latin America. Although constitutions have been changed to permit at least one successive reelection (Argentina, Bolivia, Brazil, Colombia, Ecuador), none has been changed to permit indefinite reelection. Paradoxically, the notion of term limits was invented in Latin America in the nineteenth century precisely as a mechanism to prevent presidents from overextending their stay in office. Some countries such as Mexico went as far as to abolish all forms of reelection. In the 1990s many presidents tried to relax term limits, and some succeeded in doing so, but only to the point of allowing one reelection. Indefinite reelection was never granted. Attempts by Carlos Menem in Argentina (1989–99) and Álvaro Uribe in Colombia (2002–10) to obtain permission to seek a third term were rejected by the courts, public opinion, or sectors within the ruling parties. In Peru, the attempt by Fujimori to get a third term did succeed, but the battle destabilized the country, ultimately prompting Fujimori to resign from office shortly after election to his third term.

From a strictly electoral standpoint, ending term limits does not imply ending democracy. A number of analysts agree that if politicians compete electorally on relatively equitable terms, the issue ends up being settled by citizens.[38] Reelection could even serve as a mechanism to improve accountability. The argument is that presidents seeking reelection are more accountable to the electorate than lame-duck presidents who are not running and who therefore need not worry about courting voters.[39] Patricio Navia has even argued that the problem is not unlimited reelection but excessive presidential power; efforts are needed to curb presidents' hold on power by strengthening the independence of other centers of power and curtailing executive abuse of prerogatives.[40]

However, we feel that the longer a president remains in power, the greater the risk of erosion of separation of powers, the independence of the judicial branch, the neutrality of the electoral authorities, and even the autonomy of civil groups and business firms that interact with the state. In other words, time is causally linked to increases in presidential powers: the longer the president stays in office, the more appointments and contracts he or she makes, and this makes societal and business groups more willing to comply with the preferences of the executive branch.[41]

The debate about term limits could be evaluated empirically. The evidence suggests that a lack of term limits lessens the probability of alternating power. Statistical studies of developing democracies, chiefly in Africa, where unlimited presidential terms are fairly common, show a high rate of probability that sitting presidents will continue to be reelected.[42] Statistical estimates for Latin America are scarcer, but it seems that the upshot is similar: incumbents are rarely defeated. A historical data series that dates from the mid-nineteenth century notes that only two sitting presidents failed to win reelection: Hipólito Mejía, in the Dominican Republic in 2004, and Daniel Ortega, in Nicaragua in 1990.[43]

A number of factors make presidential continuation probable in the absence of term limits. Essentially, incumbents can deploy an arsenal of tools to remain competitive, or at least, to lessen the competitiveness of their rivals: state resources to indulge in widespread clientelism; agenda-setting powers in the legislature; appointments in the judicial branch and the entire state bureaucracy; information technologies and means of physical coercion to threaten both voters and activists, especially within the ruling party.[44] In other words, time allows presidents to augment their institutional powers, even if they lose some electoral competitiveness, as tends to occur with governments that stay in office too long. These institutional powers can be used to undermine rivals inside and outside their parties. If even countries with strong institutional checks and balances suffer the problem of the "incumbent's advantage," in countries with weaker mechanisms of accountability such advantage becomes too formidable.

In short, theory and empirical evidence suggest that in countries with weak institutions of accountability, alternation of power is not easily achieved solely by means of electoral competition. It also requires some exogenous factor: either a devastating economic crisis, a major blunder by the authorities, or strict term limits. An election may be the best mechanism to select candidates to lead the country, but further elections alone do not ensure that others can compete equitably and eventually replace an incumbent. To be sure, the electoral process must be designed so as to offer safeguards for the opposition. This involves providing adequate information, open debate, identification of the country's key issues, equitable access to resources, and a level playing field with respect to political competition. And yet this long list of safeguards might not be sufficient to ensure alternation in power. Time is simply on the side of incumbents, especially if checks and balances are weak or declining. Longevity in office allows incumbents to accumulate more and more institutional powers, even if they lose some electoral power. Because eliminating term limits empowers presidents excessively and lessens the chance of leadership renewal within the ruling party, it seriously undermines the probability of ending a president's term. For this reason, we feel that abolishing term limits in 2009 was one of the most decisive, pro-incumbent turning points in the history of *chavismo* in Venezuela.

The Somewhat Optimistic View

Despite the barriers to political change in place, change is not out of the question. Two factors will inevitably exert pressures for possible change. One is economic and the other is strictly political. A brutal recession caused by the triple blow of a decline in world oil demand, misguided macro- and microeconomic policies, and mismanagement of Petróleos de Venezuela, S.A., has weakened the underpinnings of the system Chávez has built. As of this writing, Venezuela was in the midst of a major economic crisis. Afflicted by a potent combination of stagflation, indebtedness, declining exports, and scarcity of consumer and capital goods, Venezuela could very well be suffering one of the worst economic crises in the world. Combined with ineffective handling of key issues of interest to citizens such as personal insecurity, electricity shortages, and unemployment, these maladies have taken a serious toll on the government's approval ratings. These woes could very well generate the kind of discontent that could decidedly affect Chávez's longevity in office. They have already produced the highest surge in the ranks of the opposition since 2003, allowing it to win the popular vote in the legislative elections of September 2010 with 52 percent of the votes (6.1 million voters), up from 45 percent (or 5.1 million votes) in the 2009 referendum.

Yet, Chávez could still respond to declining political competitiveness by attempting even greater domination of the citizenry through social and political means, thus preventing the regime's downfall (see discussion in chapter 4). In other words, if an economic downturn makes a hybrid regime less competitive, the regime may feel tempted to become more autocratic.

It is conceivable that international pressure against the regime might resurface if Chávez turns politically more restrictive, and the oil income shortfall continues to the point of endangering his social-power diplomacy. A combination of economic downturn and heightened international criticism could lead to domestic political conflict.

This brings our analysis to a vital question: what factors stand to wear down and erode the institutional control Chávez now commands? Two political factors could contribute to erosion: increasing chasms between moderates and radicals within *chavismo,* and the endurance of a unified opposition that continues to win the battle against the tendency to abstain, especially on the part of the *ni-nis.* It is unlikely for a hybrid regime to move toward a more democratic system in the absence of internal moderate forces willing to open up the system. If the movement to open the system is left to radical *chavistas,* the government is likely to remain opposed to political opening. Now that the opposition has regained strength, it is conceivable that moderates within *chavismo*—interested in a rapprochement with the opposition so as to avoid unnecessary tension— might resurface as well, reproducing the felicitous interaction of moderate incumbents and moderate opponents that some political scientists have famously argued is a precondition for regime liberalization.[45]

The debate between moderates and radicals within *chavismo* has been described as one between the "*chavismo* without Chávez" forces and the "there's no *chavismo* without Chávez" forces. The current loci of this confrontation are the armed forces and, to a lesser extent, state governors—and perhaps in the future the legislature, now that, following the September 2010 elections, it will have opposition representation again. In the armed forces, the presence of Cuban technicians holding influential positions has created uneasiness, especially in the higher ranks. It is difficult to gauge how deep-seated these concerns may be, but there is some tangible evidence of profound divisions between Venezuelan and Cuban personnel. Retired *chavista* generals have made declarations of their distrust of Cuban technicians, and there are rumors that the resignation of the country's vice president, also a general of considerable influence, was related in some way to the Cuban influence.

With respect to state governors, exacerbated centralism and delays in processing revenue owed to the states have generated discontent even among regional *chavista* governors, not just opposition governors. The governor of the state of Lara, considered one of the country's most influential, decided to withdraw from the PSUV and support another revolutionary organization in 2010.

The future prospects for moderate *chavistas* hinge on the capacity of the opposition to stay united. There is no question that one of their most amazing political feats for the 2008 and 2010 elections was to offer a large menu of "unified candidacies," meaning designating no more than one candidate for any one open seat. For the 2010 election, Chávez thought he could disunite the opposition leadership and discourage opposition voters by changing the electoral law in his favor. The new Organic Law of Electoral Processes (or LOPE, by its Spanish acronym) changed the electoral system to give more "nominal," that is majority based, seats to districts that are heavily *chavista* and produced pro-government gerrymandering in districts that voted for the opposition in 2008 and 2009. This law was designed to ensure that the opposition wins far fewer seats in Congress than their actual share of the vote. Yet, Chávez's move backfired: the law ended up encouraging opposition leaders to unite even more, and opposition voters to vote in record numbers. In April 2010, building on lessons from the 2006 presidential elections and the 2008 midterm elections for governors and mayors, the opposition formed the Democratic Unity Table (Mesa de la Unidad Democrática, MUD) to run for the September 2010 elections. This Mesa coordinated the right number of candidacies per contested seat.

If this trend toward a unified (that is, one able to coordinate strategies) and non-abstaining opposition continues, moderate *chavistas* may begin to play out, in a credible way, the balance between radicals in office and the opposition. Although the government (through the 2009 electoral law) ensured that the opposition, despite winning the popular vote in 2010, obtained less than 40 percent of Congress, it nonetheless proved unable this time around to stop the rebirth of pluralism within an important branch of government. This was perhaps the first victory in favor of pluralism since Chávez came to office. The task of the opposition from this point on is to avoid balkanization, which is always a risk given the heterogeneity of the opposition and the myriad tactics employed by Chávez to split the opposition. If it avoids balkanization, the opposition might strengthen moderate *chavistas,* and this could pave the way for a more substantive opening of the political system.

Reflections

Mythologists, humanists, paleontologists, and cryptozoologists who study dragons agree that despite some variations, dragons share common characteristics that distinguish them from other species, real or imagined. Dragons are creatures of formidable size that often display supernatural powers. They have reptile-like (and thus tough) skins. They spew fire at their enemies. They often have bird or bat wings, or can at least slither like serpents. And they protect certain treasures while destroying others, even feasting on the most precious products in the land, sometimes the country's most beautiful virgins.

For us, the Chávez regime fits this image almost to a T. Chávez's ability to return triumphant from the dead (after 1992 and again after 2002–03), not to mention to transform one of Latin America's most consolidated democracies into a politically tough regime and still win elections, conveys certain supernatural powers that other more ordinary political leaders and movements lack. His belligerence toward enemies, both at home and in Washington, burns like fire. His ability to change policy direction so quickly and to cover so much ground politically, often packing the agenda to the point where not even his ministers can keep track, suggests that this dragon must also have wings that allow him to move fast and high. His obsession with targeted spending to protect his bipolar constituency suggests that this dragon, too, cares about treasures. And his approach to the oil sector, destroyed by his appetite for more and more resources to spend, reveals that this creature feasts voraciously on the best meals in the land.

But not all dragons share these frightening aspects. In Chinese mythology, for instance, dragons symbolize auspicious powers and can even be signs of good luck. Chinese dragons don't typically disgorge fire; they are actually afraid of fire. Instead, they spew water and mist, thus creating much needed rain, which earns them a reputation as purveyors of good things. The Chávez regime, we also argued, encompasses some of these more benign elements. Certainly, this is how the *chavistas* see it. For them *chavismo* is the essence or at least the symbol of dreams coming true, whether it is getting an education, a much needed job, a state contract, a special favor, or a personal sense of empowerment.

In many ways, the Chávez regime is neither one dragon nor the other, but a combination of both. It is a hybrid regime that has adapted very Latin American traditions—aggressive populism, nationalist anti-Americanism, statist economic policies, militarism, and an impatience with inequality—to modern times. This allowed the regime to conduct nothing less than a political revolution at home, at least by Venezuelan standards, where historically, political extremism was the exception rather than the norm. While the regime's approach to economics, in contrast to politics, has been more akin to recycling than inventing, even exacerbating mistakes made by previous administrations, Chávez has nonetheless managed to maintain a bipolar coalition that has proved hard to defeat electorally and is unmatched by any president in the history of elections in Venezuela since 1958.

A perfectly benign or a perfectly malevolent dragon would not have been capable of such a feat. The formidable barriers facing this dragon, stemming from those who defended the status quo and others who hoped for a better future, required a not-so-gentle dragon. And the opportunities available, in terms of institutional and economic resources, were just too abundant for this dragon to be exclusively monstrous. Chávez consolidated power by combining both popular support and popular betrayal, together with a good dose of cheating. It is a hybrid regime, with unquestionable Latin-tropical roots.

For the opposition—which as of this writing is just as numerous as the *chavistas*—there is no question that this dragon has only one face. Since 1999 the opposition has been searching for ways to defeat or at least tame the monster, but only recently have optimal conditions come to the fore, namely the rise of economic and governance chaos (a change in exogenous conditions) and the opposition's own realization of the need for electoral unity, a less extreme rhetoric, and a concerted campaign against abstentionism (a change in endogenous conditions).

Scholars who study dragons are also baffled by an additional mystery: Why have so many cultures that had little or no contact with each other come to develop the notion of dragons?[46] Dragons have been recorded in Greek mythology, in European Christianity, in Viking legends, in Inuit art, in China's folklore, in the Middle East, in India, and in pre-Columbian America. Different versions of this strange creature occur in various cultures.

Likewise, we feel that the *chavismo* phenomenon—or a version of it—can also arise in other cultures. Obviously, exact replicas are unlikely, but we identified conditions under which citizens elsewhere may come to yearn to see a dragon on their horizon—instability (in economics), insecurity (in the workplace and in the streets), incapacity (of state bureaucracies), intolerance (by followers), and party decay. Once those dragons appear, we have argued in this book, the landscape changes dramatically. The dragon becomes the sole, domineering figure in the land. If you happen to be part of the treasures that the dragon protects, you cheer. If, on the other hand, you become the target of their fires or appetite, you are likely to curse forever the moment you wished for a dragon to come true.

Notes

Chapter One

1. See Thomas Carothers, "The Backlash against Democracy Promotion," *Foreign Affairs* 85, no. 2 (March/April 2006): 55–68; Larry Diamond, "Thinking about Hybrid Regimes," *Journal of Democracy* 13, no. 2 (April 2002): 21–35.

2. See Thomas Carothers, "The End of the Transition Paradigm," *Journal of Democracy* 13, no. 1 (January 2002): 5–21; Marina Ottaway, *Democracy Challenged: The Rise of Semi-Authoritarianism* (Washington, D.C.: Carnegie Endowment for International Peace, 2003); Andreas Schedler, ed., *Electoral Authoritarianism: The Dynamics of Unfree Competition* (Boulder: Lynne Rienner, 2006); Steven Levitsky and Lucan Way, "The Rise of Competitive Authoritarianism," *Journal of Democracy* 13, no. 2 (April 2002): 51–65; Beatriz Magaloni, *Voting for Autocracy: Hegemonic Party Survival and Its Demise in Mexico* (Cambridge University Press, 2006).

3. See Kenneth Roberts, "Neoliberalism and the Transformation of Populism in Latin America: The Peruvian Case," *World Politics* 48 (October 1995): 82–116; Maxwell Cameron, *Democracy and Authoritarianism in Peru: Political Coalitions and Social Change* (London: Palgrave Macmillan, 1994); Carlos Iván DeGregori, "Peru: The Vanishing of a Regime and the Challenge of Democratic Building," in *Constructing Democratic Governance*, 2nd edition, edited by Jorge I. Domínguez and Michael Shifter (Johns Hopkins University Press, 2003).

4. See Nora Lustig, "Poverty, Inequality and the New Left in Latin America," research paper (Washington, D.C.: Woodrow Wilson Center, Latin America Program, October 2009) (www.wilsoncenter.org/topics/pubs/LAP_090716_Lustig Bulletin ENG_1.pdf).

5. See Jorge I. Domínguez and Rafael Fernández de Castro, eds. *Contemporary U.S.-Latin American Relations: Cooperation or Conflict in the 21st Century?* (New York: Routledge, 2010).

6. Michael Penfold, "Federalism and Institutional Change in Venezuela," in *Federalism and Democracy in Latin America*, edited by Edward Gibson (Johns Hopkins University Press, 2004).

7. For more on the role of party crisis and the entry of new forces, see Javier Corrales, "The Backlash against Market Reforms," in *Constructing Democratic Governance in Latin America*, 3rd ed., edited by Jorge I. Domínguez and Michael Shifter (Johns Hopkins University Press, 2008).

8. See José Antonio Gil Yepes, "Public Opinion, Political Socialization, and Regime Stabilization," in *The Unraveling of Representative Democracy in Venezuela*, edited by Jennifer L. McCoy and David J. Myers (Johns Hopkins University Press, 2004).

9. Macartan Humphreys and Martin Sanbu, "The Political Economy of Natural Resource Funds," in *Escaping the Resource Curse*, edited by Macartan Humphreys, Jeffrey Sachs, and Joseph Stiglitz (Columbia University Press, 2007); James Robinson, Ragnar Torvik, and Thierry Verdier, "Political Foundations of the Resource Curse," *Journal of Development* 79 (2006): 447–68.

10. See, for example, Daniel Levine, *Conflict and Political Change in Venezuela* (Princeton University Press, 1973); Terry Lynn Karl, *The Paradox of Plenty: Oil Booms and Petro States* (University of California Press, 1997); Moisés Naím, *Paper Tigers and Minotaurs: The Politics of Venezuela's Economic Reforms* (Washington, D.C.: Carnegie Endowment for International Peace, 1993); *Unraveling of Representative Democracy in Venezuela*, edited by McCoy and Myers; Jonathan Di John, *From Windfall to Curse? Oil and Industrialization in Venezuela, 1920–2005* (Pennsylvania State University Press, 2009).

11. Michael Ross, "How Mineral-Rich States Can Reduce Inequality," in Humphreys and others, *Escaping the Resource Curse*, edited by Humphreys, Sachs, and Stiglitz; Kurt Weyland, "Politics and Policies of Latin America's Two Lefts: The Role of Party Systems vs. Resource Bonanzas," paper presented at the annual meeting of the American Political Science Association, Chicago, August 30, 2007.

12. Robert A. Dahl, *Polyarchy: Participation and Opposition* (Yale University Press, 1971).

13. United Nations, Economic Commission on Latin America and the Caribbean, *Social Panorama of Latin America, 2009* (Santiago, Chile: 2009).

14. Norberto Ceserole, *Caudillo, Ejército, Pueblo: La Venezuela del Presidente Chávez* [Strong-man, army, people: The Venezuela of President Chávez] (Madrid: Ediciones Al-Andaluz, 1999) (also available at www.analitica.com/bitblioteca/ceresole/caudillo.asp).

Chapter Two

1. Guillermo O'Donnell, *Modernization and Bureaucratic-Authoritarianism: Studies in South American Politics* (University of California, Institute of International Studies, 1973).

2. Nancy Bermeo, *Ordinary People in Extraordinary Times: The Citizenry and the Breakdown of Democracy* (Princeton University Press, 2003).

3. Javier Corrales, "In Search of a Theory of Polarization," *European Review of Latin American and Caribbean Studies*, no. 79 (2005): 105–18.

4. Francisco Monaldi and Michael Penfold, "Institutional Collapse: The Role of Governance in Explaining Venezuela's Economic Decline 1975–2005," in *Venezuela: Anatomy of a Collapse*, edited by Ricardo Hausmann and Francisco Rodríguez (Pennsylvania State University Press, forthcoming).

5. Michael Penfold, "Electoral Dynamics and Decentralization in Venezuela," in *Decentralization and Democracy in Latin America*, edited by Alfred Montero and David Samuels (University of Notre Dame Press, 2004), pp. 155–79.

6. Daniel Hellinger, "Political Overview: The Breakdown of Puntofijismo and the Rise of Chavismo," in *Venezuelan Politics in the Chávez Era: Class, Polarization, and Conflict*, edited by Steve Ellner and Daniel Hellinger (Boulder: Lynne Rienner, 2004).

7. Michael Coppedge, "Venezuela: Popular Sovereignty versus Liberal Democracy," in *Constructing Democratic Governance in Latin America*, edited by Jorge I. Domínguez and Michael Shifter (Johns Hopkins University Press, 2003), pp. 165–92; Javier Corrales, "Power Asymmetries and the Rise of Presidential Constitutions," paper presented at the annual meeting of the American Political Science Association, Philadelphia, 2006.

8. Douglass C. North, William Summerhill, and Barry R. Weingast, "Order, Disorder, and Economic Change: Latin America versus North America," in *Governing for Prosperity*, edited by Bruce Bueno de Mesquita and Hilton L. Root (Yale University Press, 2000), pp. 17–58; Adam Przeworski, *Democracy and the Market: Political and Economic Reforms in Eastern Europe and Latin America* (Cambridge University Press, 1991). For a version of this argument applied to the Venezuelan case see Francisco Monaldi and Michael Penfold, "Institutional Collapse: The Role of Governance in Explaining Venezuela's Economic Decline, 1975–2005," in *Venezuela: Anatomy of a Collapse*, edited by Hausmann and Rodríguez.

9. Miriam Kornblith and Vinay Jawahar, "Elections vs. Democracy," *Journal of Democracy* 16, no. 1 (January 2005): 124–37.

10. See Corrales, "In Search of a Theory of Polarization."

11. For a detailed account, see Brian Nelson, *The Silence and the Scorpion: The Coup against Chávez and the Making of Modern Venezuela* (New York: Nation Books, 2009).

12. Social spending for political purposes in 2004 reflects both the amounts deployed to defend the regime on the occasion of the August referendum and the upcoming gubernatorial and mayoralty elections held in October.

13. Javier Corrales, "Strong Societies, Weak Parties: Regime Change in Cuba and Venezuela in the 1950s and Today," *Latin American Politics and Society* 43, no. 2 (2001): 81–112.

14. For a discussion of the division within *chavismo* between radicals and moderates, see Steve Ellner, *Rethinking Venezuelan Politics* (Boulder: Lynne Rienner, 2008).

15. The opposition wondered about the spectacular, hard-to-explain surge of 11.7 percent of registered voters in a brief six-month period between April and October 2004. Newspapers reported a greater number of registered voters at one address than were likely to reside at that location.

16. By September 2006, the incumbent had sponsored three times more air-time minutes in ad campaigns than allowed by law, not including the *Aló Presidente* Sunday TV program, where Chávez addresses the nation for several hours. See "Abuso presidencial en los medios de comunicación del estado" [Presidential abuse of the

state communications media], in *Ciudadanía Activa (Caracas)* [Active citizenship], December 2006 (www.ciudadaniaactiva.org).

17. Vice President Jorge Rodríguez, in a speech given in the National Assembly on January 31, 2007, stated: "Claro que queremos instaurar una dictadura, la dictadura de la democracia verdadera y la democracia es la dictadura de todos" [It is clear that we wish to install a dictatorship, a dictatorship of true democracy and democracy is the dictatorship of all the people]. See "Jorge Rodríguez: 'Queremos instaurar la dictadura de la democracia verdadera'" at http://venezuelareal.zoomblog.com/archivo/2007/02/01/jorge-Rodriguez-Queremos-instaurar-la-.html.

18. Simon Romero, "Chávez Seeks Tighter Grip on Military," *New York Times*, May 29, 2009, p. A1.

19. Gideon Maltz, "The Case for Presidential Term Limits," *Journal of Democracy* 18, no. 1 (2007): 128–42.

20. Jennifer L. McCoy, "From Representative to Participatory Democracy? Regime Transformation in Venezuela," in *The Unraveling of Representative Democracy in Venezuela*, edited by Jennifer L. McCoy and David J. Myers (Johns Hopkins University Press, 2004), pp. 263–96.

21. This section draws on Javier Corrales and Michael Penfold, "Venezuela: Crowding Out the Opposition," *Journal of Democracy* 18, no. 2 (April 2007): 99–113.

22. See World Bank, *Making Services Work for Poor People* (Washington, D.C.: 2004).

23. Francisco Rodríguez, "An Empty Revolution: The Unfulfilled Promises of Hugo Chávez," *Foreign Policy* 87, no. 2 (2008): 49–62.

24. Michael Penfold, "Clientelism and Social Funds: Empirical Evidence from Chávez's *Misiones* Programs," *Latin American Politics and Society* 49, no. 4 (2007): 63–84.

25. Ruth Berins Collier and David Collier, "Inducements versus Constraints: Disaggregating 'Corporatism,'" *American Political Science Review* 73, no. 4 (1979): 967–86.

26. Kurt Weyland, "Neopopulism and Neoliberalism in Latin America: How Much Affinity?" *Third World Quarterly* 24, no. 6 (2003): 1095–1115.

27. José Antonio Gil Yepes, "Public Opinion, Political Socialization, and Regime Stabilization," in *Unraveling of Representative Democracy in Venezuela*, edited by McCoy and Myers.

28. See Bruce Bueno de Mesquita and others, *The Logic of Political Survival* (MIT Press, 2003).

29. Chang-Tai Hsieh, Edward Miguel, Daniel Ortega, and Francisco R. Rodríguez, "The Price of Political Opposition: Evidence from Venezuela's Maisanta," NBER Working Paper No. w14923 (Cambridge: National Bureau of Economic Research, 2009) (http://ssrn.com/abstract=1394830).

30. Alfred Stepan, "State Power in the Southern Cone of Latin America," in *Bringing the State Back In*, edited by Peter Evans, Dietrich Rueschemeyer, and Theda Skocpol (Cambridge University Press, 1985).

Chapter Three

1. Mark Weisbrot, Rebecca Ray, and Luis Sandoval, "The Chávez Administration at 10 Years: The Economy and Social Indicators" (Washington, D.C.: Center

for Economic and Policy Research, February 2009). For a similar point to the one made in the chapter, see Leonardo Vera, "Políticas sociales y productivas en un estado patrimonialista petrolero, 1999–2007" [Social and economic policy in a oil rentist state], *Nueva Sociedad*, no. 245 (May–June 2008): 111–28; Gregory Wilpert, *Changing Venezuela by Taking Power* (London and New York: Verso, 2007).

2. Sebastian Edwards and Rudiger Dornbusch, *The Macroeconomics of Populism in Latin America* (Chicago University Press, 1991); Rosemary Thorp, *Progress, Poverty and Exclusion: An Economic History of Latin America in the 20th Century* (Washington, D.C.: Inter-American Development Bank, 1998).

3. Thorp, *Progress, Poverty and Exclusion*.

4. Francisco Rodríguez Caballero, "Las consecuencias económicas de la revolución Bolivariana" [The economic consequences of the Bolivarian revolution], *Revista Nueva Economía*, no. 19 (April 2003): 85–142.

5. Ibid., p. 95 (author's translation).

6. Janet Kelly and Pedro Palma, "The Syndrome of Economic Decline and the Quest for Change," in *The Unraveling of Representative Democracy in Venezuela*, edited by Jennifer McCoy and David Myers (Johns Hopkins University Press, 2004).

7. Michael Penfold, "Clientelism and Social Funds: Empirical Evidence from Chávez's *Misiones* Programs," *Latin American Politics and Society* 49, no. 4 (2007): 63–84.

8. *Ley de Protección y Promoción de Inversiones* [Law for the protection and promotion of investment], Declaración 356, *Gaceta oficial extraordinaria*, no. 5390 [Official extraordinary gazette, no. 5390], 1999.

9. Following liberalization, between 2000 and 2002, the telecommunications sector attracted over $2 billion in foreign direct investment.

10. Rodríguez Caballero, "Consecuencias económicas."

11. According to estimates prepared by the National Budget Office of the National Assembly, the economic impact of the failed April 2002 coup was 1.36 percent of GDP; negative growth caused by the 2002–03 oil strike was 7.59 percent of GDP.

12. Venezuela did not join the OPEC-led oil embargo, and remained a U.S. supplier.

13. See Francisco Rodríguez, "An Empty Revolution: The Unfulfilled Promises of Hugo Chávez," *Foreign Affairs* (March–April 2008): 49–62; Mark Weisbrot, "An Empty Research Agenda: The Creation of Myths about Contemporary Venezuela" (Washington, D.C.: Center for Economic and Policy Research, 2008).

14. According to data provided by the Central Bank of Venezuela, the not-for-profit sector under which these beneficiaries would be included grew more than 16.5 percent in 2006, 10.9 percent in 2007, and 9.2 percent in 2008. Cooperatives were vigorously promoted to build a "socialist market" model, and were generously supported via seed capital, equipment, and state contracts; their number increased from 1,336 in 2001 to 102,568 in 2005. However, an in-depth study of a small number of co-ops showed that most were unable to replace initial capital. See Josefina Bruni-Celli, "Viabilidad económica y desempeño cooperativo" [Economic viability and cooperative performance], in *Estrategias en tiempos de turbulencia: Las empresas venezolanas* [Strategies in times of turbulence: Venezuelan companies], edited by Michael Penfold and Roberto Vainrub (Caracas: Ediciones IESA, 2009).

15. Javier Corrales, "Hugo Chávez: Uso, abuso y desuso de las instituciones políticas" [Hugo Chávez: Use, abuse, and discontinued use of political institutions], in *Nuevos liderazgos y democracia en América Latina* [New leadership and democracy in

Latin America], edited by Jesús Tovar (Mexico City: Autonomous National University of Mexico, forthcoming).

16. See Francisco Monaldi and others, "Political Institutions and Policymaking in Venezuela: The Rise and Collapse of Political Cooperation," in *Policymaking in Latin America: How Politics Shapes Policies,* edited by Ernesto Stein and others (Washington, D.C., and Cambridge, Mass.: Inter-American Development Bank and Harvard University, David Rockefeller Center for Latin American Studies, 2010), pp. 371–417.

17. For example, Ana Julia Jatar, "Guiso a la Chavezca" [Scandal à la Chávez], *El Nacional,* April 8, 2008, p. 4, estimates private gains of close to $80 million in the placement of public debt made by the power and light company EDC following its nationalization in 2007. Other transactions undertaken by the Ministry of Finance and PDVSA followed similar procedures.

18. Francisco Olivares, "CAAEZ: Sólo Militares" [CAAEZ: Only the military], *El Universal,* July 9, 2008, p. 4.

19. For a brief overview of Venezuela's boom-bust cycles (described as "ax-relax-collapse" cycles), see Javier Corrales, "The Repeating Revolution: Chávez's New Politics and Old Economics," in *Leftist Governments in Latin America,* edited by Kurt Weyland, Raúl L. Madrid, and Wendy Hunter (Cambridge University Press, 2010).

20. Based on data from Miriam Kornblith and Thaís Maingón, "Contenidos y formas de la acción estatal en el período 1936–1980" [Content and forms of state intervention from 1936 to 1980], *Cuadernos del Cendes* 4 (1984): 67–94.

21. "El patrón bolivariano," [The Bolivarian pattern] *VenEconomía Opina* (online newsletter), October 3, 2008.

22. Teodoro Petkoff, "A Watershed Moment: Venezuela," Andean Working Paper (Washington: Inter-American Dialogue, 2008).

23. Barbara Stallings and Robert Kaufman, "The Political Economy of Latin American Populism," in *The Macroeconomics of Populism in Latin America,* edited by Sebastian Edwards and Rudiger Dornbusch (University of Chicago Press, 1991).

24. Suhelis Tejero Puntes, "Sector público absorbe a 41.400 trabajadores por estatizaciones" [Public sector absorbs 41,400 workers through state takeovers], *El Universal,* August 24, 2008 (www.eluniversal.com/2008/08/24/eco_art_sector-publico-absor_1014380.shtml).

25. "Venezuela: Gobierno afirma que la nómina de PDVSA ha crecido 266.66%" [Venezuela: The Government asserts that PDVSA's payroll expanded by 266.66%], *ABNInfolatam* (online newsletter), July 19, 2009.

26. Oscar Echevarría, *La economía venezolana, 1944–1994* [The Venezuelan economy, 1944–1994] (Caracas: Editorial Arte/Fedecámaras, 1995).

27. Jonathan Di John, *From Windfall to Curse? Oil and Industrialization in Venezuela, 1920–2005* (Pennsylvania State University Press, 2009).

28. *Doing Business* (online database of World Bank), 2008 (www.doingbusiness.org).

29. Felipe Pérez Martí, "Revisión, rectificación y reimpulso económico" [Revision, correction, and new economic impulse] (Caracas: Ministry of Popular Power through Communication and Information, 2008).

30. Di John, *From Windfall to Curse?*

31. Charles Lindblom, *Politics and Markets: The World's Political-Economic Systems* (New York: Basic Books, 1977).

32. "Jesse Chacón deja su cargo por arresto de su hermano" [Jesse Chacón resigns because of his brother's arrest], *El Universal,* December 7, 2009, p. 7.

33. According to one account, the fiscal cost of the financial crisis in these small banks caused by the fraudulent extraction of public and private deposits came to over $7 billion. See Juan Carlos Zapata, "El fin de la historia bonita" [The end of the lovely story], *El Mundo Economía & Negocios*, February 26, 2010, p. 26.

34. Ibid.

35. The parallel rate would presumably be held down by issuing dollar-denominated debt, or allowing PDVSA to sell foreign exchange on the unofficial market in order to expand the amount of local currency available to cover the cost of operations.

36. Katiuska Hernández, "Gobierno ha expropriado 174 empresas este año" [The government has expropriated 174 firms this year], *El Nacional* (Caracas), September 20, 2010.

37. Stratfor, "Venezuela: Guri Dam Drops to Lowest Level," May 7, 2010.

38. Javier Corrales, "The Repeating Revolution: Chávez's New Politics and Old Economics," in *Latin America's Leftist Turn*, edited by Kurt Weyland, Raúl L. Madrid, and Wendy Hunter (Cambridge University Press, 2010).

39. Adam Przeworski and others, *Democracy and Development: Political Institutions and Well-Being in the World, 1950–1990* (Cambridge University Press, 2000).

Chapter Four

1. Manuel Hidalgo, "A Petro State: Oil, Politics and Democracy in Venezuela," Working Paper Series 49/2007 (Madrid: Real Instituto Alcano, 2007); Manuel Hidalgo, "Hugo Chávez's Petro-Socialism," *Journal of Democracy* 20, no. 2 (April 2009): 78–92; Francisco Monaldi and Michael Penfold, "Institutional Collapse: The Role of Governance in Explaining Venezuela's Economic Decline, 1975–2005," in *Venezuela: Anatomy of a Collapse*, edited by Ricardo Hausmann and Francisco Rodríguez (Pennsylvania State University Press, forthcoming); Leonardo Vera, "Políticas sociales y productivas en un estado patrimonialista petrolero, 1999–2007" [Social and economic policies in an oil rentist state], *Nueva Sociedad*, no. 245 (May–June 2008): 111–28. For a classic perspective on this topic see Asdrúbal Baptista and Bernard Mommer, *El petróleo en el pensamiento económico venezolano* [Oil in Venezuela's economic thought] (Caracas: Ediciones IESA, 1992).

2. Thomas Friedman, "The First Law of Petropolitics," *Foreign Policy* (March–April 2006) (www.foreignpolicy.com/articles/2006/04/25/the_first_law_of_petropolitics).

3. Jeffrey Sachs and Steve Werner, "Natural Resource Abundance and Economic Growth," NBER Working Paper 5398 (Cambridge, Mass.: National Bureau of Economic Research, 1993); Osmel Manzano and Roberto Rigobón, "Resource Curse or Debt Overhang?" NBER Working Paper 8390 (Cambridge, Mass.: National Bureau of Economic Research, 2001); Francisco Rodríguez and Jeffrey Sachs, "Why Do Resource-Rich Economies Have Slower Growth Rates? A New Explanation and an Application to Venezuela," *Journal of Economic Growth* 4, no. 3 (1999): 277–303; Xavier Sala-i-Martin and Arvind Subramanian, "Addressing the Natural Resource Curse: An Illustration from Nigeria," NBER Working Paper No 9804 (Cambridge, Mass.: National Bureau for Economic Research, 2003).

4. Macartan Humphreys, Jeffrey Sachs, and Joseph Stiglitz, eds., *Escaping the Resource Curse* (Columbia University Press, 2007).

5. Michael Ross, "Does Oil Hinder Democracy?" *World Politics* 53, no. 3 (April 2001): 325–61; Nathan Jensen and Leonard Wantcheckon, "Resource Wealth and Political Regimes in Africa," *Comparative Political Studies* 37, no. 7 (2004): 816–41.

6. Sala-i-Martin and Subramanian, "Addressing the Natural Resource Curse"; Jonathan Isham and others, "The Varieties of the Resource Experience: How Natural Resource Export Structures Affect the Political Economy of Economic Growth," unpublished paper (Washington, D.C.: World Bank, 2003); Michael L. Ross, "The Political Economy of the Resource Curse," *World Politics* 51, no. 2 (1999): 297–322; Paul Collier, *The Bottom Billion* (Oxford University Press, 2007).

7. Stephen Haber and Victor Menaldo, "Do Natural Resources Fuel Authoritarianism? A Reappraisal of the Resource Curse," Working Paper no. 351 (Stanford University, 2008).

8. Thad Dunning, *Crude Democracy: Natural Resource Wealth and Political Regimes* (Cambridge University Press, 2008); James Robinson, Ragnar Torvik, and Thierry Verdier, "Political Foundations of the Resource Curse," *Journal of Development Economics* 79 (2006): 447–668.

9. Terry Lynn Karl, "Petroleum and Political Pacts," *Latin American Research Review* 22, no. 1 (January 1987): 63–94.

10. Sala-i-Martin and Subramanian, "Addressing the Natural Resource Curse."

11. For an application of the concept of the stakes of power holding, see Douglass C. North, William Summerhill, and Barry R. Weingast, "Order, Disorder, and Economic Change: Latin America versus North America," in *Governing for Prosperity*, edited by Bruce Bueno de Mesquita and Hilton L. Root (Yale University Press, 2000), pp. 23–29.

12. Sala-i-Martin and Subramanian, "Addressing the Natural Resource Curse."

13. Haber and Menaldo, "Do Natural Resources Fuel Authoritarianism?"; Dunning, *Crude Democracy.*

14. Juan Carlos Rey, *Problemas socio-políticos de América Latina* [Socio-political problems of Latin America] (Caracas: Aleneo de Caracas, 1980); Daniel Levine, *Conflict and Political Change in Venezuela* (Princeton University Press, 1973); Diego Bautista Urbaneja, *Pueblo y petróleo en la política venezolana del siglo XX* [People and petroleum in Venezuelan politics of the twentieth century] (Caracas: Centro de Formación y Adiestramiento de Petróleos de Venezuela, 1992).

15. Terry Lynn Karl, *The Paradox of Plenty: Oil Booms and Petro States* (University of California Press, 1997).

16. Rey, *Problemas socio-políticos de América Latina*; Levine, *Conflict and Political Change in Venezuela.*

17. Moisés Naím and Ramón Piñango, eds., *El caso Venezuela: Una ilusión de armonía* [The case of Venezuela: An illusion of harmony] (Caracas: Ediciones IESA, 1984).

18. Monaldi and Penfold, "Institutional Collapse."

19. For a review of politics and the policy process surrounding the effort to internationalize PDVSA, see César Baena, *The Policy Process in a Petro State* (London: Ashgate Publishing, 1999).

20. For a description of the budgetary process during this period, see José Manuel Puente, Germán Ríos, and Abelardo Daza, "The Political Economy of the Budget Process in Venezuela," Research Network Working Paper (Washington, D.C.: Inter-American Development Bank, 2007).

21. See Bernard Momer, "Subversive Oil," in *Venezuelan Politics in the Chávez Era: Class, Polarization, and Conflict*, edited by Steve Ellner and Daniel Hellinger (Boulder: Lynn Rienner, 2003), pp. 131–46.

22. Luis Giusti, in "Oil and Revolution: Viewpoints," *ReVista, Harvard Review of Latin America* 8, no. 1 (Fall 2008): 24.

23. Michael Penfold, "Clientelism and Social Funds: Evidence from Chávez's *Misiones*," *Latin American Politics and Society* 49, no. 4 (winter 2007): 63–84.

24. Yolanda D'Elia, and Luis Francisco Cabeza, "Las misiones sociales en Venezuela" [The social missions in Venezuela], Working Paper Series (Caracas: Latin American Institute for Social Research Press, 2008). See also Luis Pedro España, *Detrás de la pobreza: Diez años después* [Behind poverty: Ten years on] (Caracas: Universidad Católica Andrés Bello, 2009).

25. D'Elia and Cabeza, "Las misiones sociales en Venezuela."

26. España, *Detrás de la pobreza*.

27. Francisco Rodríguez, "An Empty Revolution: The Unfulfilled Promises of Hugo Chávez," *Foreign Affairs* (March–April 2008) (www.foreignaffairs.com/articles/63220/francisco-rodrÃ%C2%ADguez/an-empty-revolution).

28. Ramón Espinasa, "The Performance of the Venezuelan Oil Sector, 1997–2008: Official versus International and Estimated Figures," paper presented at the Conference on Energy Cooperation and Security in the Hemisphere Task Force, University of Miami, Center for Hemispheric Policy, October 2008.

29. Ibid.

30. This section draws on Javier Corrales, "The Repeating Revolution: Chávez's New Politics and Old Economics," in *Leftist Governments in Latin America*, edited by Kurt Weyland, Raúl Madrid, and Wendy Hunter (Cambridge University Press, 2010).

31. Benjamin Smith, "The Wrong Kind of Crisis: Why Oil Booms and Busts Rarely Lead to Authoritarian Breakdown," *Studies in Comparative International Development* 40, no. 4: 55–76, reaches a similar conclusion, but for different reasons. See also Collier, *Bottom Billion*.

32. Karl, *The Paradox of Plenty*; Fernando Coronil, *The Magical State: Nature, Money, and Modernity in Venezuela* (University of Chicago Press, 1997).

33. Levine, *Conflict and Political Change in Venezuela*; Karl, "Petroleum and Political Pacts."

34. Deborah Norden, "Party Relations and Democracy in Latin America," *Party Politics* 4, no. 3 (1998): 432–34; Monaldi and Penfold, "Institutional Collapse."

35. Collier, *Bottom Billion*; Moisés Naim, *Paper Tigers and Minotaurs* (Washington, D.C.: Carnegie Endowment for International Peace, 1993); Henry A. Dietz and David J. Myers, "From Thaw to Deluge: Party System Collapse in Venezuela and Peru," *Latin American Politics and Society* 49, no. 2 (summer 2007): 59–86.

36. On addiction to rents in Venezuela, see Aníbal Romero, "Rearranging the Deck Chairs on the Titanic: The Agony of Democracy in Venezuela," *Latin American Research Review* 21, no. 1 (1997): 7–36.

37. Hugo J. Faría, "Socialismo democrático contra socialismo totalitario" [Democratic socialism versus totalitarian socialism] (www.hacer.org/current/Vene221.php; accessed July 22, 2010); Hugo J. Faría, "Hugo Chávez against the Backdrop of Venezuelan Economic and Political History," *Independent Review* 12, no. 4 (2008).

38. Stephan Haggard and Robert R. Kaufman, *The Political Economy of Democratic Transitions* (Princeton University Press, 1995); Inter-American Development Bank, "The Politics of Policies: Economic and Social Progress in Latin America, 2006 Report" (Washington, D.C., and Cambridge, Mass.: IDB and Harvard University, David Rockefeller Center for Latin American Studies, 2006).

39. Adam Przeworski and others, *Democracy and Development: Political Institutions and Well-Being in the World, 1950–1990* (Cambridge University Press, 2000).

40. Guillermo O'Donnell, "Delegative Democracy," *Journal of Democracy* 5, no. 1 (January 1994): 55–69.

41. Javier Corrales, "Reform-Lagging States and the Question of Devaluation: Venezuela's Response to the Exogenous Shocks of 1997–98," in *Exchange Rate Politics in Latin America*, edited by Carol Wise and Riordan Roett (Brookings Institution Press, 2000), pp. 123–58.

42. Damarys Canache, "Urban Poor and Political Order," in *The Unraveling of Representative Democracy in Venezuela*, edited by Jennifer L. McCoy and David J. Myers (Johns Hopkins University Press, 2004), pp. 33–49.

43. Joan Nelson, *Fragile Coalitions: The Politics of Economic Adjustment* (New Brunswick, N.J.: Transaction, 1989); Adam Przeworski, *Democracy and the Market: Political and Economic Reforms in Eastern Europe and Latin America* (Cambridge University Press, 1991); Stephan Haggard and Steven B. Webb, *Voting for Reform: Democracy, Political Liberalization, and Economic Adjustment* (Oxford University Press, 1994); Susan Eckstein, ed., *Power and Popular Protest: Latin American Social Movements*, updated and expanded edition (University of California Press, 2001).

44. Barbara Geddes, 1995, "The Politics of Economic Liberalization," *Latin American Research Review* 30, no. 2 (1995): 195–214.

Chapter Five

1. See Javier Corrales, "Using Social Power to Balance Soft Power: Venezuela's Foreign Policy," *Washington Quarterly* 32, no. 4 (2009): 97–114, and Carlos Romero and Javier Corrales, "Relations between the United States and Venezuela, 2001–2009," in *Contemporary U.S.–Latin America Relations: Cooperation or Conflict in the 21st Century?* edited by Jorge I. Domínguez and Rafael Fernández de Castro (New York: Routledge, 2010), pp. 218–46.

2. The famous 1959 "Betancourt Doctrine" called for not recognizing regimes installed by military force. By the late 1960s the doctrine had been abandoned as autocracies became prevalent worldwide.

3. Elsa Cardozo, *Cuatro escritos, cuatro momentos: La política exterior venezolana en la segunda mitad del siglo XX* [Four writings, four moments: Venezuela's foreign policy in the second half of the 20th century] (Caracas: Universidad Metropolitana, 2007).

4. For a discussion of soft-balancing, see Robert A. Pape, "Soft Balancing against the United States," *International Security* 30, no. 1 (2005); T. V. Paul, "Soft Balancing in the Age of U.S. Primacy," *International Security* 30, no. 1 (2005): 46–71; Andrew Hurrell, "Hegemony, Liberalism, and Global Order: What Space for Would-Be Great Powers?" *International Affairs* 82, no. 1 (2006): 1–19.

5. Stephen M. Walt, "Can the United States Be Balanced? If So, How?" paper delivered at the annual meeting of the American Political Science Association, Chicago, September 2–5, 2004.

6. Daniel H. Nexon, "The Balance of Power in the Balance," *World Politics* 61, no. 2 (April 2009): 330–59, provides a thorough review of hard- and soft-balancing, arguing that hard- and soft-balancing can be difficult to distinguish. See also Stephen G. Brooks and William C. Wohlforth, "International Relations Theory and the Case

against Unilateralism," *Perspectives on Politics* 3, no. 3 (2005): 509–24; Keir A. Lieber and Gerard Alexander, "Waiting for Balancing: Why the World Is Not Pushing Back," *International Security* 30, no. 1 (2005): 109–39; Robert Kagan, "The September 12 Paradigm: America, the World and George W. Bush," *Foreign Affairs* 87, no. 5 (September–October 2008).

7. Mark E. Williams, "International Relations Theory and Venezuela's Soft Balancing Foreign Policy," paper presented at the meeting of the Latin American Studies Association, Montréal, 2007; Mark E. Williams, "The New Balancing Act: International Relations Theory and Venezuela's 'Soft Balancing' Foreign Policy," *The Revolution in Venezuela*, edited by Jonathan Eastwood and Thomas Ponniah (DRCLAS/Harvard University Press, forthcoming); Gregory Wilpert, *Changing Venezuela: The History and Policies of the Chávez Government* (New York: Verso, 2007).

8. Corrales, "Using Social Power to Balance Soft Power."

9. Reality of Aid Management Committee, "South–South Development Cooperation: A Challenge to the Aid System?" report (Quezon City, Philippines: IBON Books, 2010) (www.realityofaid.org/userfiles/roareports/roareport_08b0595377.pdf#).

10. Richard Feinberg, "Chávez Conditionality," *Latin Business Chronicle* (online magazine), June 4, 2007 (www.latinbusinesschronicle.com/app/article.aspx?id=1296).

11. Sean W. Burges, "Building a Global Southern Coalition: The Competing Approaches of Brazil's Lula and Venezuela's Chávez," *Third World Quarterly* 28, no. 7 (2007): 1343–58.

12. United Nations Conference on Trade and Development, "FDI: Venezuela," *World Investment Report 2007: Transnational Corporations, Extractive Industries and Development* (New York and Geneva: UNCTAD, 2007).

13. Includes petro-states for which data are available: Iran, Oman, Qatar, Saudi Arabia, Syria, United Arab Emirates, Yemen, Algeria, Angola, Republic of Congo (Brazzaville), Egypt, Gabon, Libya, and Nigeria. Kuwait, with 47 percent of outward FDI, was excluded.

14. Maruja Tarre Briceño, "Abandonados en grandes ligas: Chávez quiere ahora codearse con los grandes de la política mundial" [Abandoned in the big leagues: Chávez now wants to hobnob with the international big shots], *El Universal*, August 24, 2008.

15. Gustavo Coronel, "Pedigüeños de todo el mundo: Absteneos!" [Claimants from around the world: Abstain!], *Las Armas de Coronel* (blog), August 4, 2007 (http://lasarmasdecoronel.blogspot.com/2007/08/pediguenos-de-todo-el-mundo-absteneos-ya.html).

16. Natalie Obiko Pearson and Ian James, "Venezuela Offers Billions to Countries in Latin America," Associated Press, August 28, 2007.

17. Andrés Oppenheimer, "Alan García, Chávez y las casas del ALBA" [Alan García, Chávez, and the ALBA houses], *El Nuevo Herald* (Miami), March 16, 2008. See also James M. Roberts and Edward Enrique Escalante, "Fighting for Freedom in Rural Peru: 'ALBA Houses' Threaten Democracy," Backgrounder 2173 (Washington, D.C.: Heritage Foundation, August 18, 2008).

18. On Cuba's medical diplomacy, see Julie Feinsilver, "Cuba's Health Politics: At Home and Abroad," Council on Hemispheric Affairs, n.d. (www.coha.org/cuba%E2%80%99s-health-politics-at-home-and-abroad).

19. Jorge I. Domínguez, *To Make a World Safe for Revolution: Cuba's Foreign Policy* (Harvard University Press, 1989).

20. Ernesto Guevara, "Vietnam and the World Struggle for Freedom: Message to the Tricontinental; published April 1967," in *Che Guevara and the Cuban Revolution: Writings and Speeches of Ernesto Che Guevara*, edited by David Deutschmann (Sydney: Pathfinder/Pacific and Asia, 1987), p. 359.

21. Joseph Poliszuk, "The Argentinean Bribe," *El Universal*, May 14, 2010; Malú Kikuchi, "Argentina: Paralela y para . . . lelos" [Argentina: Parallels for . . . idiots!], *HACER Latin American News* (online magazine), July 1, 2010 (www.hacer.org/latam/?p=3923).

22. Richard Gott, *In the Shadow of the Liberator: Hugo Chávez and the Transformation of Venezuela* (New York: Verso, 2000).

23. "Presidente de Venezuela: Hugo Rafael Chávez Frías" [The president of Venezuela: Hugo Rafael Chávez Frías], *Gobierno en Línea* [Government online], República Bolivariana de Venezuela [Bolivarian Republic of Venezuela], official website (www.presidencia.gob.ve).

24. Carlos Blanco, *Revolución y desilución: La Venezuela de Hugo Chávez* [Revolution and disillusion: The Venezuela of Hugo Chávez] (Madrid: Catarata, 2002).

25. Ivan G. Osorio, "Chavez Bombshell?" *National Review Online*, January 8, 2003 (www.nationalreview.com/articles/205441/chavez-bombshell/ivan-g-osorio); see also Johan Freitas and Luis Garcia, "9/11: Chavez Financed Al Qaeda, Details of $1M Donation Emerge," December 31, 2002 (www.freerepublic.com/focus/news/814934/posts).

26. Pape, "Soft Balancing against the United States."

27. The idea of U.S. intervention in the coup is based on two arguments. First, the United States knew of the coup at least from April 6 and yet it did not warn the Venezuelan government (see "CIA Documents Show Bush Knew of 2002 Coup in Venezuela" (www.democracynow.org/2004/11/29/cia_documents_show_bush_knew_of). Second, the White House issued an early statement that may be interpreted as supporting the coup. See also Eva Golinger, "The CIA Was Involved in the Coup against Venezuela's Chávez," Venezuelanalysis.com, November 22, 2004: "On April 12, 2002, White House spokesperson Ari Fleischer stated: '. . . Government supporters, on orders from the Chavez government, fired on unarmed, peaceful protestors. . . .' On that same day, U.S. Department of State spokesperson Philip T. Reeker claimed: '. . . Venezuelan military and policy refused orders to fire . . . and refused to support the government's role in such human rights violations'" (http://venezuelanalysis.com/analysis/800).

28. Wilpert, *Changing Venezuela by Taking Power*, pp. 169–74.

29. Susanne Gratius, "Venezuela: Assessing Democracy Assistance," report, Project on Assessing Democracy Assistance, FRIDE (online magazine), July 23, 2010 (www.fride.org/publication/792/venezuela).

30. Shannon quoted in Mark P. Sullivan, *Venezuela: Issues in the 111th Congress*, CRS Report for Congress (Washington, D.C.: Congressional Research Service, November 17, 2009), p. 15; see also n. 37.

31. See Harold Trinkunas, "Venezuela's Strategic Culture: Findings Report 1" (Miami: Florida International University, Applied Research Center, and U.S. South Command, 2009).

32. Pew Global Attitudes Project, "Global Unease with Major World Powers: Rising Environmental Concern in 47-Nation Survey" (Washington, D.C.: Pew Research Center, 2007).

33. See Javier Corrales, "China and Venezuela's Search for Oil Markets, or Why Venezuela Is Trapped, for Now," in *Latin America Facing China: South–South Relations beyond the Washington Consensus*, edited by Alex Fernández and Barbara Hogenboom (New York: Berghahn Books, 2010).

34. Saudi Arabia understands, as does any large commodity supplier, the relationship between rising prices and declining demand. If the price of oil rises excessively, the appeal of alternative fuels increases and the demand for oil declines—an outcome that is not in a producer's interest. The Saudis prefer to set affordable prices for oil, whereas Venezuela and Iran—both of them experiencing declining oil production—prefer price maximization. For a statement of Saudi Arabia's oil policy, see Prince Turki Al-Faisal, "Don't Be Crude: Why Barack Obama's Energy-Dependence Talk is Just Demagoguery," *Foreign Policy* (September–October, 2009).

35. Nima Gerami and Sharon Squassoni, "Venezuela: A Nuclear Profile," report (Washington, D.C.: Carnegie Endowment for International Peace, December 18, 2008) (www.carnegieendowment.org/publications/index.cfm?fa=view&id=22568); Roger Noriega, "Hugo Chávez's Criminal Nuclear Network: A Grave and Growing Threat," AEI Outlook Series (website of the American Enterprise Institute for Public Policy Research), October 2009 (www.aei.org/outlook/100079).

36. Elodie Brun, *La Place de l'Iran dans la politique étrangère du Venezuela* [The position of Iran in Venezuela's foreign policy], paper presented at the conference "Iran in Latin America: Threat or Axis of Annoyance," Woodrow Wilson International Center for Scholars, Washington, D.C., July 10, 2008. There is some concern that Iran is helping Venezuela explore the nuclear option. There are rumors that Iranian scientists and engineers are prospecting for uranium ore in the granite bedrock under the southeastern jungles of Venezuela, a region rich in mineral deposits.

37. Ian James, "Venezuela-Russia ties deepen despite US pressure," Associated Press, September 18, 2008; Ricardo Adrián Runza, "La construcción de una comunidad de seguridad en América del Sur a la luz de la adquisición de armamento" [The construction of a security community in South America in light of the acquisition of armaments], Policy Paper 20, Program of Cooperation on Regional Security (Bonn and Berlin: Friedrich Ebert Foundation, July 2008) (http://library.fes.de/pdf-files/bueros/la-seguridad/50503.pdf).

38. Aaron Wodin-Schwartz, "Venezuela's Relations with Iran and Russia," umpublished paper, George Washington University, 2008; Stockholm International Peace Research Institute (SIPRI), data generated using importer/exporter TIV (Trend Indicator Values) tables at SIPRI website (http://armstrade.sipri.org/armstrade/page/values.php).

39. Michael Klare, *Rising Powers, Shrinking Planet: The New Geopolitics of Energy* (New York: Metropolitan, 2008).

40. Burton, "Venezuela: Documenting the Threat."

41. Roberto Giusti, "Entrevista: Yoani Sánchez, bloguera cubana" [Interview: Yoani Sánchez: Cuban blogger], *El Universal*, April 4, 2010 (http://politica.eluniversal.com/2010/04/04/pol_art_chavez-ha-sido-el-v_1818183.shtml).

42. See Javier Corrales, "Cuba's New Daddy," *Hemisphere: A Magazine of the Americas* 17 (Fall 2006): 24–29.

43. "Venecuba, a single nation?" *The Economist*, February 13, 2010.

44. Ibid.

45. Ibid.

46. María Teresa Romero, "El frágil y pendular entendimiento entre Venezuela y Colombia" [The fragile and pendular understanding between Venezuela and Colombia], ARI, no. 40, April 2008 (www.nuevamayoria.com/index.php?option=com_content&task=view&id=461&Itemid=43).

47. Chávez bragged about his ability to communicate with the FARC (the guerrilla group Revolutionary Armed Forces of Colombia), but in the end there was little result and the FARC became increasingly unwilling to accept Chávez's intermediation.

48. Cynthia J. Arnson and Arlene B. Tickner, "Colombia and the United States: Strategic Partners or Uncertain Allies?" in *Contemporary U.S.–Latin American Relations*, edited by Domínguez and Fernández de Castro.

49. Julia Buxton, "European Views of the Bolivarian Progressive Social Image: Have the Revelations of Deeper Relations with the FARC Changed Anything? Does It Matter?" paper presented at conference "Ten Years of Venezuelan Foreign Policy: Impacts in the Hemisphere and the World," held at Florida International University, Summit of the Americas Center, Miami, May 29, 2008.

50. Michael Shifter, "A New Path for Latin America," *Current History* 107, no. 706 (February 2008): 90–92.

51. Orlando J. Pérez, John A. Booth, and Mitchell A. Seligson, "The Honduran Catharsis," report, *Americas Quarterly* (web exclusive), August 5, 2010 (www.americasquarterly.org/honduran-catharsis).

52. Pew Global Attitudes Project, "Global Unease with Major World Powers."

53. Peter Hakim, "The Next President's Agenda for the Americas," paper presented at the eighth conference at the Aspen Institute, "U.S. Policy in Latin America," Washington, D.C., November 27 to December 2, 2007 (www.aspeninstitute.org/sites/default/files/content/docs/congressional%20program/Hakim_Paper.pdf); Abraham F. Lowenthal, "The Obama Administration and the Americas: A Promising Start," *Washington Quarterly* 32, no. 3 (July 2009): 119–36.

Chapter Six

1. See Thomas Carothers, "The End of the Transition Paradigm," *Journal of Democracy* 13, no. 1 (January 2002): 5–21; Thomas Carothers, "The Backlash against Democracy Promotion," *Foreign Affairs* 85, no. 2 (March/April 2006); Larry Diamond, "Thinking about Hybrid Regimes," *Journal of Democracy* 13, no. 2 (2002); Marina Ottaway, *Democracy Challenged: The Rise of Semi-Authoritarianism* (Washington, D.C.: Carnegie Endowment for International Peace, 2003); Steven Levitsky and Lucan Way, "The Rise of Competitive Authoritarianism," *Journal of Democracy* 13, no. 2 (April 2002).

2. Henry E. Hale, "Hybrid Regimes: When Democracy and Autocracy Mix," unpublished paper, George Washington University, Department of Political Science, 2009.

3. Freedom House, "Freedom in the World 2010: Erosion of Freedom Intensifies," report (Washington D.C., 2010).

4. Levitsky and Way, "The Rise of Competitive Authoritarianism."

5. Javier Corrales, "Petro-Politics and the Promotion of Disorder," in *Undermining Democracy: 21st Century Authoritarians* (Washington, D.C.: Freedom House, Radio Free Europe/Radio Liberty, Radio Free Asia, 2009) (www.underminingdemocracy.org/venezuela).

6. "Venezuela Murder-Rate Quadrupled under Chávez: NGO," Reuters, March 11, 2010 (www.reuters.com/article/idUSTRE62A44A20100311).

7. "El Tiro por la culata," *Veneconomía Opina*, August 16, 2010.

8. World Bank, *Ease of Doing Business Index*, 2010 (www.doingbusiness.org/economyrankings).

9. Francisco Monaldi and others, "Political Institutions and Policymaking in Venezuela: The Rise and Collapse of Political Cooperation," in *Policymaking in Latin America: How Politics Shapes Policies*, edited by Ernesto Stein and others (Washington, D.C., and Cambridge, Mass.: Inter-American Development Bank and Harvard University, David Rockefeller Center for Latin American Studies, 2008), pp. 371–417; Javier Corrales, "Explaining Chavismo: The Unexpected Alliance of Radical Leftists and the Military in Venezuela under Hugo Chávez," in *Venezuela: Anatomy of a Collapse*, edited by Ricardo Hausmann and Francisco Rodríguez (Pennsylvania State University Press, forthcoming).

10. Javier Corrales, "Why Polarize: Government-Opposition Relations in Venezuela," in *Revolution in Venezuela*, edited by Jonathan Eastwood and Thomas Ponniah (forthcoming); Javier Corrales, Polarización y oposición en Venezuela: ¿Existe evidencia de aprendizaje político? [Polarization and opposition in Venezuela: Is there evidence of political learning?], edited by Manuel Hidalgo (Madrid: forthcoming).

11. See Albert Hirschman, *Exit, Voice and Loyalty: Responses to Decline in Firms, Organizations and States* (Harvard University Press, 1970).

12. For instance, the National Electoral Council introduced opposition-demanded reforms such as better audits of polling stations and voting machines, and greater presence and less harassment of international observers. See also Manuel Hidalgo, "Hugo Chávez's 'Petro-Socialism,'" *Journal of Democracy* 20, no. 2 (April 2009): 78–92.

13. Article 58 requires the press to publish "timely, truthful, and impartial" content, but it is not clear how impartiality is defined. The Law of Social Responsibility in Radio and Television regulates the content of information. The law prohibits graphic depictions of violence between 5 a.m. and 11 p.m. in both media. This ensures that during prime-time broadcasting any form of repression, if it were to occur, would be considered illegal and an official investigation could be opened by the regulator. Reform of the penal code made insulting the president or other government officials, including in the broadcast media, punishable by six to thirty months in prison. Reporting that "disturbs the public peace" carries a prison sentence of two to five years. In April 2010 Oswaldo Alvarez Paz, a former presidential candidate, was jailed because he badmouthed the president during a TV program broadcast by Globovisión.

14. Andrés Cañizález, "Tiempos de revolución: Protagonismo y polarización mediáticas en Venezuela" [Revolutionary times: Media protagonism and polarization in Venezuela], in *Tiempos de cambio: Política y comunicación en América Latina* [Times of change: Politics and communication in Latin America], edited by Andrés Cañizález (Caracas: Universidad Católica Andrés Bello, 2009).

15. The survey by the Press and Society Institute (Instituto de Prensa y Sociedad) also revealed that 56 percent of journalists had suffered some sort of verbal or physical threat or attack during the previous year. The state does little to nothing to discourage such harassment. The same survey noted that only 9 percent of reporters were inclined to formally complain about threats, attacks, and harassment. See Freedom House, "Freedom of the Press in Venezuela" (www.freedomhouse.org/template.cfm?page=25 1&year=2008&country=7519).

16. Claudio Lomnitz and Rafael Sánchez, "United by Hate," *Boston Review*, July–August 2009 (http://bostonreview.net/BR34.4/lomnitz_sanchez.php).

17. Kurt Weyland, "Clarifying a Contested Concept," *Comparative Politics* 34, no. 1 (2001): 1–22.

18. See Ruth Berins Collier, "Populism," in *International Encyclopedia of Social and Behavioral Sciences*, edited by Neil J. Smelser and Paul B. Baltes (Oxford, U.K.: Elsevier, 2001), pp. 11813–16; Ruth Berins Collier and David Collier, "Inducements versus Constraints: Disaggregating 'Corporatism,'" *American Political Science Review* 73 (1979): 967–86; Robert R. Kaufman and Barbara Stallings, "The Political Economy of Latin American Populism," in *The Macroeconomics of Populism in Latin America*, edited by Rudiger Dornbusch and Sebastian Edwards (University of Chicago Press, 1991); Cas Mudde, "The Populist Zeitgeist," *Government and Opposition* 39, no. 4 (2004): 541–63; Torcuato S. Di Tella, "Populismo" [Populism], *Diccionario de ciencias sociales y políticas* [Dictionary of social and political sciences], edited by Torcuato S. Di Tella and others (Buenos Aires: Emecé Editores, 1989), pp. 564–68.

19. Collier, "Populism."

20. See Weyland, "Clarifying a Contested Concept."

21. Stephen B. Kaplan, "Globalization and Latin America: From Spendthrifts to Misers," Ph.D. dissertation, Yale University, Department of Political Science, 2009.

22. See Frances Hagopian, "Conclusions: Government Performance, Political Representation, and Public Perceptions of Contemporary Democracy in Latin America," in *The Third Wave of Democratization in Latin America: Advances and Setbacks*, edited by Frances Hagopian and Scott P. Mainwaring (Cambridge University Press, 2005); Scott P. Mainwaring, "The Crisis of Democratic Representation in the Andes," *Journal of Democracy* 7, no. 3 (July 2006): 13–27.

23. Inter-American Development Bank, *The Politics of Policies: Economic and Social Progress in Latin America*, Economic and Social Progress Report (Washington, D.C., and Cambridge, Mass.: Inter-American Development Bank and Harvard University, David Rockefeller Center for Latin American Studies, 2006), p. 119.

24. The banking scandal of 2009 highlighted the extent of the *boliburguesía* problem. One of those arrested as a result of the financial scandal, Arné Chacón, explained in a newspaper interview in 2005 that although he had no money, he had been "sold" a 49 percent stake in one of the now-liquidated banks in return for the business he would bring in: "It's perfectly normal that since I'm close to the government, they would deposit more money in my bank" (Violeta Del Portillo, "Entrevista a Chácón," *La Razón*, 2005). Both Chacón and his brother, the minister Jesse Chacón, have been close to Chávez from the time both staged a military coup as army officers in 1992. Another of the jailed bankers, Ricardo Fernández, obtained a monopoly contract to supply staple foods to Mercal, a state-owned chain of subsidized grocery stores. His banks received billions of dollars in government deposits, as well as loans from state banks. See José de Córdoba and Darcy Crowe: "Venezuelan President Hugo Chávez to Shut Banks of Billionaire Ally Ricardo Fernández," *Wall Street Journal*, December 1, 2009.

25. Corrales, "Explaining Chavismo."

26. Harold Trinkunas, "Venezuela's Strategic Culture: Findings Report 1" (Miami: Florida International University, Applied Research Center, and U.S. South Command, 2009).

27. Noam Lupu, "Who Votes for *Chavismo?* Class Voting in Hugo Chávez's Venezuela," *Latin American Research Review* 45, no. 1 (2010): 7–32.

28. Kurt Weyland, "The Rise of Latin America's Two Lefts," *Comparative Politics* 41, no. 2 (2009): 145–64.

29. Kaplan, *Globalization and Latin America*.

30. Weyland, "Rise of Latin America's Two Lefts."

31. CGD Task Force, "Helping Reforms Deliver Growth in Latin America: A Framework for Analysis," in *Growing Pains*, edited by Liliana Rojas-Suárez (Washington, D.C.: Center for Global Development, 2009); Nora Lustig, "Poverty, Inequality and the New Left in Latin America," research paper prepared for the Woodrow Wilson International Center for Scholars, Latin America Program (Washington, D.C.: Woodrow Wilson Center, 2009).

32. Robert R. Kaufman, "The Political Effects of Inequality in Latin America: Some Inconvenient Facts," *Comparative Politics* 41, no. 3 (April 2009): 359–79.

33. See Nancy Bermeo, "Does Electoral Democracy Boost Economic Equality?" *Journal of Democracy* 20, no. 4 (October 2009): 21–35.

34. Stephan Haggard and Robert R. Kaufman, *Development, Democracy and Welfare States: Latin America, East Asia and Eastern Europe* (Princeton University Press, 2009); Nancy Birdsall, *Fair Growth: Economic Policies for Latin America's Poor and Middle-Income Majority* (Washington, D.C.: Center for Global Development, 2008).

35. Scott P. Mainwaring, "State Deficiencies, Party Competition, and Confidence in Democratic Representation in the Andes," in *Crisis of Democratic Representation in the Andes*, edited by Scott P. Mainwaring, Ana María Bejarano, and Eduardo Pizarro Leongómez (Stanford University Press, 2006).

36. Diana Orces, "Problems of Political Tolerance in the Americas," in *Challenges to Democracy in Latin America and the Caribbean: Evidence from Americas Barometer 2006–2007*, edited by Mitchell A. Seligson (Vanderbilt University Press, 2008).

37. Matthew M. Singer, "With Friends Like These: Some of the Undemocratic Attitudes of Democracy's Winners," mimeograph, University of Connecticut, Department of Political Science, 2009.

38. Patricio Navia, "Limit the Power of Presidents, Not Their Term in Office," *Americas Quarterly* (blog), Spring 2009 (www.americasquarterly.org/node/536).

39. Ibid.

40. Ibid.

41. Steven Griner, "Term Limits Can Check Corruption and Promote Political Accountability," *Americas Quarterly*, Spring 2009 (www.americasquarterly.org/pros-and-cons-of-term-limits).

42. Paul Collier, *Wars, Guns, and Votes: Democracy in Dangerous Places* (New York: HarperPerennial, 2009); see also Daniel Posner and Daniel Young, "The Institutionalization of Political Power in Africa," *Journal of Democracy* 18, no. 3 (July 2007): 126–40.

43. Adam Przeworski and Carolina Curvale, "Does Politics Explain the Gap between the United States and Latin America?" in *Falling Behind: Explaining the Development Gap between Latin America and the United States*, edited by Francis Fukuyama (Oxford University Press, 2008).

44. Ibid. See also Javier Corrales, "Volatilidad económica, debilidad de partidos y neocaudillismo en América Latina" [Economic volatility, party weakness, and neocaudillismo in Latin America], *Journal of Democracy en Español* 50, no. 3 (2008): 1–35.

45. Adam Przeworski, *Democracy and the Market: Political and Economic Reforms in Eastern Europe and Latin America* (Cambridge University Press, 1991).

46. See David E. Jones, *An Instinct for Dragons* (New York: Routledge, 2000).

Index